*IGUANA IGUANA*

**Guide for SUCCESSFUL Captive Care**

**BOOKS BY FREDRIC L. FRYE:**

Husbandry, Medicine, and Surgery in Captive Reptiles (1973)
Biomedical and Surgical Aspects of Captive Reptile Husbandry (1981)
Phyllis, Phallus, Genghis Cohen & Other Creatures I Have Known (1984, 1995 Reprint with additional material)
First Aid for Your Dog (1987)
First Aid for Your Cat (1987)
Schnauzers, A Complete Owner's Guide (1988)
Mutts, A Complete Owner's Guide (1989); simultaneously published in the United Kingdom as Mongrels, A Complete Owner's Guide (1989)
Biomedical and Surgical Aspects of Captive Reptiles, 2nd Ed., in two volumes (1991)
A Practical Guide for Feeding Captive Reptiles (1991, 1993)
Captive Invertebrates: A Guide to Their Biology and Husbandry (1992)
Reptile Clinician's Handbook: A Compact Clinical and Surgical Reference (1994, 1995)

**BOOKS COAUTHORED BY FREDRIC L. FRYE:**

Iguanas: A Guide to Their Biology and Captive Care (1993)
Self-Assessment Colour Review of Reptiles and Amphibians (1995)
Colour Atlas of Comparative Veterinary Histology (1996)

**PHOTO CREDITS:**

Front cover: "Hearty." Photo credit: Fredric L. Frye; courtesy of Taryn Hook-Merdes.
Back cover: "Gucci." Photo credit: Elaine Harland; courtesy of Bryan and Kathy McDonough.

# *IGUANA IGUANA*

## Guide for SUCCESSFUL Captive Care

**Fredric L. Frye, DVM, MSc, CBiol, FIBiol**
**Fellow, Royal Society of Medicine**

Krieger Publishing Company
Malabar, Florida
1995

Original Edition 1995
(Based on *Iguanas: A Guide to Their Biology and Captive Care*)

Printed and Published by
**KRIEGER PUBLISHING COMPANY**
**KRIEGER DRIVE**
**MALABAR, FLORIDA 32950**



**Library of Congress Cataloging-in-Publication Data**

Frye, Fredric L.
Iguana iguana: guide for successful captive care/Fredric L. Frye.—Original ed.
p. cm.
Includes bibliographical references (p. ) and index.
ISBN 0-89464-892-6
1. Green iguanas as pets. I. Title.
SF459.I38F76 1995
639.3′95—dc20 95-6212
CIP

10 9 8 7 6 5 4 3 2

## CONTENTS

To Brucye, Lorraine, Erik, Bice, Noah, and Ian.

To Drs. Gordon Burghardt, A. Stanley Rand, Dagmar I. Werner, and Gordon H. Rodda and many other professionals in the field of herpetology for their magnificent contributions to our understanding of the biology and welfare of iguanas; to David Blair who has shown others how to be successful in the captive breeding of several species of iguanid lizards; and to Emeritus Professor Milton Hildebrand, a gifted and inspirational teacher and mentor who, among so many instructors that were responsible for my formal education, made the most significant impression on me.

## ACKNOWLEDGMENTS

The author wishes to express his gratitude to Robert E. Krieger and the editorial and production staffs, especially Elaine Harland, of Krieger Publishing Co. for their enthusiastic support of this project.

My wife and best friend, Brucye Frye, cheerfully and avidly copy edited each draft of the manuscript for this book and made many thoughtful suggestions to make this edition more "user-friendly" for persons unfamiliar with veterinary medical terminology. Her efforts are much appreciated.

I am grateful to my veterinary colleagues and their iguana-owning clients for sharing some of their experiences with these fascinating creatures. I wish to give special thanks to Dr. Donald Burton and his client (our mutual friend), Mrs. Helen L. Benton, for gathering and contributing clinical chemistry and hematology data from Helen's group of splendid iguanas.

Dr. Gordon H. Rodda provided many useful suggestions that were incorporated into this second edition; his insight and critical comments were beneficial and sincerely appreciated. I hope he finds this edition worthy.

# PREFACE

The material in this new edition is presented in a format similar to Frye and Townsend, *Iguanas: A Guide to Their Biology and Captive Care*. The anecdotal chapter entitled "Wendy's Observations" is retained.

The rest of the chapters, tables, and appendixes are substantially expanded and updated to include the most current information. New tables and an expanded color section enhance the more user-friendly style. Except where noted, all of the photographic images were made by the author.

# INTRODUCTION

Lizards resembling those living today have inhabited the earth since the Mesozoic Era (Age of Reptiles), around 120–190 million years ago.

These reptiles thrive in many disparate habitats. Presently, they can be found on all continents except Antarctica, although, in eons past, they lived there when this land mass had a much warmer climate and was attached to the super landmass called Gondwana.

Of the more than 3,000 species of lizards living today, some of the iguanas—especially common green iguanas, *Iguana iguana*—are the most popular reptiles kept in captivity either as pets or as study animals in North America as well as in parts of Europe and Asia. In citing the sources for most of the iguanas comprising the "pet trade," Dr. Gordon Rodda referred to the following data supplied by the World Conservation Monitoring Centre and CITES Secretariat statistics: exports of live green iguanas from just Colombia, Honduras, and El Salvador alone accounted for nearly 300,000 iguanas in 1990; the United States imported the majority of them.[1] Some iguanine lizards are listed as threatened or endangered species and are protected under one or more international treaties; consequently, they are not available in the pet trade. With increased worldwide interest in preserving the rainforests and the diversity of their flora and fauna, efforts are being made to halt the destruction of this vital biological treasure. Organizations such as The International Iguana Society and The Nature Conservancy's International Program are devoted to this goal.

Green iguanas often become docile, interact with their owners and, with proper care, these large and impressively colored lizards may live for more than 20 years. Their daily needs for space, water, food, temperature maintenance, and exercise are modest and can be easily satisfied if the owner knows what they are. Iguanas are quiet and clean animals. Thus they are frequently kept as pets in apartments, condominiums, and townhouses where larger, noisier creatures such as barking dogs or squawking parrots would be forbidden by tenant membership rules. Since iguanas can perceive red, orange, yellow, and green, their color vision can be used to advantage when inducing them to eat a nutritious, home-prepared diet.

Some common green iguanas display an amazing intelligence (for reptiles): they recognize their owners, and can be trained to use a cat litter-filled tray or other designated elimination area. With compassionate care, they usually become very tame and responsive to their owners and, when obtained as hatchlings, a degree of human-animal bonding appears to take place. One particularly striking aspect of this behavior is discussed in Chapter 9, and the potential deleterious consequences of these close relationships are considered in Chapters 2 and 7.

In this book, I provide information on how to properly care for green iguanas and, where appropriate, have included anecdotes. The personal experiences of Wendy Townsend (who coauthored the first edition of this book) also are included in Chapter 11, entitled "Wendy's Observations." I wish to assure you that all of these stores are true—as anyone who has a long-term commitment or experience with green iguanas can vouchsafe.

This book was not written to serve as a substitute for or supersede appropriate professional veterinary medical care when your iguana has health problems. However, it will guide you and help you prevent many common health-related difficulties, and it will characterize the important signs or symptoms of numerous diseases (some of which require veterinary assistance and care).

Whenever biological or medical terms are used in this book, I attempt to explain their meaning so that even a young child who is motivated to learn about green iguanas can understand the information. If some esoteric (understood by only a particular group) terms remain incomprehensible, I apologize!

Some "normal" physiological laboratory values, photographs of disease conditions, and dosages of drugs used in treating various diseases are included in this book so that when an owner of an iguana consults a veterinarian who usually does not treat green iguanas, a source of information will be available.

Dr. Donald Burton and Mrs. Helen L. Benton developed and provided the data on clinical hematology and clinical biochemistry relating to a group of particularly healthy and well-kept green iguanas. Helen and her numerous iguanas (20, as of this date of publication) have been grand sources for invaluable information that ordinarily would have been difficult or even impossible to obtain. When a clinician investigates a population of humans or domestic animals, the controlled conditions under which the data are obtained usually impose little or no stress on those whose blood and other body fluids are being analyzed. However, when dealing with even the most tame nondomestic animal, the process of just capturing and restraining and then gathering specimens imposes stress on it; the diet, captive husbandry practices, and other variables that cannot always be controlled also can affect results of tests. Even changes of laboratory personnel, equipment, and chemical test reagents introduce variables that cannot always be predicted. However, Helen Benton's iguanas were kept in exemplary captive conditions and soon adjusted to being transported to the site of specimen collection and were not intimidated by the personnel and laboratory equipment involved in the testing (which were consistent). Thus, this recently developed information regarding a population of healthy, essentially tame, captive common green iguanas is as nearly free from extraneous artifactual data as it could possibly be (see Appendix A).

## THE LAZY IGUANA

by Fredric L. Frye

When asked to clean up his room,
"*I don't wanna*", said the iguana, "*it's not my place*".
Then help with the yard.
"*I don't wanna*", said the iguana, "*it's not my place*".
How about pitching in with the dishes?
"*I don't wanna*", said the iguana, "*it's not my place*".
Please take out the trash.
"*I don't wanna*", said the iguana, "*it's not my place*".
Will you help serve dinner?"
"*I don't wanna*", said the iguana, "*it's not my place*".
Well then, help watch for the DEADLY ANACONDA!
"*I don't wanna*", said the iguana, "*it's not my place*".
Say, now, if you are not going to do
ANYTHING to help, just what ARE you
going to do?
"*I'm going to take a nice long nap; I really can't take the frantic pace*".

AT THIS TIME, ALONG CAME THE DEADLY ANACONDA, AND—
SNAP!!
HE FOUND THE IGUANA'S *PLACE*!

[1]According to a U.S. Fish and Wildlife Service survey, approximately 800,000 iguanas were imported into the United States in 1993.

# CHAPTER 1

## UNDERSTANDING GREEN IGUANAS

### IGUANAS IN GENERAL

The most recent taxonomic classification of iguanine lizards lists eight genera within the family Iguanidae: The Galapagos marine iguana, *Amblyrhynchus cristatus*; the Fiji banded iguana, *Brachylophus faciatus* (*B. vitiensis*); the land iguanas, *Conolophus pallidus* and *C. subcristatus*; the spiny-tailed iguanas, *Ctenosaura pectinatus*, *C. defensor*, *C. hemilopha*, and *C. similis*; the ground and rock iguanas, *Cyclura* sp.; the desert iguana, *Dipsosaurus dorsalis*; the common green iguana, *Iguana iguana*; and the rock-dwelling chuckawallas, *Sauromalus obesus*, *S. ater*, *S. australis*, *S. hispidus*, *S. slevini*, and *S. varius* (Blair 1991; Etheridge 1982). Many smaller iguanine lizards also exist; and although some taxonomists may disagree with this redefinition of the iguanas, for this discussion it is sufficient. See Table 1.1.

Previously, a distinction was made between common green iguanas bearing one or more small "horns" on their dorsal rostrum from those that do not possess these modified scales. Those possessing horns were referred to as *Iguana iguana rhinolopha*, and those lacking these nasal adornments were referred to as *Iguana iguana*. Many, if not most, authorities today ascribe to only a single classification: *Iguana iguana*. These two morphs can and do crossbreed and yield fertile "hybrid" offspring, some of which bear rostral hornlike scales and some of which do not bear rostral hornlike scales.

The common green iguana was first described as "*Lacerta iguana*" by the great 18th-century zoologist and father of the science of taxonomy (classification of species), Carolus Linnaeus (1707–1778) in his *Systema Naturae* in 1758. One hundred and forty years later, the scientific nomenclature was augmented to include *Iguana* (*Hypsilophus*) *rhinolophus* as a subspecies from Veracruz, Mexico; but, at present, this assignment of subspecies status to *Iguana iguana rhinolopha* is disputed by some taxonomists. The common green iguana has also been known as *Iguana tuberculata*, described by Laurenti in 1768, and *Iguana viridis*, described by Spix in 1825.

The Latin American common green and spiny-tailed iguanas and the Fiji banded iguanas dwell in ecological communities consisting of rain forests and sparsely wooded savannahs with rocky outcroppings. The distribution of these iguanas nearly half a world apart further supports the

**TABLE 1.1 Global Distribution of Iguanine Lizards**

| Common name | Genus | Number of species | Geographic range |
|---|---|---|---|
| Marine iguana | *Amblyrhynchus* | 1 | Galapagos Islands |
| Banded iguanas<br>Crested iguana | *Brachylophus* | 2 | Fiji and Tonga Islands |
| Land iguanas | *Conolophus* | 2 | Galapagos Islands |
| Spiny-tailed iguanas | *Ctenosaura* | 9 | Mexico, Panama, and Colombian islands |
| Ground and rock iguanas | *Cyclura* | 7 | Caribbean islands |
| Desert iguana | *Dipsosaurus* | 1 | Southwestern United States and Mexico; islands in the Gulf of Mexico |
| Green iguana | *Iguana* | 1* | Mexico to southern Brazil and Paraguay; Lesser Antilles |
| Chuckawallas | *Sauromalus* | 6 | Southwestern United States and Mexico; islands in the Gulf of Mexico |

Modified from Etheridge, 1982.
*The classification of *Iguana i. rhinolopha* as a separate subspecies is now questioned by some taxonomists.

role that plate tectonics plays in the dispersion of flora and fauna over the earth's surface. The desert iguana and chuckawallas inhabit more xeric (dry) desert life zones; the chuckawallas prefer rocky masses with numerous cracks and crevices in which to take refuge from predators. The Galapagos ground iguanas live on the islands in the Galapagos archipelago; and the other ground and rock iguanas are native to several islands throughout the Caribbean and Gulf of Mexico regions and on some of the eastern Central and South American shores. These lizards occupy several major ecological niches: rain forest, woodland, savannah, and desert; arboreal (trees); and marine aquatic (saltwater). They have been remarkably successful in their exploitation of all these diverse habitats.

Many of these lizards have a dorsal crest of prominent dermal spines that courses along the midline from the neck to near the tail base, but it is greatly reduced in the desert and spiny-tailed iguanas, and the chuckawallas lack it entirely. Except for the chuckawallas and, to a lesser extent, the spiny-tailed and desert iguanas, most of these lizards are characterized by an extendable dewlap that serves several important purposes: for thermoregulation, it assists in heat absorption and radiation; and during courtship and combat rituals, it is displayed like a palette upon which sexually significant colors are exhibited. The common green, Fiji, ground, and rock iguanas, which are laterally compressed, appear slightly flattened from side to side; the desert iguanas are cylindrical; and the chuckawallas and spiny-tailed iguanas, which are dorsoventrally compressed,

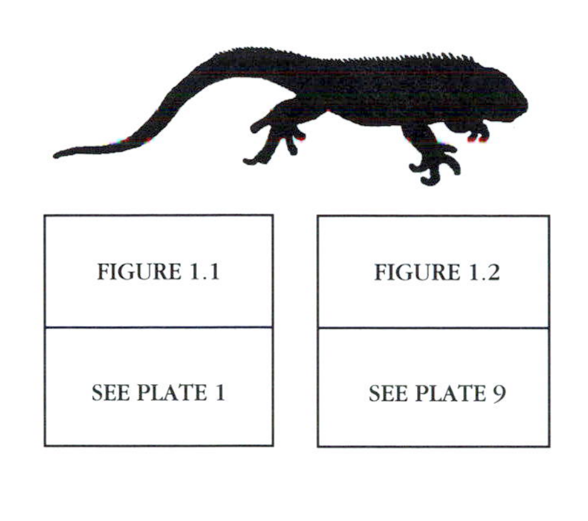


appear wider than tall when viewed from above. In the chuckawallas and spiny-tailed iguanas, this flattened shape enhances the ability of these creatures to seek refuge in fissures and crevices between large boulders where they inflate their large lungs (thereby greatly increasing their body diameter), thus making it difficult to extract them from the cracks. This preference to seek refuge in cracks and crevices is termed *thigmotaxis*, and these lizards are described as being *thigmotactic*.

In addition to their two lateral eyes, iguanas possess a parietal ("third") eye on the dorsal midline of the skull, immediately behind the level of the two lateral eyes (Figures 1.1 & 1.2). Rather than being employed as a primary visual organ, this effective sense organ serves as a "dosimeter" of radiant solar energy; it helps regulate the amount of time that iguanas spend exposed to direct sunlight while they bask. Also, it is intimately associated with the maturation of the sex organs, thyroid gland, and probably other endocrine glands (Stebbins and Cohen, 1973). The parietal eye probably only responds to shadows rather than transmitting discrete images to the brain. This ability could be of survival value by warning the iguana of attack by a predatory bird overhead. Consequently, when approached from above and behind in bright light, even a tame iguana may flinch as a shadow covers the top of its head.

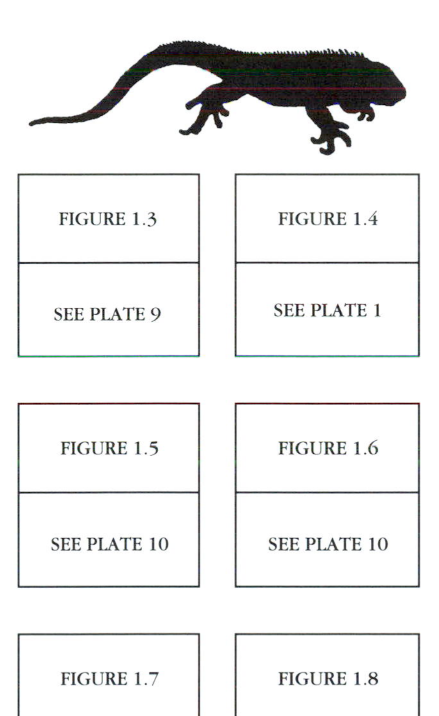


Obvious sexual dimorphism (sex-linked—often hormone-dependent—differences) are present in some iguanas. The sex of even hatchlings often can be differentiated by someone who is experienced with iguanas.

In comparison to mature female green iguanas, mature males have the following: a more robust body build; significantly larger head, neck, dewlap, and jowls; more highly developed dorsal spinal crest (Figures 1.3 & 1.4); more highly developed femoral pores (Figures 1.5 & 1.6); greater cross-sectional diameter of the tail base; bilateral hemipenial bulges, which often can be seen on the underside of the tail (Figures 1.7 & 1.8); and more vivid coloration during mating season. Also, adult male green iguanas tend to have a slightly shorter body than mature females of the same snout-to-vent length (SVL). These gender differences relate to their mating habits (see Chapter 10). Figures 1.9 & 1.10 illustrate some superficial features and the forelimb and hindlimb appendages and skull features of a male green iguana.

In comparison to mature male green iguanas, mature females have the following: a more slightly built body; a narrower head and neck; greater length between the forelimbs and the hindlimbs (in order to accommodate developing eggs); shorter and thinner dorsal spines; less robust neck and jowls; and a slimmer round tail. They retain the color that they had in their youth throughout much of their lives, tending to remain green or silvery green most of the year, although some females display a pale bronze or orange color on their limbs during part of the year. Figure 1.11 illustrates the internal anatomy of a female green iguana.

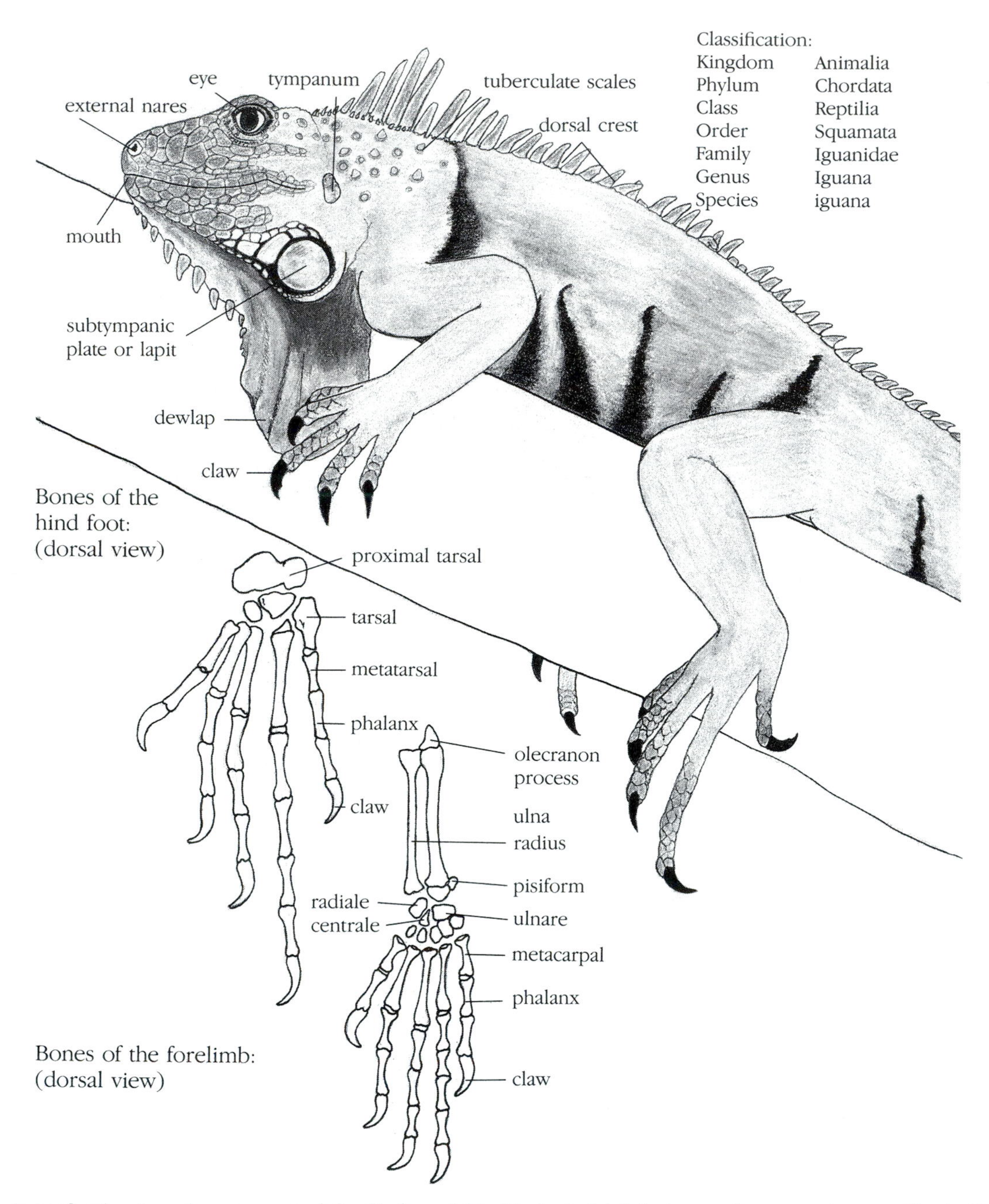


**Figure 1.9.** Superficial external anatomy and forelimb and hindlimb skeletal features of a green iguana. Illustration by Wendy Townsend.

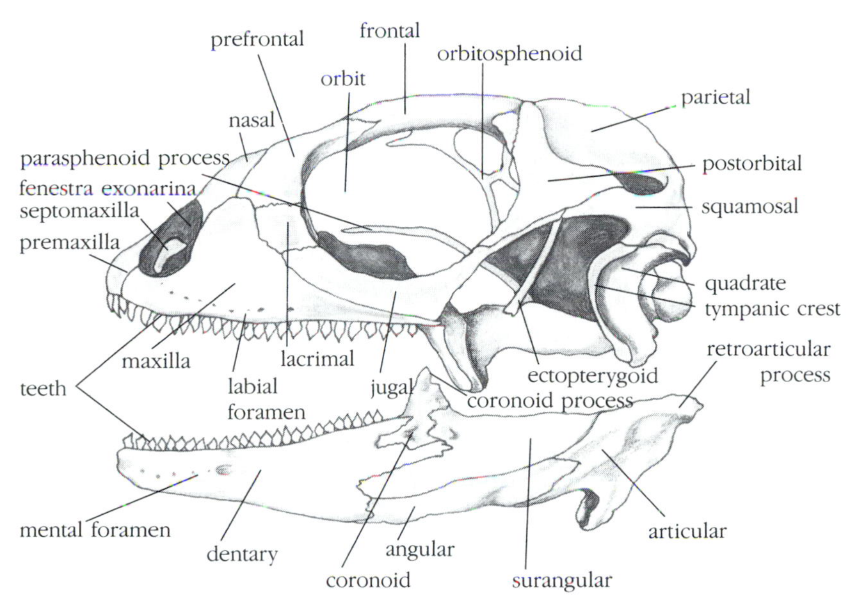


**Figure 1.10.** Anatomical features of the skull of a green iguana. Illustration by Wendy Townsend.

As is the case with other scaly reptiles, iguanas periodically molt or "shed" their old worn-out epidermis. Skin shedding is consistent with growth, occurring frequently with the rapid increase in size of young iguanas. Sloughing of the skin becomes less frequent as growth slows, but never ceases entirely because the outer epidermis is always subjected to wear and tear and thus must be renewed from time to time.

Although green iguanas are mostly vegetarian, their dietary preferences change substantially as they grow toward young adulthood. As youngsters, they eat mostly vegetables; however, if given the opportunity, they also eat animal-based food. Under natural rain forest habitats, the vegetable items are composed of tender leaves, blossoms, tendrils, and miscellaneous fruits. The animal-based food consists of small invertebrates such as spiders, insects and their larvae, and other creatures that the small hatchlings can overpower and ingest. Soon, however, green iguanas become accustomed to—and actually prefer—feeding upon more vegetable-based matter, particularly tender leaves and tropical fruit. This change in dietary preference largely coincides with migration from the ground, or near the soil, into foliage growing farther from the ground. Once they are fully grown, the majority of the green iguanas' food consists of leaves, blossoms, tendrils, and fruits. Being opportunistic, if they encounter eggs, nestling birds, small mammals, arachnids, caterpillars, and other invertebrates, they often eat them; but these items represent only a minor amount of the total diet. The change in diet makes sense when you understand that the requirement for protein diminishes markedly once growth slows.

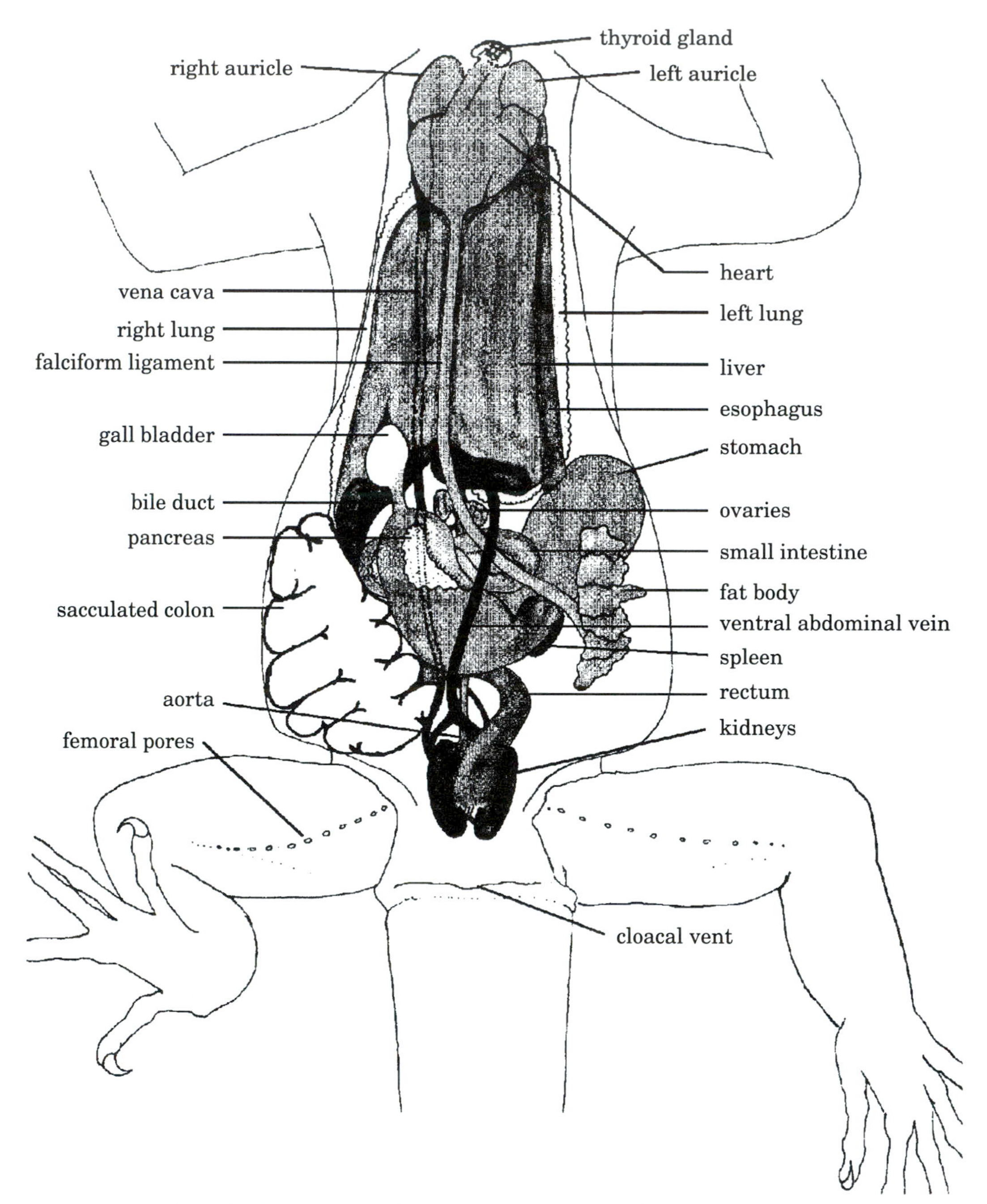


**Figure 1.11.** Diagram of the internal anatomy of a female green iguana.

Sexual maturity can occur from the second to the fifth year, depending upon whether the iguana grows to maturity in its native habitat or in captivity; maturity may occur earlier in captivity.

Successful breeding programs involving the following iguanas have been reported: for the common green iguana, *Iguana iguana* (Banks, 1984; David Blair's current efforts); for the Fiji banded iguana, *Brachylophus faciatus* (Arnett, 1979); for the rhinoceros iguana, *Cyclura cornuta* (Tonge and Bloxam, 1984); for *C. nubila* and *C.* sp. (Duval undated, cited by Tonge and Bloxam, 1984; Haast, 1969; Shaw, 1969; Burchfield, 1973; Peters, 1982; and Roman, 1978).

Some of these breeding attempts were initiated to increase local populations of wild iguanas which had been severely depleted due to uncontrolled habitat destruction, hunting pressure, and egg removal from nests. Conservation of iguanas should be more easily accomplished in their natural habitats than in even the most sophisticated artificial captive environments. Another goal for these breeding programs is to encourage the indigenous people to establish and maintain sufficient viable populations of iguanas so that they can be cropped periodically for their eggs, meat, and skins. In either case, enough unrelated iguanas must be included so that genetic diversity can be maintained.

Some of these captive breeding programs produced positive results for the first few years and generations, but later revealed that the quality of breeding animals and their progeny, if any, had rapidly diminished to the point where reproductive output ceased altogether. Once inbreeding is permitted, the "gene pool" becomes concentrated with a marked increase in the incidence of deleterious genetic traits, and soon there is a noticeable decrease in vigor. In his paper on captive breeding of the common green iguana at the Royal Melbourne Zoo in Australia, Banks (1984) suggested that the detrimental effects of inbreeding successive generations, originating from a single pair of iguanas that may have been siblings, were surprisingly swift and serious. The incidence of infertility, egg-hatching failure, embryonic and fetal developmental abnormalities, and other problems rose in a directly parallel fashion with the coefficient of inbreeding. These experiences confirm the absolute necessity for genetic diversity when attempting to breed iguanas in captivity or under wild conditions.

The balance of the information in this book will relate specifically to the common green iguana, *Iguana iguana*, because many of the other iguanines are either not readily available to the pet trade or are threatened with extinction due to habitat loss and/or overexploitation.

## SELECTING A GREEN IGUANA

Before actually obtaining a green iguana, you must decide whether you are willing to provide care for an animal that, possibly for the next 20 or more years, will be dependent upon you for its every need. Those little bright green hatchling iguanas that you see scampering from one end of the pet shop's cage to the other will, with suitable care, grow into impressive lizards that measure well over 4 feet from nose to tail tip. Iguanas are creatures native to the tropical rain forests. Are you willing and able to give such an animal the appropriate captive environment and nutritious food it requires—and your time interacting with it—so that it can achieve its inborn potential? If the answer is affirmative, then it is important for you to learn how to reach your goal efficiently and in a way that is practical so that both you and your pet iguana benefit.

The most often asked question regarding the acquisition of a new iguana probably is whether to purchase a hatchling or a well-started juvenile or adult. With increasing numbers of captive-bred youngsters being sold through the pet trade, it is often possible to select a healthy, unparasitized, and "head-started" iguana of about 1–3 months of age. By this age, the juvenile iguana should be eating well and already growing vigorously.

The prospective owner often is faced with choosing from a tank containing anywhere from 5 to 35 little green iguanas that may or may not have been actually *bred* in captivity. Many exporters are still obtaining their stock by capturing wild females and collecting their eggs or removing naturally deposited iguana eggs from nests and incubating them artificially. Both of these practices are inherently undesirable because they reduce the natural population within a given locality and, furthermore, increase the likelihood that hatchlings produced under such conditions will be exposed to a diversity of pathogenic bacteria, fungi, viruses, and parasitic organisms that may have accumulated in overcrowded holding pens that may never have been properly sanitized between batches. Also, because the hatchlings may be strictly segregated from older healthy iguanas, they may not have had an opportunity to acquire the normal intestinal microflora by which they process cellulose and digest nutrients.

The following are characteristic of a healthy iguana:

- Well-rounded, fleshy hind limbs and tail
- Green, lustrous skin
- Alertness
- An upright posture

The iguana that is eating, is reasonably active, is exploring its boundaries by tongue-flicking, and is not hyperactive or fearful, is a good choice.

**Protruding pelvic bones, bloated belly, yellow-green and wrinkled skin (often punctuated by black specks or patches), and nasal or ocular discharges are signs that the hatchling iguana is not in optimum condition and may actually be diseased. Fecal stains and/or accumulations of urates around the cloacal vent are signs of inherent health problems.**

There is nothing intrinsically wrong with obtaining an iguana when it is an adult if it is healthy and parasite free. Many adult iguanas available from reptile dealers are previous pets whose owners tired of them or could no longer keep them, or they outgrew their cages. These pre-owned iguanas can make excellent pets because they usually are healthier than newly arrived wild-caught animals; and, since they have usually adapted to the conditions of captivity, they are accustomed to being handled and are somewhat "domesticated." Wild-caught iguanas have survived the trauma of being captured and may have been held in enclosures that were not hygienic; been kept with other iguanas that had not been segregated by size, sex, territorial dominance, or state of health; and not been shipped until there were enough to fill an order from a pet distributor or wholesale dealer. Some of these may not have been fed or given fresh water for several weeks prior to the time that they ended up in the dealer's shop. Consequently, many wild-caught iguanas arrive at their final destination burdened by intestinal and/or external parasites, (lizard) malaria, wounds, abscesses, other "lumps and bumps," and malnutrition-related conditions such as deformed jaws, limb bones, and spines. When large numbers of iguanas are housed together, they crawl over one another. Their sharp claws, which are often covered with feces, may penetrate the skin of other iguanas and, in doing so, cause infections (especially by *Salmonella*; see Chapter 7).

**Routine microscopic examination of a newly acquired iguana's feces should be done because this fecal examination is the best means for determining whether or not an iguana is free of harmful parasites.** Many veterinarians provide this service. It is especially crucial when any newly acquired iguana (especially one whose previous living conditions are questionable) is to be brought into the vicinity of resident iguanas already in a collection. Of course, each and every newly acquired animal should be quarantined until it is determined that it is not harboring pathogens harmful to the resident iguanas. Generally, a 6-week to 12-week quarantine is recommended. During this time, the newly arrived iguana is examined thoroughly and subjected to whatever laboratory tests that are deemed necessary. For instance, it is wise to have the blood from any new wild-caught iguana examined for the presence of malarial parasites. This test, which is inexpensive and requires taking only a minute quantity of blood from the iguana's tail vein, can be performed by a veterinarian whose practice includes reptiles. Although potentially harmful to other iguanas, the organism responsible for this type of malaria is **not** transmissible to humans.

Except for an iguana that has a clearly serious disorder, adopting a physically imperfect iguana should not be disregarded. Many "damaged" iguanas can be rehabilitated and can make excellent pets. Usually, "rehabilitation" simply means providing the iguana with appropriate husbandry and a nutritious diet, and perhaps a veterinarian who is competent with reptiles. Sometimes, imperfect iguanas can be obtained through classified ads, adoption committees of local herpetological society chapters, and the herpetological "grapevine." Stories about adopted "damaged" iguanas are included in Chapter 11.

## BASIC BEHAVIOR OF GREEN IGUANAS

Various aspects of the green iguana's behavior are found scattered throughout this book and are not confined to a single chapter. This section, presented in a glossary format, is a quick reference describing some of the basic behavioral repertoire that the captive green iguana is observed to "do" on a somewhat regular basis (although some of these behaviors also have been observed in wild iguanas). Some behavior is associated only with hatchlings. Some behavior is characteristic of mature iguanas. Some of these behaviors may be modified by the exigencies related to being in captivity. This book is directed at persons keeping *captive* green iguanas rather than those observing wild ones, but if the reader wishes to learn more about wild iguanas, several excellent references are listed in the Bibliography.

### Stacking

FIGURE 1.12

SEE PLATE 9

Very young *caged* iguanas, from newly hatched babies to those several months old, often will pile on top of each other to a point where they may be several iguanas deep (Figure 1.12). **Stacking behavior is not normal; it is caused by overcrowded captive conditions.** Although the combined weight of several iguanas may not pose much of a problem to those on the bottom of the pile, the sharp claws of iguanas (which often are covered with feces) may penetrate the skin of cagemates and result in infections. Generally, stacking can be prevented by providing adequate space in which iguanas can disperse and stake out their own domains and where they can feed, obtain water, bask, and exert their territorial prerogatives.

### Closing of One or Both Eyes

While basking, iguanas may alternately close one eye and keep watch with the other. Eye closing, in addition to being a protective measure, is a response to both displays by other iguanas and to human touch. Submission, toleration, or fear may be indicated.

### Eye "Bulging"

Iguanas may push their eyes out from under closed lids for a few moments, and then rub them on a branch or similar surface. Presumably, this is to remove pieces of shedding skin or to scratch an itch. **If the eye (or**

**eyes) continue to bulge, the iguana should be examined by a veterinarian who has experience with treating reptiles.** An inflammation of the mucous membranes surrounding the eye or one or more glands that serve the eye may indicate a disease process, even a tumor. Surgery of the eye and its supportive structures is both possible and practical; however, because these structures are served by a well-developed vascular supply, surgical intervention for conditions related to the eyes may be accompanied by considerable hemorrhage which can be difficult to control without specialized equipment and expertise.

### Sleeping

Iguanas go to sleep when the sun goes down, closing both eyes and extending their limbs back against their bodies in a relaxed position. They awake at sunrise and do not enjoy being disturbed or handled during the night. However, when basking on a branch or other resting surface, they may fall asleep, particularly after they have eaten a large meal.

### Tongue Flicking and Tongue Licking

Tongue testing is comparable to sniffing and has a sensory function. Iguanas explore new or unfamiliar things in their environment by lightly touching them with their tongues. They also frequently reaffirm familiar objects, food, human hands, and particularly other iguanas by tongue testing. Iguanas clean their teeth and lips by both licking and wiping them on branches or on other surfaces.

### Cautious Exploratory Behavior

This behavior is associated with the passage of what the iguana probably perceives to be a potential threat. The male iguana will creep along, evaluating his surroundings by visual scanning and much tongue testing. The subadult female iguana exhibits similar behavior when entering a territory that may be occupied by an adult male iguana and is perhaps both cautious and submissive.

### Mouth Opening

This is usually part of a defensive or aggressive display, often accompanied by expulsion of air, primarily but not exclusively, in a hiss to warn other iguanas. When overheated or exerted, iguanas will pant. **If a confined iguana is seen panting, its living arrangements may not permit a sufficient temperature gradient between warmer and cooler areas within the cage; adjustments must be made, as overheating is dangerous for an iguana.** Iguanas also yawn, opening the mouth widely and then shutting it abruptly. This is entirely normal behavior.

### Sneezing

It is entirely normal for iguanas to sneeze frequently. Glands in their nasal cavities secrete concentrated salt solution which is expelled through this sneezing activity (see Chapter 5). The sneezing of *clear* fluid from the nostrils is not a cause for concern; however, **if the nasal discharges contain mucus or are discolored, the affected iguana should be examined and evaluated by a veterinarian.**

### Head Bobbing

Head bobbing is a major means of communication and is intended primarily, but not exclusively, for other iguanas. The head is tossed upward and brought down in sequences varying in degree and number, depending on the nature of the display. Head bobbing is generally associated with territorial assertion of dominance. Both male and female iguanas bob, but males do it more often and with greater exaggeration and variation. Isolated iguanas will head-bob, but less frequently than those kept in pairs or groups. Other head movements, such as shaking, are associated with courtship or irritants.

Many iguanas respond to their owners' head bobbing by vigorously "answering" with their own. **Some of my clients have described how their adult male iguanas have attacked them, inflicting wounds serious enough to require emergency medical and surgical attention, after they bobbed their heads trying to communicate with their pets who had recently been exposed to strong, unfiltered natural sunlight.**

Some adult male green iguanas, when confronted by their own image in a mirror or in a highly reflective surface such as the inside of their glass or plastic terrarium, may behave as if they are in the presence of another male iguana and display a rich repertoire of head bobs, open-mouth threats and hisses and may even rush at the image as if to attack it. Several owners have related stories of how their large male iguanas have attacked their own images and, in doing so, have broken heavy plate-glass mirrors. An 8–12-pound adult iguana has the body mass to do considerable damage when it is provoked!

### Dewlap Extending and Dewlap Retracting

Extensions of the hyoid bones stiffen and support the leading edge of the dewlap in both genders; however, this thin-skin-covered structure is much more highly developed in adult male iguanas than it is in adult female iguanas. When extended, the dewlap (of both genders) increases the surface area for thermal absorption and dissipates heat when iguanas are overheated.

During territorial displays, or when threatened, iguanas extend their dewlaps to impart a more imposing appearance to the head and neck;

because the dewlaps of male iguanas are more highly developed than those of females, these displays are far more impressive in adult males. In an attempt to become obscure to a potential attacker or predator, an iguana may retract its dewlap in order to minimize its appearance. For these reasons, these same motions also may be displayed when an iguana's own image is reflected from a mirror or other reflective surface such as the inside of its glass- or shiny plastic-walled cage.

### Lateral Body Flattening

Not to be confused with inflation of the body (which occurs when an iguana is captured or restrained), lateral flattening—usually accompanied by raising the dorsal crest and extending the dewlap—gives the iguana a larger appearance and is both a combative and defensive display.

### Tail Twitching and Tail Lashing

A fight between mature male iguanas includes initial twitching of the tail with intermittent lashes. Nervous iguanas also may twitch the tips of their tails. **Frightened or cornered iguanas strike out pointedly with defensive lashes. Such a tail strike directed against a person's face, especially near the eyes, can inflict serious, even devastating, corneal injury.**

### Color Changes

An iguana's color can change within minutes and occurs in response to temperature fluctuation, physical condition, social status, and "mood." At the onset of basking, an iguana's overall color darkens and lateral bands become more prominent. As the body temperature increases to higher levels, coloration lightens, the head becoming pale gray or nearly white in extreme heat. This is a protective mechanism because lighter shades reflect rather than absorb radiant thermal energy. **Chilled, sick, injured, depressed, or defeated iguanas are darker than their normal color. Active dominant iguanas usually have a lighter color than lower ranked iguanas living under identical environmental conditions.**

Most female green iguanas retain their green color when mature (see frontispiece), but a few assume a golden orange skin hue. Color changes related to maturity alone are more often associated with males as they begin to produce the male sex steroid (Rodda, 1992). Six or eight weeks prior to and during courtship, male iguanas acquire bright gold or orange colors over much of the body (see frontispiece). Lone males may exhibit these vivid colors more subtly. Interestingly, after mature male iguanas have been surgically castrated, they change back—and retain—the bright green skin color more characteristic of hatchlings. A similar return of "immature" skin hue is observed in adult females that have had their ovaries removed. Therefore, it is likely that much (if not all) of the golden-orange color typical of sexual maturity is influenced by sex hormone(s)—testosterone in males and estrogen (and possibly progesterone) in females.

The injection of some therapeutic agents can also induce skin color changes, usually seen as a very dark or even jet black pigmentation at and around the site of injection. The blackening of small areas of skin also is caused by some skin infections (see Chapter 7) and by endoparasitism (see Chapter 8). Two chemical agents which induce these immediate skin pigment alterations are the anesthetic ketamine hydrochloride (Ketaset®, Ketalar®, etc.) and the antibiotic enrofloxacin (Baytril®). Usually, these skin color changes are transient and disappear after a few minutes to an hour or two. However, because of their acidity or alkalinity, some drugs can cause severe irritation and even necrosis of the tissues into which they are deposited. For that reason, some drugs, such as enrofloxacin, should be diluted with sterile saline to as much as 50% before injection; the equivalent dose in milligrams/kg of body weight is injected, but the volume is doubled. This has proven to be a method by which injection-related irritation and inflammation can be reduced or eliminated entirely. These drugs should be administered by *deep intramuscular* injection.

### Skin Shedding

FIGURE 1.13

SEE PLATE 11

Shedding of skin is consistent with growth, occurring frequently as young iguanas rapidly grow. Sloughing of the old epidermis becomes less frequent as growth slows, but never stops completely. Rather than coming away as a single inverted slough (as occurs in snakes), senescent iguana skin is shed in patches (as occurs in most lizards) (Figure 1.13). Some iguanas eat pieces of their shedded skin (dermatophagy). This is considered to be normal behavior.

### Geophagy and Lithophagy (Eating Earth and Stones)

As iguanas move along the ground tongue testing various surfaces, they sometimes nibble on or eat dust, sand, rocks, debris, or other foreign matter. **Excessive ingestion of foreign material can be an indication of malnutrition or some dietary deficiency (or maybe boredom). This behavior should be discouraged; it can be corrected by feeding the iguana a highly nutritive fiber (mostly leafy greens) diet which simulates the one found in the rain forest.** Not only is such a diet highly nutritious, it also provides the iguanas with something to occupy their time. Conversely, if a small amount of nutritionally dense artificial diet which contains an iguana's daily requirement of food is offered, the iguana may consume the entire portion in a few minutes, leaving an enormous amount of time for boredom and, consequently allowing atypical and potentially destructive behavioral activity to develop. Providing iguanas with living edible plants from which they can browse at will in the cage or captive enclosure is a far more ethologically enlightened method of husbandry, and will help prevent geophagy and lithophagy.

When weather and the owner's conditions permit, outdoor cages are more suitable than even the most elaborate indoor quarters. When kept under semi-natural housing, iguanas rarely display geophagy or lithophagy because their available time is spent eating, basking, and interacting as they would in the rain forest.

### Coprophagy (Eating Stools)

The consumption of stools is unusual in most reptiles, but it is entirely normal behavior in green iguana hatchlings. This is how they acquire the vital fermentative bacteria and protozoa that actually digest the cellulose-rich plant material that they ingest. **Coprophagy becomes abnormal behavior when it occurs in older iguanas (which should already possess an adequate intestinal microflora).** These older iguanas usually do not eat their own feces, but rather those of other creatures who have defecated within the enclosure.

Most, but not all, intestinal roundworms, tapeworms, and flukes are relatively host-specific. However, there is an obvious opportunity for the *horizontal* transmission of disease (transmission of disease-causing bacteria, fungi, viruses, protozoa, and worms from one infected or infested iguana to its cagemates, particularly if they are of the same or closely related species). Many parasitic worms and protozoa are characterized by their direct or indirect multihost life cycles and may be furnished with the required host when one animal consumes the stools of another.

Coprophagy in adult iguanas should and can be discouraged by practicing good hygiene, avoiding overcrowded conditions, and quarantining all new arrivals until their health can be assured.

### Everting Hemipenes

Mature male iguanas are observed everting one or both hemipenes, partially or entirely, and discharging a moist, whitish, substance which may have shreds of partially dried material mixed with it. This firm waxy material is a mixture of desquamated cells from the lining of the hemipenial sheaths, glandular secretions, and, in some instances, semen. Many male iguanas respond to the scent or chemical cue(s) contained in these plug-like objects by increased head-bobbing, dewlap displays, etc.; these displays can occur when the males are exposed to their own plugs or to another iguana's plugs (H. Benton, personal communication). Hemipenial discharges occur almost daily in some males; others pass this secretion seasonally, as a prelude to, or during courtship. Some owners have observed their adult male green iguanas masturbating on inanimate objects such as stuffed toys, gloves, or cushions. In one instance, a male iguana's favorite "love" object was a stuffed toy velociraptor inspired by the movie *Jurassic Park*. Excessive male sexually aggressive behavior is discussed in Chapter 9.

### Escape, Defense, and Fearful Behavior

An iguana will flatten its body, shrink behind a branch or other cover, and remain motionless in an attempt to become obscure to a potential threat. If caught, escape efforts include "freezing up" and/or twisting, rotating, and writhing. Similar behavior is discussed in Restraint in Chapter 1. An iguana, like many other lizards, can shed or "autotomatize" part or most of its tail in response to a threat of capture or predation. Located along the tail vertebrae are "break planes" or points where the tail can be cast off. Usually, there is little or no hemorrhage from the blood vessels serving the tail because the arteries go into immediate vascular spasm, thereby preventing blood loss. When tail autotomy occurs, the shed tail wiggles violently for a few minutes thus distracting the erstwhile predator. When the predator's attention is drawn to the writhing tail, the iguana is often able to escape. Soon, the stump from which the old tail had grown heals over, and it begins to regrow a new tail. Often, the new appendage is regrown within a year, although it may be shorter with a less prominent scale pattern and color than the original (see Tail Disorders in Chapter 9). With successive bouts of autotomy, the regrown tail becomes ever shorter and less attractive, but it still can function as a balance structure.

### Body Jolting

Healthy, contented iguanas are occasionally observed making this seemingly involuntary movement consisting of a brief, strong twitch while sitting upright. Although alarming to observe, it is apparently no cause for concern.

### Pacing

**Sometimes an iguana displays signs of its rejection of captivity by constant pacing along the edges of its cage, digging into the substrate or rubbing its nose on the walls or boundaries of its enclosure. If it persists in any of these behaviors, it is likely that something within the iguana's immediate captive environment is either lacking or distressing.** Insufficient hiding or refuge areas, intimidation by a socially dominant cage mate, or even something within the iguana's view may be causes for anxiety. Simple observation and experimentation and housing adjustments made by the owner may reduce or entirely eliminate the restlessness and help the iguana relax and adapt to captivity.

### Territorial Behavior

Territoriality is an inborn trait in wild and captive iguanas, especially in subadult and adult male iguanas. This behavior serves to preserve the species in its most vigorous state by selecting the breeding males who are most fit to pass their genetic endowment down to their offspring. **It is only when territoriality becomes excessive that corrective measures should be taken.** For example, some dominant males bully, harass, and even bite lower-ranked males so often that the lower-ranked males are injured and driven away from food sources and basking sites.

Male-on-male territorial displays are characterized by head bobbing, dewlap extension, hissing, skin color changes, and feigned threats to bite or actual biting. Under natural rainforest conditions, these ritualized disputes rarely result in severe injury to either combatant because there is ample room for each to escape. (However, bites can be serious if they involve soft tissues, and limb fractures can result if one of the jousting males is forced from his perch and falls.) In the restricted space often afforded captive iguanas, the ability of a submissive male iguana to escape badgering is limited, and the psychic stress that attends such subjugation and frequent challenges for basking space, food resources, and females diminishes the lower-ranked male's health.

When appropriate nesting sites are scarce, some female green iguanas have been observed exhibiting milder forms of territoriality by standing their ground and defending their nesting site when other females attempted to deposit their egg clutches in the same limited egg-depositing place.

In the rain forest there is infrequent competition for food, as this would be energetically wasteful and particularly unnecessary for herbivorous iguanas who can usually find adequate forage within their range—even if this range is not ideal from a dominant territorial perspective. Of primary concern to male iguanas, both captive and wild, are available perches and basking areas, both for basking and male "displaying." Each iguana seeks the "perfect" spot. Optimum digestion of food occurs at the higher temperatures available in the best perches and basking areas, and this enables peak utilization of nutrients which promotes faster growth and superior fitness. In turn, the larger, healthier iguanas have a higher likelihood for survival; and the fittest males secure choice mating territories and enough females to ensure their contribution to the genetic "pool" from which future generations will be drawn.

### Cannibalism

Although it would seem totally counterproductive to the survival of a species for it to engage in feeding upon its young, some iguanas do—

particularly the spiny-tailed iguana, *Ctenosaura similis* (Fitch and Henderson, 1978; Mitchell, 1986; Mora, 1991). It has been suggested that cannibalism offers several advantages: it eliminates potential competitors and it benefits some members of a population during times of food scarcity in the wild when the young would find it difficult to survive (Mora, 1991). **Although not a common problem, cannibalism can occur with the green iguana, especially under conditions of overcrowding and/or population stress and also where small hatchlings are kept in the presence of large, aggressive males.** If given an opportunity, both male and female iguanas may consume the eggs of their own or another species; very rarely, however, will a female iguana eat her own eggs.

For additional information on the rich behavioral repertoire of iguanine lizards, refer to Auffenberg, 1982; Carpenter, 1982; Distel and Veazey, 1982; Drummond and Burghardt, 1982; Dugan, 1982; Dugan and Wiewandt, 1982; Gibbons and Watkins, 1982; Ryan, 1982; and Werner, 1982.

## HANDLING

The quality of the rapport between the pet iguana and the keeper depends upon the following:

- The quality of the iguana's "psychological" environment (specifically privacy, which is enhanced by providing a hiding box)
- The keeper's knowledge of an iguana's natural behavior
- The frequency and type of interaction between the keeper and the iguana

The relationship you have with your iguana will be affected by how often you interact, whether or not your movements are intimidating, and the way you touch your pet.

Excepting physical contact during basking, mating, and territorial disputes, mutual touching is not noted to be a large part of an iguana's usual communications. So, for the captive iguana, the human touch may be perceived as anything from an attack to a minor annoyance. Still, it is apparent that once tame, pet iguanas like being gently stroked on some areas of their bodies; therefore **between you and your iguana, touch is a major means of communication.** Teach your pet to associate human hands not only with feeding, but also with the pleasant sensation of being caressed. You can convey kindness and reassurance of your familiarity through your touch. This is easily done! Realize that the pet iguana is sentient, can experience fear, and is aware of its captivity. Care for your pet, and the right touch will follow naturally. Once an iguana is accustomed to interaction with people, the question, "How much handling is too much?" is determined by its behavior. Generally, tame iguanas can be handled frequently (if done considerately) as long as the iguana is healthy, is at ease, and is feeding regularly.

## LIFTING AND CARRYING

When picking up a green iguana, it is helpful to understand the arboreal adaptions of this lizard. In nature, green iguanas are most secure at heights, usually resting on the elevated branches of a tree. The lengthy digits of the rear limbs and the claws are ideal for climbing. Each claw can be described as having a "lock-release" mechanism. When iguanas descend a tree trunk or branch, they ease themselves down by alternately locking in and releasing the claws. Even the tail presses against the tree for stability and does not hang uselessly. If the iguana becomes insecure in its position or feels threatened, it will tighten its grip on a surface (including your hand or arm) by digging in with its claws. This is important to remember when approaching an iguana, especially a hatchling. As the iguana grows, its claws become large and sharp defensive instruments. They can be clipped at intervals, or protective caps called Soft-Paws® (which are designed to keep cats from damaging persons and objects with their sharp claws) can be applied (Rossi, 1984). Also see Care of Claws, Chapter 9. The limbs and toes of a baby iguana are particularly fragile, and care must be taken when lifting it from the branch, clothing, upholstery, or other surface to which it is clinging.

Ease a finger under each hand or foot to disengage the claws from the surface while keeping the other hand in front of the iguana's head. **Iguanas do not like to be grabbed around the neck or midsection from above.**

Be a passive handler. Allow your iguana to climb onto you by easing your hand anteriorly (toward its head) under the forelimbs (Figure 1.14a).

If your iguana turns away or tries to avoid you, persist with patience. Gently corner the iguana, making it necessary for it to climb onto you. At this point, if your pet is nervous and jumpy, you will need to hold onto it. **Never grab an iguana, large or small, tame or wild, by the tail.** The idea is to let the iguana feel it is being supported rather than being caught.

If an iguana feels caught, it will usually writhe and wriggle in an attempt to get free. In this case, do not drop the iguana, but maintain a firm but gentle hold on the thoracic and pelvic regions with the limbs pinioned (as described in Restraint in this chapter) until the iguana becomes calm (Figure 1.14d).

Once the iguana is at ease, slowly release your hold, and encourage it to climb from one hand to the other or to sit on your shoulder. Your shoulder is an attractive place to an iguana. The top of your head is even better. To discourage the iguana from climbing on your face to get to the top of your head (which it will eventually try to do), place your hand between the iguana's face and yours.

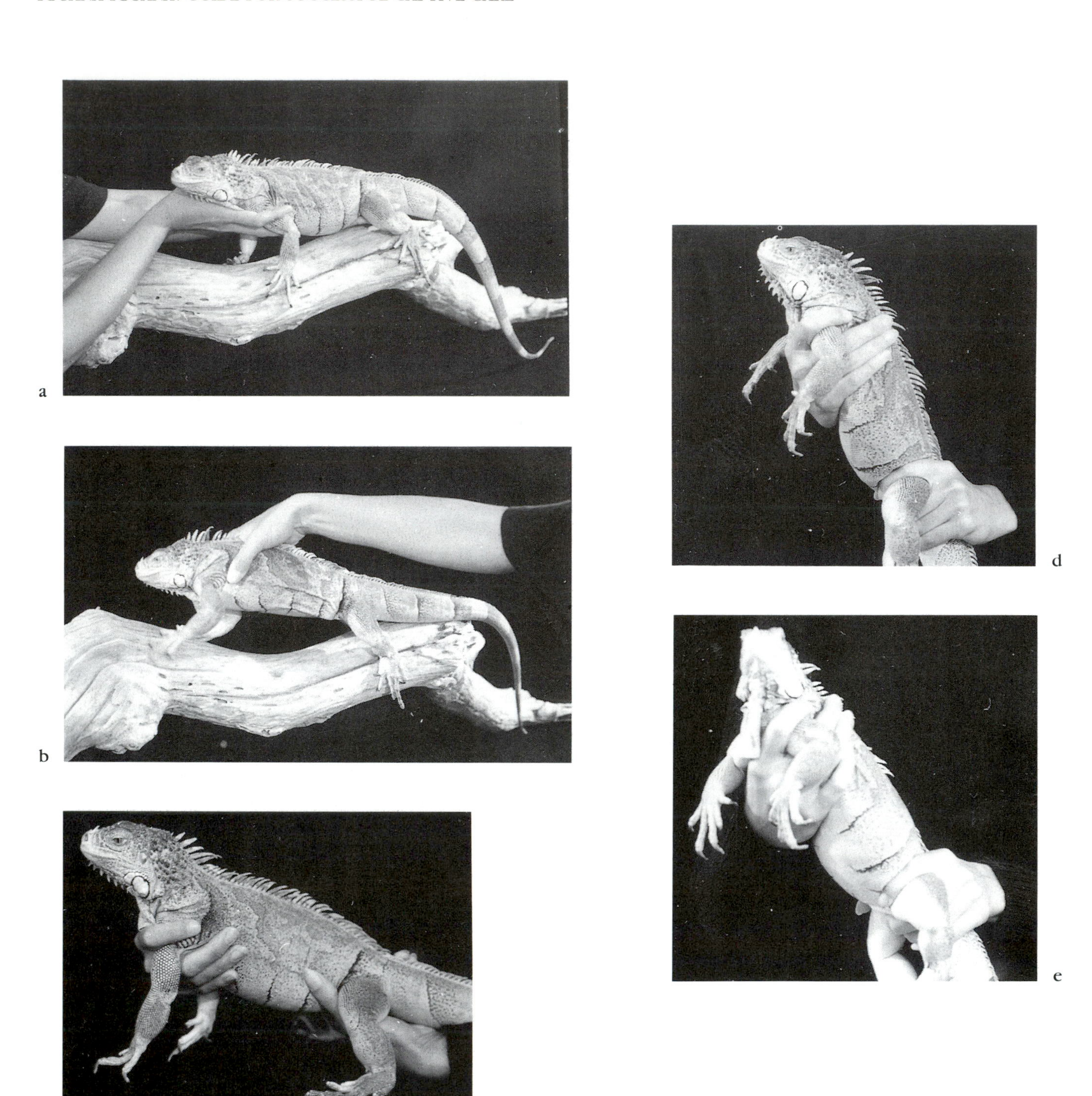

**Figure 1.14a–e.** Sequence of photographs illustrating handling and safe restraint of an iguana. Note how the iguana grasps the branch when it is picked up from above. The limbs of iguana in 1.14d are held firmly so that it cannot struggle free; however the legs are not folded over its spine (which could result in limb injuries). Photo credit: Wendy Townsend.

## RESTRAINT

Green iguanas bear sharp claws on each of their digits, and they possess powerful tails with which they can flail predators and anyone who handles them carelessly. Their claws can inflict severe lacerations on the arms, neck, and face of the unwary person, but protective soft plastic caps can be applied to the sharp tips of larger iguanas' claws so that they can no longer scratch so severely. They often become accustomed to being handled and are tolerant of manipulation, but it is important to know how to properly restrain these powerful iguanas so that neither they nor their human handler is injured.

Generally, it is the claws and tail that are employed in defense. When tail lashing and scratching have failed to dissuade a handler, and when given the opportunity, a defensive iguana may try to bite. Although iguanas are almost exclusively vegetarians, their teeth can inflict severe wounds. **Therefore, the four limbs must be held against the iguana's body with the head directed away from the handler in such a way that the claw-tipped feet and sharp teeth cannot be used in defense.**

If an iguana is clinging to a wire mesh screen or woven cloth surface, carefully disengage its claws before lifting it. If it is merely plucked from the screen or fabric, its claws may be torn out or its toes may sustain fractures. ***IT IS EXTREMELY IMPORTANT WHEN GRASPING AN IGUANA'S LIMBS NOT TO EXERT EXCESSIVE FORCE ON THE LOWER PORTION OF THE LIMBS, i.e., THE HANDS OR FEET, BECAUSE IT IS RELATIVELY EASY TO CAUSE FRACTURES OF THE UPPER SEGMENTS (THE ARMS OR THIGHS, RESPECTIVELY).*** All that is necessary is to pinion the limbs against the body wall.

If all else fails and an agitated iguana must be restrained, wrap it up in a cloth towel so that its limbs, neck, and body are held firmly, leaving only its head and tail exposed. If required, its limbs can be strapped against its body wall with cloth or gauze, or, alternatively, the entire iguana can be confined to a length of stockinette or even a toeless cotton sock. Sticky adhesive, masking, duct, or transparent tapes should not be used because the adhesive removes the superficial epidermis where it is in contact with the skin.

A method that I have described for short-time restraint (Frye, 1973, 1981, 1991a, 1994a) relies upon a nervous response, called the *vago-vagal* effect, which slows the iguana's heart rate, lowers its blood pressure, and induces a brief period of nonchemical torpor (Figure 1.15a & b). It can be applied repeatedly without ill effects. One iguana, which I used to teach the technique to veterinary students, was subjected at least twice weekly for over 4 years by about 20 students during each session. He finally got so accustomed to being used for this maneuver that as soon as he was removed from his cage and placed on the lecture demonstration table, he would relax, close his eyes and, seemingly, go to sleep all by himself! The

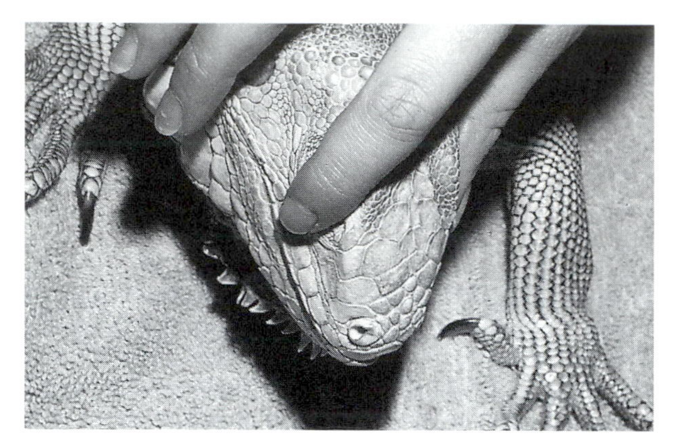

**Figure 1.15a.** Inducing the vago-vagal reflex requires application of mild, steady digital pressure to the closed eyes for 30–45 seconds.

**Figure 1.15b.** This recumbent iguana is reacting to the vago-vagal reflex, which is used to induce short-term restraint. This maneuver is used for nonpainful procedures, such as obtaining motion-free X-ray photographs.

vago-vagal maneuver is safe and effective, but the technique should not be employed by untrained persons because, if applied incorrectly, delicate structures could be injured.

## BITING

Iguanas have powerful jaw muscles and many small, sharp teeth lining the upper and lower jaws. A large iguana is capable of giving a painful, damaging bite—but so is a cat or a dog. Green iguanas are generally nonaggressive. Unless you have a wild-caught or untamed iguana, you probably will not be bitten. A newly acquired young iguana may try to bite defensively or when it is hungry; some iguanas can be provoked into biting if they are persistently annoyed. Mature male iguanas have been observed biting on objects (including other iguanas and human hands) that have recently been in contact with either a mature receptive female or another mature male iguana. Such behavior is probably due to the presence of pheromones generally associated with sexual activity. You should always wash your hands thoroughly after handling each iguana (especially sexually mature male iguanas).

**Bite attempts are usually both predictable and avoidable. If your pet iguana bites you, it will be because you threatened or angered it.**

In our coauthored book, Wendy Townsend cautioned against kissing an iguana or approaching its head too closely with your face because the iguana may mistake your show of affection as a threat to its safety, and it may defend itself by biting. Several of my clients have sustained serious facial injuries when they failed to heed this warning. Whether or not these iguanas were used to being kissed, it is likely that the stress of being taken out of their homes, as well as enduring whatever illnesses they were suffering from, left them more than unreceptive to kissing. Also, the mere presence of a face with two large eyes so close to them may have been perceived as an immediate threat.

Although iguanas possess well-ordered brains (at least for reptiles), they still are not intellectually "gifted." Some people who become fond of their iguanas inevitably feel the need to bestow a few kisses on their pets. This is certainly understandable, but remember that this human expression of affection is likely to be perceived as an act of aggression rather than affection by an iguana either unaccustomed to such contact or under duress. When owners enthusiastically smother their tiny new pets with kisses, the iguanas usually close both of their eyes and then become motionless, probably waiting to be eaten. In time, most iguanas lose their fear of being close to the human face.

To prevent biting, I recommend a more gradual approach to familiarizing your pet iguana with yourself via the following:

- Always speak softly.
- Handle it gently and regularly.
- Hand-feed your iguana to increase its confidence in you.
- Reserve kisses for thoroughly tame iguanas.

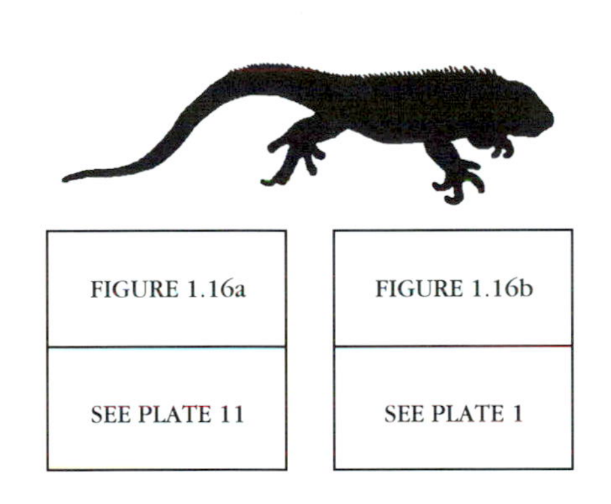

FIGURE 1.16a

SEE PLATE 11

FIGURE 1.16b

SEE PLATE 1

FIGURE 1.16c

SEE PLATE 2

## HAND FEEDING

**Hand feeding is an excellent way to hasten acclimation.** When your iguana accepts food from your hand, a rewarding, mutually satisfying association occurs (Figure 1.16a, b & c). Most hand-fed iguanas come to expect such treatment and may not feed as heartily when simply left with a meal, no matter how appetizing.

## "DIFFICULT" IGUANAS

"Difficult" iguanas are those that have been mishandled, deeply traumatized, or taken from the wild as adults. Such iguanas may never become good pets, but, as captives, they deserve proper care nevertheless. Most prospective iguana keepers will want to avoid acquiring "difficult" iguanas which are characterized by a defensive or fearful response to human presence. Still, there are some people who feel compassion for mistreated or unfortunate living things (no matter how wretched they may seem to others) and feel challenged to "rehabilitate" or otherwise provide a kind environment for such animals.

## Observed Behavior of "Difficult" Iguanas

"Difficult" iguanas possess individual personalities. Some become more sociable towards people than others. A particularly aggressive adult male may acquire a specific dislike for certain people; and, whenever these people enter a room where the iguana can see them, there is an immediate hostile response consisting of overtly aggressive head bobbing, dewlap displays, and a sudden open-mouth rush towards the perceived enemy. These are **not** sham feints; the iguanas performing these aggressive acts can and will deliver severe bites if given the opportunity.

For some "difficult" iguanas, trust of human hands has never been established (perhaps due to insufficient or improper contact). The "out-of-control" iguana that flees headlong, crashing into the walls of its enclosure, is terrified; a hiding box is particularly crucial for it. When picked up, the frightened iguana typically goes through several behavioral postures. After writhing or spinning in an attempt to escape, it will "freeze," suddenly becoming pliant and motionless. Wide, unblinking eyes, a retracted dewlap, and an absence of tongue flicking are usually noted. Nervous twitching of the tail may be the only movement. It may change from being immobile to making a frantic attempt to escape, lunging away from the handler. If this fails, it may become defensive by extending its dewlap, puffing up its body by inhalation, and expelling the air in a hiss. Tail lashing and attempts to bite may accompany this defensive behavior.

A "difficult" iguana may not adapt to even the most innovative captive husbandry: the cage may be large and furnished with luxuriant living foliage; it may be warm and properly humid; the diet may be perfect; the cage mates may be compatible; yet it incessantly paces the inner perimeter and abrades its nose against the interior of the cage. This "difficult" iguana may eventually accept captivity, but if it does not, it may be more humane to try to find it another home, preferably one offering outdoor housing. I can recall two "difficult" male iguanas—one in Florida and another in California—that were eventually relocated to new owners who were willing and able to provide them with large enclosures planted with living, edible foliage; both iguanas soon calmed down and, when provided with adult females, sired young.

## Suggestions for Handling "Difficult" Iguanas

- Let the iguana feel supported rather than caught, when holding it, by becoming gently—but firmly—like a somewhat confining branch.
- Try to calm the iguana by stroking its dewlap area.
- Encourage the iguana to tongue flick your finger (an association between human scent and a nonharmful, pleasant touch may form), while being careful of bite attempts.

- Schedule handling sessions for the convenience of the handler, but keep in mind that they should be somewhat regular, not excessively long, and not within an hour of the iguana's mealtime. For example, try two 10-minute sessions daily for 2 or 3 weeks. (This is also a good handling schedule for newly acquired iguanas.)

### Suggestions for Feeding "Difficult" Iguanas

- At feeding time, do not **capture** the iguana, but do try to hand-feed it.
- Hold a little of the food between the dish and the iguana.
- Move closer to the iguana with the food, and wait a minute.
- If the iguana won't accept the offer, or flees, put the food down and slowly withdraw your hand.
- Back away from the enclosure until the iguana eats voluntarily. You may have to leave the room.

# CHAPTER 2

## HUSBANDRY

### HOUSING

#### Basic Considerations

To avoid having to purchase and set up progressively larger tanks to accommodate an iguana's increasing size, initially invest in a glass or plexiglass tank of no less than a 220-liter (55-gallon) capacity. Other options are to construct a cage of similar volume, or to purchase and convert a used commercial showcase or similar glass-fronted container.

When constructing an enclosure, vinyl-coated steel hardware cloth with half-inch mesh is recommended for all parts of a cage that are to be screened (for example, a lid or door). Chicken wire will not confine a small iguana, and regular window screening is not satisfactory because the small iguana will inevitably catch one or more of its claws in its fine woven mesh.

Generally, iguanas should not be kept in the same enclosure with other animals, particularly birds and other reptile species (even other lizards), because of the possibility of transferring pathogenic bacteria or protozoa between them. Also, interspecies intimidation or even predation can occur when various animals of different species, classes, or body sizes are mixed. Lastly, combining different species usually complicates the task of maintaining cage hygiene.

As male iguanas mature and develop their territorial hierarchies, they become quite aggressive to any other iguanas of their species, even hatchlings (which they have been known to attack and eat). Therefore, **mature males should not be housed with other smaller iguanas of either sex unless it has been determined that the smaller male or female is recognized and accepted by the male**. Most females are tolerant of each other, but may display aggression at the time they deposit their eggs if adequate nesting material and space are not provided.

The size and conformation of accommodations for keeping captive iguanas depend upon the following:

- The kind and gender(s) of iguanas that will be housed together.
- The size of the animals at present and the size attained at maturity.
- The number of iguanas that will be sharing the cage or enclosure.
- Whether the enclosure will be an indoors or outdoors structure.

- The climatic conditions to which the iguana will be exposed throughout the year, taking into careful account extremes of hot and cold weather. Generally, they prefer an environmental temperature of from 28 °C to 36 °C (82 °F to approximately 97 °F).

### Outdoor Enclosures

Ideal outdoor housing arrangements for a captive iguana must have a ground area where it can eat, drink, and toilet. Broad-leaf trees such as mulberry (particularly the weeping variety) or hibiscus are perfect because not only do they provide shade and basking areas but, in addition, their leaves, blossoms, and fruit (pods in hibiscus) are edible and nutritious for iguanas. At least a sturdy *nonresinous* tree branch or similar structure upon which the iguana can climb and bask in the sun is essential. Large dog houses or similar shelters can be used to provide additional shade as well as privacy.

When planning an outdoor enclosure, ask yourself: Could a free-roaming dog, raccoon, opossum, or coyote gain access to the yard? Smaller iguanas periodically fall prey to pet or feral cats and, depending on the location, the possibility of an iguana being carried off by a raptor such as a hawk or owl is not out of the question. If these mishaps are even remotely likely to happen, you should construct a particularly sturdy enclosure with some provision for screening out cats, foxes, weasels, skunks, raccoons, hawks, owls, crows, ravens, magpies, and bluejays. At any rate, only large iguanas with at least a 36-cm (14-inch) snout-to-vent length (SVL) should be allowed to roam an open outdoor area unattended.

Because they are usually incapable of reducing their deep-core body temperature if overheated except by seeking shade or resorting to a modified kind of panting respiration, iguanas are subject to hyperthermia (abnormally high body temperature) and death if exposed to sustained temperatures exceeding 39 °C (102.2 °F). In very warm climates, outdoor enclosures must be shaded to prevent heat stress.

### Indoor Cages

Indoor caging accommodations can be nearly as satisfactory as outdoor quarters if they are equipped with the following:

- A system for controlling light and temperature
- An appropriate ultraviolet light source
- A heat lamp or other heat-producing device
- A feeding platform or other arrangement from which the iguana can eat food uncontaminated by litter materials
- A water pan for drinking and/or bathing
- A hiding box for privacy
- Suitable doors that are sufficiently large to permit servicing

## Providing a Visual Barrier

It is important that a visual barrier be included at the periphery of the cage or enclosure in order to prevent the iguana from striking and/or rubbing its nose as it explores its captive surroundings. A barrier can consist of opaque tape, Mylar® film, construction paper, paint, etc. The width of the barrier depends on the size of the iguana(s) and the individual circumstances of the caging. Generally, a barrier of from 15–45 cm (6–18 inches) is sufficient to block the view through a large transparent terrarium or enclosure. The barrier should be affixed to the outside of the tank so that the interior can be cleaned without disturbing the opaque surface. If an iguana persists in digging or nose rubbing, it is likely that something is either lacking or distressing within its enclosure. Insufficient hiding or refuge areas, intimidation by a dominant cage mate, or even something within the iguana's view may cause anxiety. Careful observation and experimentation with housing adjustments are likely to resolve the problem and help the restless iguana adjust to captivity.

## Providing Light and Heat

Iguanas are natives of tropical zones and will not thrive—or even survive—if they are subjected to low environmental temperatures. If the daytime or nighttime temperatures are expected to drop below 23.3 °C (74 °F), all outdoor and indoor enclosures must be provided with supplementary heating in the form of radiant heat from overhead nonilluminating infrared heat lamps, ceramic devices (e.g., Pearlco® bulbs), or other form of warmth; heating pads; or subsurface circulated warmth such as closed-circuit water heating coils. (See Sources For Reptile-Related Products at the end of this book.)

All lighting fixtures and heating devices must be installed so that the iguanas cannot come into direct contact with them and so that water cannot be accidentally splashed on hot surfaces. All electrical wiring must be well insulated and installed according to existing building codes.

Regardless of the brand and size of the artificial source of ultraviolet illumination, it is highly desirable to select a tube or bulb that is coated on its inner surface with 2096 light-emitting phosphor (Barnard et al., 1991). Presently, Sylvania produces a 15-watt fluorescent tube that has this phosphor. Barnard et al. recommend that iguanas be exposed to a photoperiod of 12 hours light and 12 hours dark using these tubes.

Pearlco® bulbs are ceramic devices that produce only heat. They have a considerably longer service life than conventional heat lamps and therefore are more economical because of their enhanced efficiency. The savings in electrical rates and the longer service-life of these ceramic devices will help pay for the initial price difference between a less expensive (and less efficient) conventional spotlight and this more expensive (but more efficient) nonilluminating ceramic product.

Whatever types of heating devices are used, they should be fitted into metallic reflectors which help direct the bulbs' thermal output onto a narrower cone of focused warmth. Also, they should be suspended approximately 0.5–1.0 meter (19.5–39 inches) above the indoor or outdoor enclosure, depending on the rated capacity.

Automatic light timers are readily available and are ideal for controlling incandescent lighting and photoperiod; special electronic rheostatic controllers designed for fluorescent tubes are expensive and difficult to obtain except on special order. A thermostat is used to control the other heat-producing devices.

A small domestic heating pad can be used. For large areas, a bigger waterbed heater, a hog-farrowing blanket (designed to provide additional warmth for newborn piglets), or heat tapes can be substituted.

Heating pads should be covered by a large piece of artificial turf to prevent thermal burns. When used with a terrarium or other small cage, the domestic electrical heating pad should be placed **beneath** the cage bottom rather than inside the cage.

An area of approximately 0.75 square meter (2 square feet) warmed by a 100-watt standard light bulb, a 75-watt red spot bulb, a 40–60 watt Pearlco® ceramic heating device fitted into an aluminum reflector, or a subsurface heating pad set at approximately 33 °C (92 °F) can support two adult iguanas.

### Examples of Outdoor and Indoor Enclosures

The following diagrams (Figure 2.1 & 2.2) and information are examples of various environments (adapted from Frye and Townsend, 1993).

- A 4-foot Vitalite® (or equivalent fixture) hangs over the dog house, approximately 46–61 cm (18–24 inches) above the iguanas' basking sites. These fluorescent fixtures are placed as close to the iguanas as possible, but are not within their reach. They can be mounted immediately above the hardware-cloth-covered ceiling of the cage; the beneficial ultraviolet radiation is not diminished significantly by being transmitted across the woven wire "cloth." The fixtures are mounted outside the cage which prevents the iguanas from actually coming into physical contact with them.
- Two red incandescent spotlights (one 75 watts, the other 250 watts) are suspended from plant hooks secured in the ceiling above the woven hardware-cloth top of the cage. Alternatively, one of these light-emitting heat bulbs could be replaced with a nonilluminating ceramic fixture such as a Pearlco® bulb rated at

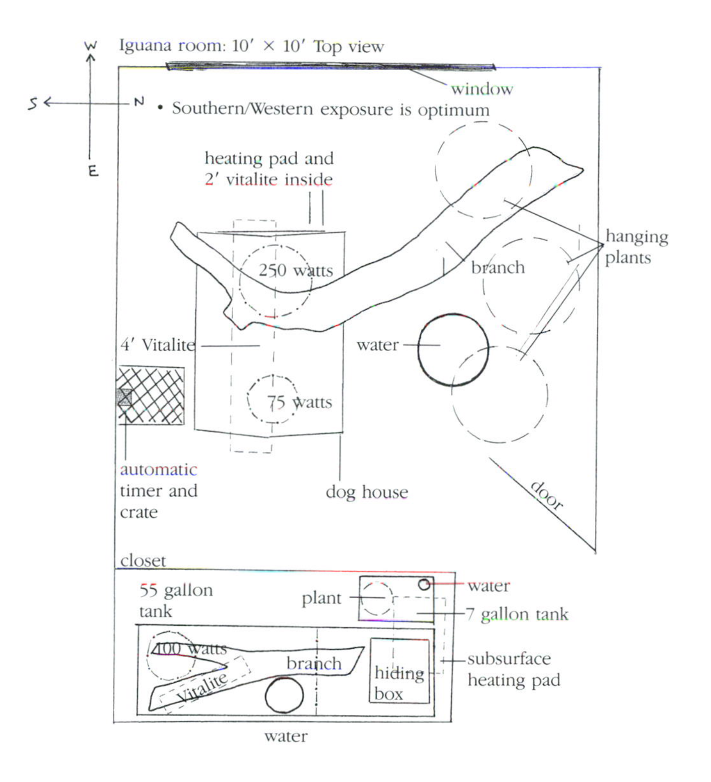


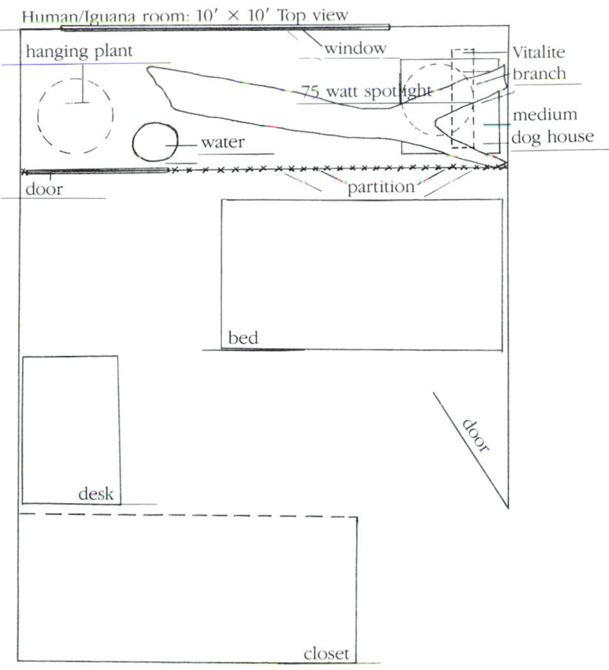


An easily built chicken wire and two-by-four partition with a walk-in door designates the iguana area. The floor of the lizard's area can be covered with artificial turf and newspapers.

Shows the same dimensions as iguana room on left. A relatively small room but up to 3 large iguanas and one person can share the space comfortably. This is a great arrangement for a child—to share his or her room with such fascinating pets!

Human/Iguana room: front view. Lighting cords are affixed to first the ceiling and then the wall after being pushed through the screening.

**Figure 2.1.** Diagrams of indoor enclosures that were designed by Wendy Townsend for her iguanas.

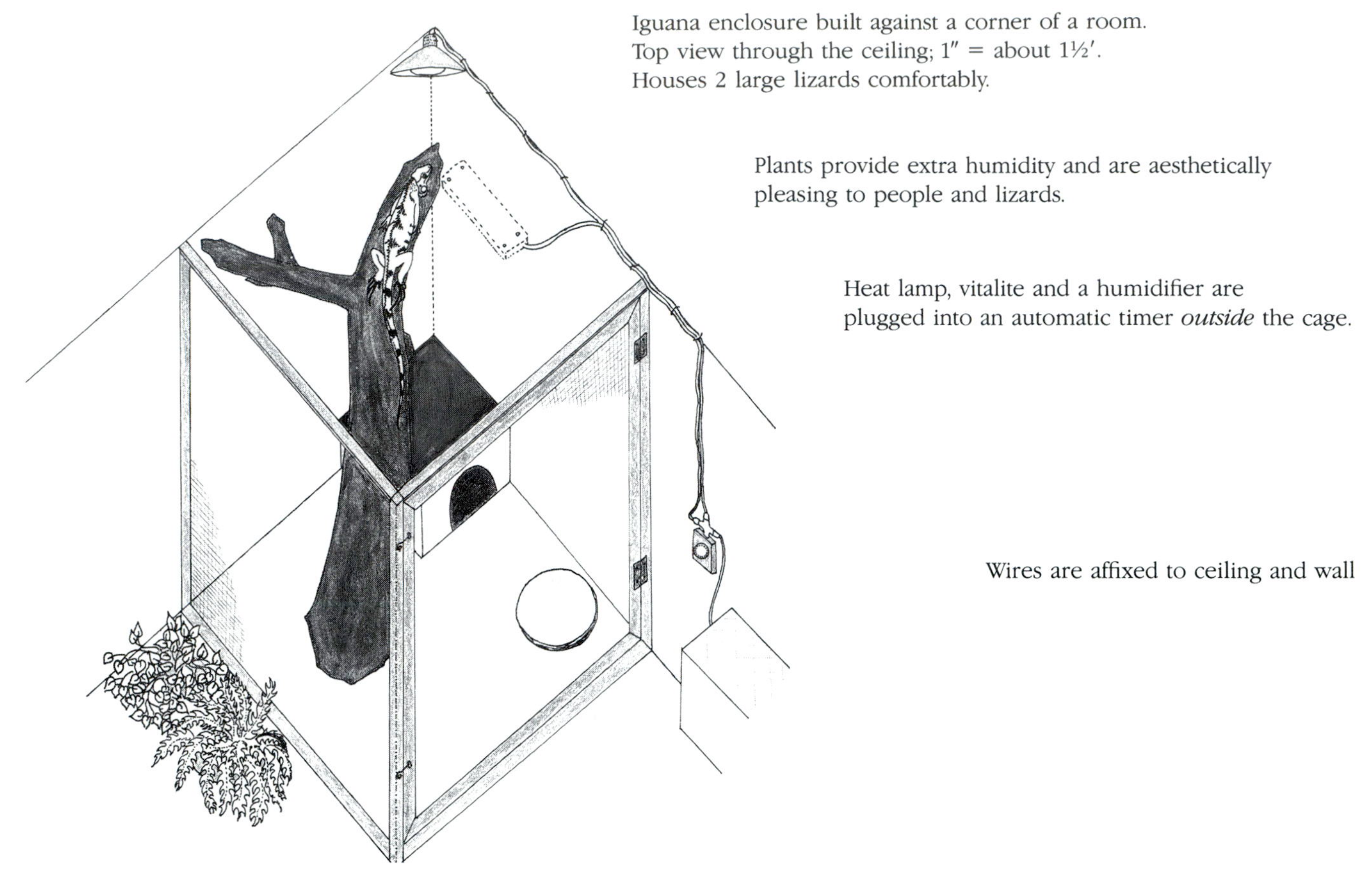


**Figure 2.2.** A relatively simple indoor set-up that utilizes existing floor, ceiling, and two walls to form a large enclosure. Illustration by Wendy Townsend.

from 40–100 watts, depending on the required thermal output. Be careful not to provide *too much* heating capacity.

- On warm days, the window is kept open, and the iguanas receive about an hour of unfiltered sunshine through the window screen; this unfiltered ultraviolet light is necessary for the iguanas to synthesize their own vitamin $D_3$ naturally. (The invisible portion of the spectrum of natural sunlight is partially filtered by window glass and by most clear plastic.)
- A 2-foot full-spectrum fluorescent fixture hangs inside the dog house; a radiant heating pad set on a low temperature is on the floor.
- A standard 100-watt light bulb (or a 20–40-watt Pearlco® ceramic bulb in a reflector fixture) and a 2-foot Vitalite® rest on the upper metal screen of a 220-liter (approximately 55-gallon) tank in the closet or on a stand.

- If the screen is made of plastic rather than woven metal wire, it will eventually deteriorate because of the effects of the ultraviolet light; therefore, replace woven plastic cloth with aluminum or a woven metallic wire product.
- One part of a heating pad set on a low temperature is placed underneath the large tank, and the other part is under a portion of a 28-liter (approximately 7-gallon) tank which houses a hatchling iguana.
- Small pieces of scrap wood should be used as spacers or risers at the corners of each tank so that they are elevated and are not actually touching the heating pads.
- All incandescent lights and heating pads are connected to an automatic timer which is enclosed by a plastic milk crate kept against the wall by the dog house. Plastic safety plugs are inserted in or tape is placed over unused wall sockets.
- The roof and the floor of the dog house are covered with artificial turf.
- There are both a large water bowl and a few newspapered toilet areas.
- A 2.7-meter (9-foot) long, 20-cm (8-inch) thick branch rests partly on the floor and partly on the dog house.
- Three giant pothos plants hang from the ceiling; they are misted periodically, as are the iguanas. Another small pothos plant is in the 28-liter (7-gallon) tank for the hatchling. Although pothos is a mildly noxious plant (like its *Philodendron* cousins), many iguanas eagerly eat its leaves.

Four large iguanas, one male and three females, share the room. They alternate using the inside of the dog house as they please.

Three smaller iguanas, two females and one male, live within the 225-liter (55-gallon) tank, protected from the largest male. The hatchling is taken outside at least every other day for no less than 15 minutes of sunshine, as no Vitalite® is set up for his tank. Periodically, the iguanas in the large tank also go out for some sunshine. Although the iguanas in the closet and in the room are all aware of each other, the closet doors provide a visual barrier; therefore stress due to territorial activity is minimized. Eventually, the two smaller females will be recognized by the male and will be allowed to occupy the room. The small male will neither grow significantly bigger nor be tolerated by the larger male. (This little male's name is Peanut, and his story is included in Chapter 11.) He is frequently given free range of the apartment as a break from his limited quarters. Depending upon the season, and changes in the iguanas' social behavior and needs, the red spot lights are moved to different warm perches. A large, covered cat box full a damp sand and sphagnum moss is available for gravid females to excavate their nests.

Numerous indoor housing arrangements can be devised by using an existing room and modifying it for sheltering one or several adult iguanas. However, smaller iguanas (less than about 30-cm or 12-inch SVL) should be kept safely in terraria until they outgrow their quarters; then they can be moved.

When setting up an indoor room, determine if an iguana could climb any furniture or drapery to get to an open or poorly screened window and escape. If it could escape, rearrange the room, keeping in mind that iguanas can leap a fair distance.

One of the most innovative "caging" systems that I have seen in an apartment was one that Taryn Hook-Merdes created for her single adult female and two adult male iguanas who would not tolerate each other within a shared territory. A bedroom was divided with a vertical panel that was secured to the floor and ceiling so as to make two habitats of nearly equal dimensions (Figure 2.3). The vertical panels were painted with a mural of rainforest images by Ms. Hook-Merdes's sister, Mara. Without disturbing them, humans could observe the iguanas on either side of the floor-to-ceiling divider through small glass viewing ports built into the divider. Each half of the room was furnished with carpeted "cat trees" which had been equipped with plastic-embedded, thermostatically con-

**Figure 2.3.** An innovative indoor environment for three mature iguanas (2 males and 1 female) that was created by dividing an apartment's bedroom. Note the carpeted cat "trees," heat-producing spotlights over basking sites, overhead full-spectrum ultraviolet tubes, hanging plants, and the decorated room divider that separates the two aggressive and territorial males. Each half of the divided room is equipped with its own humidifier. A tape recorder plays rain forest sounds which can be heard in both rooms.

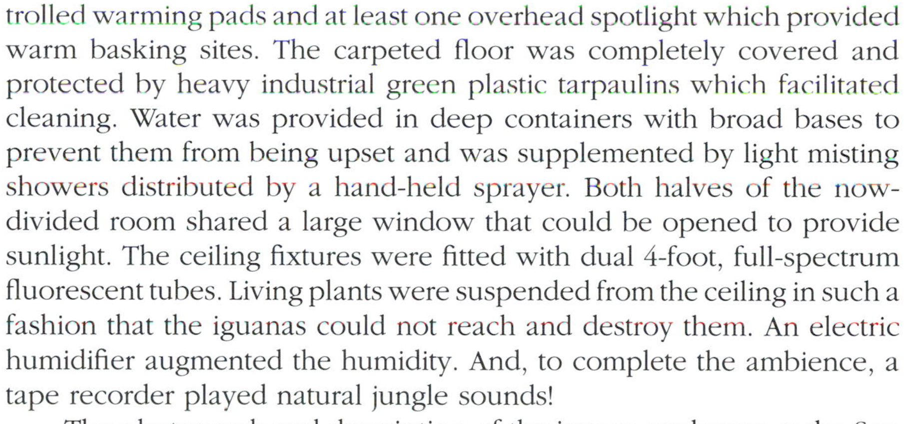

trolled warming pads and at least one overhead spotlight which provided warm basking sites. The carpeted floor was completely covered and protected by heavy industrial green plastic tarpaulins which facilitated cleaning. Water was provided in deep containers with broad bases to prevent them from being upset and was supplemented by light misting showers distributed by a hand-held sprayer. Both halves of the now-divided room shared a large window that could be opened to provide sunlight. The ceiling fixtures were fitted with dual 4-foot, full-spectrum fluorescent tubes. Living plants were suspended from the ceiling in such a fashion that the iguanas could not reach and destroy them. An electric humidifier augmented the humidity. And, to complete the ambience, a tape recorder played natural jungle sounds!

FIGURE 2.4

SEE PLATE 2

The photograph and description of the iguana enclosure at the San Diego Zoological Gardens exemplifies an excellent captive environment for iguanas (Figure 2.4). Obviously, this kind of enclosure is not possible in the typical household; however, such an arrangement can be scaled down to fit individual housing situations. For instance, a modest outdoor aviary-type enclosure does not occupy much area, can be constructed in an attractive manner, and, when thoughtfully designed, actually enhances the landscaping.

### Is a "Cageless" Setup Indoors Desirable?

However well pet iguanas adjust to their confines, they don't especially like enclosures and may spend considerable time pacing and digging at the boundaries as long as they can see that they are confined. Therefore, I recommend that a "cageless" setup be planned for iguanas that have not adapted well to captivity. Once out of a cage, the pacing ceases. Because iguanas do not require vast amounts of open space to be "happy," they usually remain within a designated area which they have selected; such an area includes heat, security, and food.

**WARNING: IF YOU DECIDE TO ALLOW YOUR PET IGUANA TO ROAM FREELY, YOU ALSO MUST PREVENT IT FROM CONTAMINATING ANY AREAS WHERE FOOD FOR HUMANS IS PREPARED OR CONSUMED.**

You should not become overly concerned, but be aware of **any** potential hazard to your pet.

There are leashes and adjustable harnesses (Figure 2.5) that have been specifically designed for restraining iguanas and similar large lizards during outdoor excursions. These devices, which are both humane and practical, are highly recommended and are readily available from pet dealers and mail-order reptile equipment sources (see Sources For Reptile-Related Products at the end of this book).

Though iguanas spend most of their time quietly basking or remaining within their "area," they will leave a favored spot to go elsewhere to drink, eat, or eliminate. They might decide to explore beyond their usual

**Figure 2.5.** A soft adjustable leash can help restrain your iguana when it is taken outdoors.

boundaries. Therefore, if your precious collection of glass ornaments is accessible to iguanas, whose fault is it if something is damaged? To avoid unfortunate accidents keep fragile or valued objects out of reach.

When pet iguanas stray from their usual area, they may be looking for a secure place to hide. If there is no suitable hiding place within their own designated area, they may pace and/or dig at the area's boundaries, especially if they can see a corner or a shelf someplace else that seems attractive. Bird houses or cardboard boxes make good hiding places for small iguanas. Dog houses and airline shipping crates (available in different sizes) make excellent hiding places for larger iguanas. If necessary, these containers can be placed on an appropriate raised surface over a heating pad or other adjustable source of mild to moderate warmth to make them a refuge into which an iguana will readily retreat for security.

Toward the end of daylight, even in an artificially illuminated environment, green iguanas begin to seek out what they perceive to be a safe place to sleep. In the wild, this would be a branch high off the ground draped by the foliage of other branches. Before settling upon the right sleeping place, your iguana(s) might seek out particular cabinets, closets, shelves, or even drapery valances and cornices that look appealing. Some owners allow their iguanas to share their bed with them. The disadvantages of this sleeping arrangement are discussed in Chapter 10.

Iguanas have good spatial recollection and sense of direction. In an apartment or home, they remember having seen spaces behind closed doors, beneath the covers of a partially made bed, etc., and will persist at getting into a desired location. So, if your iguana wanders off and you can't find it, search in all the "wrong" places!

## WATER

Whatever the accommodations are, there must be provision for adequate fresh water at all times. Much of an iguana's metabolic requirement for water is obtained from the moisture contained in the leafy vegetation and soft fruits upon which it subsists, but it also will drink considerable volumes of fresh water. It is not an iguana's nature to drink from standing vessels of water; rather, it is accustomed to imbibing drops of rain water or condensed mist from leaves in its immediate environment. However, some captive iguanas will learn to drink from water dishes. (This will be discussed in greater detail later in this chapter.)

Ideally, large enclosures should be fitted with a drainage system so that thorough cleansing of the cage can be facilitated. The inner surfaces of the cage should be treated to make them impervious to water; this treatment should be nontoxic, and the entire enclosure should be completely aired so that any noxious fumes or vapors are permitted to "outgas" and escape.

## PHOTOPERIOD

Because they are native to near-equatorial latitudes, **most iguanas and their immediate lizard cousins require a daily photoperiod (amount of light relative to amount of dark) of approximately 12-14 hours of light to 10-12 hours of dark.** This is now recognized as an important factor in maintaining these animals in health and enhancing the likelihood of captive breeding. **Keeping green iguanas in 24 hours of light daily is harmful: it will lead to declining health and will inhibit reproduction.**

Automatic light timers are ideal for conveniently maintaining an established photoperiod. They are inexpensive and readily available at hardware stores.

## VENTILATION

Although the green iguana originates from relatively humid habitats, **artificial habitats must afford adequate air circulation so that the interiors of the cages never become overly moist and fetid.** A few small, screened holes at the lower portion of the cage and a few more at the top permit a natural upward air flow that carries surplus moisture upward and out from the cage. Appropriate exhaust fans can handle the necessary air flow in large enclosures.

## WASTE MANAGEMENT

Iguanas are clean animals and have no distinct body odor that is discernible to humans. They lift their tails clear during defecation, but may later scatter feces, food, or anything else in their path of activity. A vacuum cleaner is invaluable for periodic cleanings and does not bother the iguanas. While iguanas cannot be disciplined to toilet like a cat or dog, they will generally use a particular place repeatedly. A tray of sand, kitty litter, alfalfa pellets, or strategically placed newspapers will facilitate cleaning chores. Remember, if newspaper is used to cover a toileting area, important paper documents must not be left unattended where they can be similarly soiled—few iguanas have learned to read! Droppings that miss the newspapers should be picked up with paper towels and disposed of in the toilet; the residue is easily removed with a bleach solution and sponge.

Some iguanas prefer to employ their waterbowl or your bathtub for a toileting site. **All wastes and the water from the iguana's water bowl should be disposed of in the toilet (*not* the kitchen sink).** Feces, urinary wastes, uneaten food, remnants of shed skin, moist cage-litter materials, etc. provide a fertile medium in which disease-causing bacteria and fungi can thrive, and fecal wastes from worm-infected iguanas can serve to transmit parasites from one iguana to another.

Professional and sophisticated amateur herpetologists follow a routine cage cleaning and renovation program on a regular basis. This program also provides an opportunity to record feeding and elimination by individual animals so that any abnormalities in intake or output become immediately apparent. One or two bowel movements daily, depending upon the iguana's growth, can be considered normal and healthy elimination.

All utensils that are employed for cleaning cages should be thoroughly cleansed after each use before being used in another cage. A solution of common household bleach (sodium hypochlorite) is recommended for this purpose because it is highly effective against a wide variety of disease-causing organisms. Generally, use the manufacturer's recommended dilutions for sanitation purposes. Similarly, all nondisposable plates used for feeding must be sanitized and rinsed well with fresh water before being returned to the cage.

If an outdoor enclosure is used to house iguanas, it is generally a good husbandry practice to move the site where food is offered daily so that there is no accumulation of uneaten food. Exposing these sites to unfiltered sunlight has a sanitizing effect.

It may seem that good iguana husbandry requires a great deal of time and effort. Depending upon the number of iguanas being kept, the basic maintenance routine is soon established, becomes second nature, and requires only a modest amount of time. While a lot of time is spent "playing" with iguanas, taking them out for sunshine, letting them swim in the bathtub, and also just sitting and watching them, you should expect to spend a minimum of 45 minutes every day maintaining the environment, feeding, and interacting with your iguana.

## ENVIRONMENTAL TEMPERATURE

All reptiles possess a critical high temperature beyond which they will perish. **Iguanas thermoregulate by behavior and can only warm up or cool down by moving close to or away from a given heat source.** Maintaining an iguana at or near its critical high temperature is stressful and should be avoided. Any enclosure for iguanas should afford a temperature gradient, giving them options. Although iguanas will move to shade or water to cool down, no object or surface that an iguana could possibly come into contact with should exceed 38 °C (100 °F) because it can be unwittingly burned. Green iguanas should be kept so that their warmest daytime temperature during the summer months is maintained at approximately 27–34 °C (80–94 °F). Some variance during the 12–14 hour day is desirable: the morning and later afternoon temperatures should be cooler than the midday temperature; this variance will encourage the iguanas to alter their activity patterns to include basking.

With outdoor enclosures, maintaining these optimal temperatures is relatively simple if sufficient shade is provided. Iguanas housed in outdoor habitats and exposed to natural sunlight and frequent natural or artificial rain showers are more likely to eat more enthusiastically and reproduce more readily.

Iguanas kept indoors will require more elaborate housing utilizing overhead heating lamps and/or subsurface heaters, full-spectrum ultraviolet illumination, and artificial incandescent lights to furnish "hot spots" in which they can bask and thermoregulate adequately to meet their temperature requirements. Several of these basking spots should be provided if more than one iguana is occupying the cage in order to help prevent disputes over favored territory where they can seek warmth.

## HUMIDITY

Because the native habitats of green iguanas are rain forests, the need for maintaining adequate humidity is important. **A high relative humidity of 85-95% is optimum for green iguanas.** When maintained in an environment with low relative humidity, iguanas may experience difficulty in shedding and may retain skin remnants around their toes (Figure 2.6) and tail. Also, because some moisture is normally lost when breathing, iguanas kept in dry air tend to lose more water; this must be replenished by drinking water and/or ingesting moisture-laden food.

FIGURE 2.6

SEE PLATE 11

High-moisture cage environments tend to foster the growth of pathogenic bacteria and fungi; therefore it is essential that the cage be maintained in a hygienic manner. Leftover food, feces, and urinary wastes must be removed promptly, and any (soiled or unsoiled) particulate litter must be changed frequently. For instance, alfalfa pellets are useful as cage litter because, when they are ingested, they can be digested as nutritive fiber, but they decompose quickly and become a medium for fungal and bacterial growth if they become moist and feces-contaminated.

The most practical means for providing appropriate humidity for green iguanas in large indoor cages is to employ an electric humidifier which will increase or maintain atmospheric moisture without creating an overly damp and fetid environment. In smaller cages, the air can be humidified by placing a shallow container of water over a heating source, such as a subcage heating pad.

Outdoor enclosures may be sprayed daily or twice daily to simulate natural rain showers.

Living plants increase the relative humidity of the cage air (and, as an additional benefit, provide security for juvenile iguanas). Small potted plants will be promptly trampled and "loved to death" by a large iguana, so select large hanging plants. Three or four leafy hanging plants, such as wandering Jew (*Zebrina pendula*) or golden pothos (*Epipremnum aureum*), are excellent for humidifying an area where large iguanas are living. Although pothos is mildly noxious to many mammals, many captive iguanas avidly consume it. (For one lizard species, the Solomon Island prehensile-tailed skink, *Corucia zebrata*, pothos is actually a staple item and forms the major part of the diet.) Only safe plants should be used for humidifying the cage environment. Consult Table 4.1 for a list of toxic plants to be avoided.

## CAGE-LITTER MATERIALS

Under natural conditions, tropical iguanas walk on the forest floor and move about on a surface consisting of fallen leaves in various stages of decomposition, rotting branches and logs, a myriad of fungi, and composted soil. Outdoor habitats should attempt to mimic these broadly outlined parameters.

Indoor enclosures pose more difficulties, but can be furnished so that they meet the requirements for the iguanas, are practical to construct and maintain, and are aesthetically pleasing. However, you must be careful to avoid creating a "natural" habitat that also is a hazard to its inhabitants. For instance, fine sand and small pebbles are easily swallowed along with food items and can result in gastrointestinal upset, obstruction, and eventual death of the animals that ingest them. The terms *geophagy* (earth or soil eating) and *lithophagy* (stone eating) refer to the habit some iguanas have of ingesting foreign materials. As iguanas move along the ground tongue testing various surfaces, they sometimes nibble on or eat dust, sand, or soil. This behavior may signal a mineral deficiency. An iguana who repeatedly ingests these materials should be evaluated by a veterinarian because swallowed dust, sand, and soil can form gastrointestinal obstructions. Similarly, swallowed ground corncob litter, clay kitty litter, wood shavings, etc. can, if swallowed, also cause blockages.

**While cat litter or sand is suitable for use in a litter tray or pan in the iguana's toilet area, they are *not* recommended as a cage substrate. Instead, use clean newspaper, butcher's wrap, paper toweling, artificial turf-type indoor-outdoor carpeting, or, best of all, pelleted ground alfalfa, which, although not aesthetically attractive, is both digestible and nutritious.** However, pelleted ground alfalfa or other plant-based cage substrates *must* be changed whenever they become moistened or soiled with fecal matter because these conditions support the growth of pathogenic fungi and bacteria.

It is often the manner in which food is presented that enhances the likelihood of accidental litter ingestion. Placing soft wet food items such as fresh fruit and vegetables directly on sand or pebbles may result in these litter materials being taken in with the food. It is preferable to place food in a shallow platter, paper plate, bowl, or suspended platform secured to a branch so that it can be eaten without adherent particulate materials being mixed with it. In outdoor enclosures, food can be presented on a bed of fresh grass or clean edible leaves.

## FURNISHING THE CAGE

Living trees, large branches, or artificial trees should be provided so that green iguanas will have ample places to rest, bask, and display social interactions among themselves. Carpeted "cat trees" can be substituted for actual trees or tree limbs (see Figures 2.1 & 2.2). Tree trunks, branches, etc. must be well secured so that they will not topple over and crush the inhabitants. **The type of tree or branch is vitally important: avoid resinous trees such as pine, fir, cedar, redwood, or eucalyptus because their saps can be toxic or noxious to iguanas. Avoid smooth-surfaced tree varieties such as manzanita and madrone because, although they are nonresinous, their bark is so smooth and slick that iguanas may lose their grip, fall and break their bones.** Most hard fruit woods are ideal, as are rough-barked oaks, because they offer a good gripping surface for the iguanas' sharp claws. If there is sufficient space, potted mulberry (*Morus*), *Hibiscus*, or

*Eugenia* plants should be placed in the cage and grown as shrubs or low-stature trees. The mulberry and hibiscus (which are deciduous) lose their foliage in the late fall or early winter and remain bare of leaves for several months before refoliating in the spring. Both varieties are highly nutritious and eagerly browsed by green iguanas. Any branch that has been lying on the ground should be discarded, as well as decaying or brittle branches which might break under the weight of a large iguana. Sturdy dead tree trunks or branches should be sanitized with household bleach, rinsed thoroughly with water, and dried completely before being installed in the cage.

# CHAPTER 3

## FEEDING AND NUTRITION

### WATER REQUIREMENTS

The necessity to drink water depends largely upon the moisture content in the dietary items, "insensitive" water loss to the environment through the respiratory system, and the nature of an animal's urinary and fecal wastes. For example, iguanas fed diets containing soft fruits, melons, and other foods containing a low percentage of dry matter excrete soft, moisture-laden stools; iguanas whose diets consist mainly of high dry-content food items such as leaves, excrete much drier feces and chalky urinary wastes from which much of the moisture has been extracted.

Much of an iguana's body water is derived from the moisture contained in its food, but most iguanas will drink an additional volume of water if it is presented in an acceptable form and manner. Many iguanas refuse to drink voluntarily from containers of standing water because in the wild, green iguanas drink moisture as raindroplets or dewdroplets. Captive iguanas usually drink water only by lapping dewlike drops from misted foliage, but many can be trained to imbibe fresh water from shallow vessels. Both hatchling and newly acquired iguanas should be "shown" their water bowl daily during the first few weeks of captivity. If you splash the surface of the water with a finger while the iguana is nearby, it probably will approach the bowl and drink from it.

Frequently, captive iguanas will soak for prolonged periods in their water containers, but, contrary to popular opinion, they do *not* absorb appreciable amounts of water in a spongelike fashion during this activity. Soaking often promotes bowel activity by inducing them to defecate in their water container (which can facilitate cleaning chores). Some iguana owners actually encourage their pets to use the bathtub as a toilet. (As long as the bathtub is sanitized afterward with household bleach or another effective disinfectant, there are no reasons—except aesthetic ones—why this technique should not be continued.) Bathing also is apparently pleasurable to iguanas. A sturdy water bowel that will not tip easily and that can accommodate at least half the iguana's body should be made available. Change dirtied water promptly, remember to clean and rinse the bowl or bathtub thoroughly, and avoid contaminating other surfaces with the dirty water. Whether dirty or not, replace the water at least daily.

Iguanas possess highly specialized extrarenal sodium-, potassium-, and chloride-secreting "**salt glands**." These glandular structures produce a concentrated (hypertonic) secretion, thus aiding in the conservation of precious water stores by removing excess salts (electrolytes) without the loss of significant amounts of water. Dried salt crystals are sometimes observed around the nostrils (Figure 3.1). Sneezing of this concentrated salt solution is entirely normal behavior for an iguana. When certain foods such as celery tops, swiss chard, or bok choy, are eaten by iguanas, they add electrolytes and, therefore, increase the rate and volume of salt that is sneezed.

FIGURE 3.1

SEE PLATE 3

## Dehydration

A relative or absolute deficiency of *metabolically* available water often leads to dehydration and the accumulation of insoluble sodium, potassium, and ammonium urate salts within the kidneys and other tissue sites. **When gently pinched, the skin of a dehydrated iguana will remain elevated for a few moments.**

Replacement fluid should be administered at a volume of 15–25 ml/kg every 24 hours. However, because a dehydrated iguana may already have dangerously elevated potassium levels in its plasma, the fluid used to rehydrate it should not be Ringer's solution; rather, physiological saline solution should be administered by intravenous or intracoelomic injection. In cases of severe dehydration, when intracoelomically injected fluid may not be absorbed rapidly enough and it is impossible to employ intravenous injections, the fluid can be administered directly into the bone marrow cavity of one of the thigh bones. This route of fluid administration is described as *intramedullary*, and it is usually reserved for profoundly dehydrated or critically ill patients for whom other routes are impractical or contraindicated. Later, after the iguana has been stabilized, Ringer's solution can be injected if a laboratory analysis determines that the plasma-potassium concentration is deficient.

## Relationship of Water to Urinary Bladder Stones and Gout

Concentrations of urates may promote the formation of urinary bladder stones (which occasionally reach enormous size). Because there is an intimate relationship between water and the excretion of nitrogenous urinary waste products, it is important to understand the fate of nitrogen-rich (usually animal protein) food after it has been eaten. The end products of nitrogenous foods are salts of uric acid, particularly sodium, potassium, and ammonium urate. These urate salts are the biochemical residues resulting from the reaction of uric acid with sodium, potassium, and ammonium ions in the body fluids. In carnivorous reptiles, the uric acid level in the blood rises dramatically a day or two after eating an animal protein meal and then quickly returns to a prefeeding level. In herbivorous (and, to some extent, omnivorous) reptiles such as green iguanas, whose proteinaceous nitrogen is derived from plant sources, uric acid reaches the peak level more slowly, then takes a longer time to return to the prefeeding level. Therefore, an iguana who is already moderately dehydrated is placed at a greater risk of uric acid accumulation than one which is properly hydrated.

As long as the blood circulation to the kidneys is adequate to maintain the clearance of urate salts, accumulation of urates is unlikely to occur; however, because of the insolubility of these salts, iguanas have a substantial risk of developing inflammation of joints and/or internal organs due to gout after experiencing water deprivation. It is absolutely essential to provide all captive iguanas with readily available water. There are also other causes of urinary bladder stones and gout (see Chapter 6 and Chapter 9).

## HOW GREEN IGUANAS DIGEST FOOD

The common green iguana has evolved as a folivore; i.e., its alimentary (digestive) tract is adapted to process leafy vegetation. For its instructive value, let us compare and contrast the digestive tracts of a green iguana and a ruminant such as a cow, sheep, goat, or deer.

Cattle, sheep, goats, and deer are folivorous herbivores which eat grassy or otherwise leafy fodder which, when swallowed, goes directly into the first compartment of a four-chambered stomach. This first compartment is called the *reticulum* because its inner lining surface has a *reticulated* (netted) pattern. The ingesta or "cud" may be gently and repeatedly regurgitated so that it can be chewed more thoroughly, thus reducing its particle size and, thereby, increasing the available surface area upon which gastrointestinal bacteria and protozoa can act to digest the available cellulose. From the reticulum, the well-chewed leafy ingesta moves to the *rumen*, the largest and much-expanded main chamber of the stomach complex in which the majority of the fermentative processes occur. Here, the bacterial and protozoal microflora that populate the rumen further break down and process the fibrous plant material that the ruminant swallowed. Much methane gas is produced as a result of the fermentation, and this is why ruminants belch and otherwise pass volumes of gas. From the rumen, the much-processed ingesta passes into the third chamber, the *omasum*. This chamber also is divided by variable-length extensions arising in the organ's walls which serve to increase the surface area. More microbial degradation of the ingesta occurs here. Finally, the processed plant material passes into the *abomasum*, which is functionally more like the stomach in a monogastric animal such as a human or a dog. Here, the much-digested fodder—and many of the bacteria and protozoa that served so ably to digest it—are acted upon by gastric juices, acid, and enzymes to render the constituent molecules available to the ruminant. In fact, it is the gastric microflora that constitute a large proportion of the essential amino acid-containing protein that is finally absorbed by the ruminant. After leaving the abomasum, the ingesta proceeds through the small and large intestines, and eventually leaves the body as feces.

Now let us consider the anatomy and digestive processes of the green iguana. Leaf-eating iguanas only bite their food in order to grasp and cut it into small enough pieces to swallow; little or no actual chewing is involved. The food enters the esophagus and is delivered into an unchambered simple (monogastric) stomach. Here, there may be some early digestion of part of the meal, particularly items that are not of fibrous plant origin such as soft ripe fruit (plus any invertebrates and eggs, etc.). As the ingesta moves from the relatively small stomach into the short small intestine, pancreatic enzymes and some bile are added. Eventually, the relatively still-undigested fibrous, leafy material that formed the meal enters a remarkable sacculated (much-divided), functionally multichambered organ formed by an expansion of the colon. (This complex organ functions as an expanded fermentation vat or vessel for the iguana much as the rumen does for a cud-chewing ruminant.) The sacculated colon also is characterized by its internal extensions that partially divide and greatly expand and enhance the available surface area so that microflora can act upon and digest cellulose and other food constituents, making them available for absorption and assimilation.

The major difference between the ruminant's gastrointestinal tract and the iguana's gastrointestinal tract is anatomical rather than functional. In the ruminant, fermentation occurs in the *foregut*; in the green iguana, similar fermentative processes take place in the *hindgut* (see Iverson, 1980; McBee, 1971; McBee and McBee, 1982; Parra, 1978). Also, because of the short distance between the colon and the rectum, coprodeum, and anus in the iguana, there is less opportunity for absorption of nutrients to occur. Thus, there is some absorption of vital nutrients from the ingesta while it is still in the colon. This occurs across cells lining the extensions comprising the inner walls of the sacculations that serve to divide the colon into multiple minichambers. Some nutrients, such as amino acids and fatty acids, and multi-B-complex vitamins, probably continue to be absorbed as the ingesta becomes feces and passes through the relatively short rectum and coprodeum before entering the cloaca. Figure 3.2 shows a chuckawalla whose stomach and intestines contain rocks and stones. Figure 3.3 is a necropsy specimen from a young green iguana. Figure 3.4 shows the entire gastrointestinal tract from this iguana. Figure 3.5 is a specimen of an adult green iguana's opened sacculated colon.

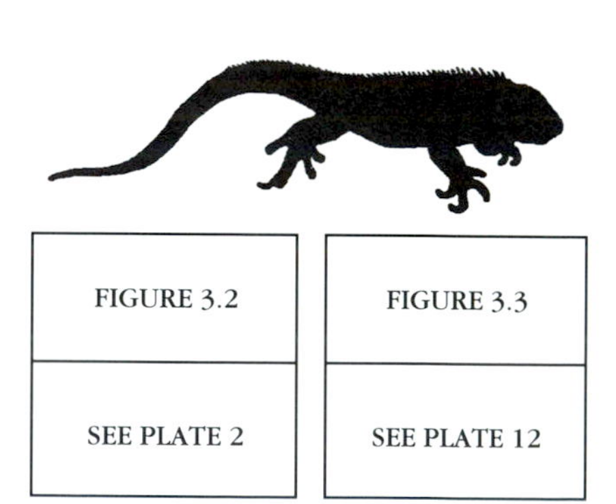


After emerging from the eggshell, infant iguanas begin to fend for themselves without any assistance from their parents. Eating usually does not commence immediately; rather, a few days to a week or more passes

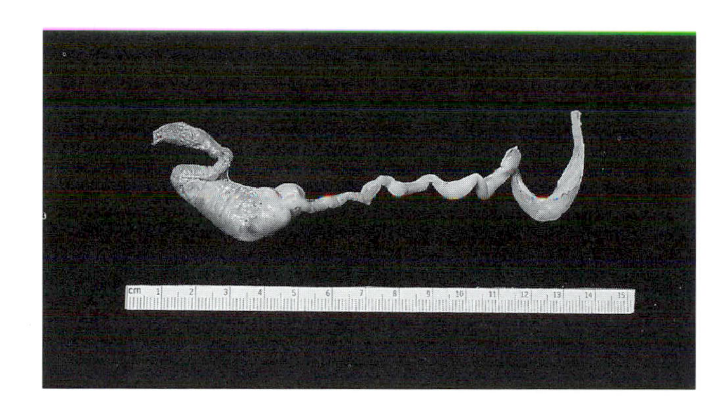

**Figure 3.4.** The entire digestive tract of the iguana illustrated in Figure 3.3. On the right are the simple stomach, very short small intestine, expanded sacculated colon, and rectum. The sacculated colon tends to be elongated in juveniles, but it soon expands and becomes rounder in adult green iguanas.

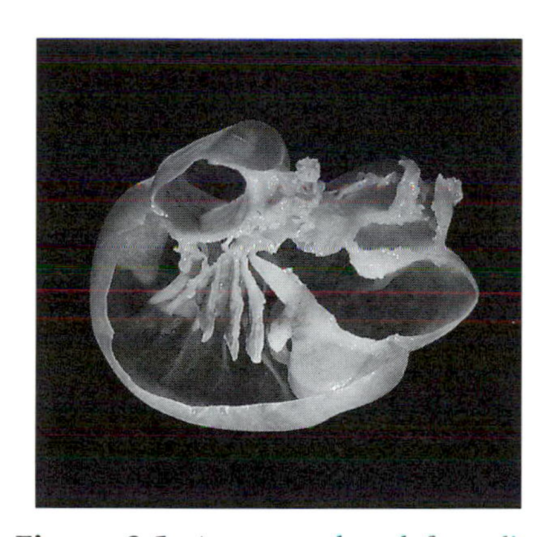

**Figure 3.5.** An opened and formalin-fixed sacculated colon from an adult green iguana. Note the multiple chambers in which microbial fermentation of cellulose occurs.

before the hatchlings begin to forage. During this time, they live on their residual stored yolk. Also, it is during these first few days of life in the wild that they ingest the fresh feces of older, conspecific iguanas. This is how they acquire the important fermentative symbiotic bacteria and protozoans that are responsible for digesting the cellulose-rich vegetable substances upon which they subsist (Troyer, 1982, 1984a, 1984b).

Many iguanas that are imported by the pet trade are hatched on so-called "iguana farms" which collect the eggs from gravid farm iguanas or collect eggs which have been deposited in wild iguana nests; these eggs are then incubated artificially. The hatchlings from these eggs probably have not been given the opportunity to have access to the fresh stools of older iguanas and, thus, may not have acquired the necessary gut microflora. This may explain why so many tiny newly hatched iguanas do not thrive, even when they are provided with an adequate diet. **Therefore, captive hatchling iguanas that have not had the opportunity to inoculate their alimentary tracts with these bacteria and protozoa which are vitally important for digestion should be given the fresh feces from healthy, older iguanas that are thriving on a green leafy diet.**

## FEEDING GREEN IGUANAS

Generally, iguanas are fed free-choice several times weekly. Young iguanas, because they are growing rapidly, need to be fed more often. Mature iguanas can be maintained on a three-to-four times per week feeding schedule.

- Hatchlings measuring from approximately 8.5 cm (3.3 in) snout-to-vent length (SVL) should be fed daily.
- Yearlings measuring approximately 17.5 cm (7 in) SVL should be fed at least five times weekly.
- Adult green iguanas (3 years old and older) measuring approximately 35 cm (14 in) SVL usually should be fed three or four times weekly.

The frequency of feeding also depends upon the activity level of the iguanas, their reproductive status, and the nutritive density or quality of the diet. The effect of the reproductive status on the appetite and nutritional requirements of mature iguanas is discussed in Chapter 10. The quality of the foodstuffs also is important when determining the amount of food to be fed. For example, a diet consisting of high water-content foods such as melons and ripe fresh fruits contains less cellulose and other nutrients than a diet whose identical weight consists of fresh green leaves or grain-rich bread.

Factors influencing the differences in nutritional quality of foodstuffs are

- Water (moisture) content.
- Energy content (calories) per unit of dry weight.
- Mineral content as a fraction of the dry weight.
- Ability of the energy content of the food to be efficiently assimilated.
- Relative content of minerals (for example, calcium:phosphorus: magnesium).

For example, the desirable relative quantity of calcium content in a food to the phosphorus content in a food is at least 2 parts of calcium to 1 part of phosphorus. Iceberg head lettuce has a low amount of calcium but a high amount of phosphorus. Therefore the desired relative amounts of calcium and phosphorus of iceberg head lettuce are reversed and, if iceberg lettuce is fed excessively to an iguana, metabolic disturbances are likely to develop. Also, because of its very high water content, extremely large amounts of lettuce must be consumed in order to obtain even minimal amounts of nutritional value.

Food items that consist primarily of easily digested and assimilated simple carbohydrates (sugars) tend to foster obesity, fermentation, and excessive intestinal gas production.

Better quality foodstuffs characteristically are composed of *complex* carbohydrates, especially cellulose, which must be processed by the microorganisms residing in the digestive tract (especially in the iguana's sacculated colon).

Iguanas will acquire a taste for almost any food offered constantly, regardless of its nutritional value or even if it has detrimental qualities (as do iceberg lettuce, brussels sprouts, corn [maize], grapes, and soaked primate chow). **Care must be taken not to begin feeding captive iguanas the wrong foods. Refer to Tables 3.1, 3.2, 3.3, 3.4, and 3.5, and "An Ideal Diet" in this chapter for guidelines in planning a nutritious diet**. If an iguana is already eating poor or deficient foods, a transition to a healthier diet should be made by mixing a little of the usual "poor" food with the new "good" food so that the iguana will eat its meal, and gradually reduce the amount of the former diet until it is totally replaced by the proper foods. Suggestions for correcting bad dietary habits by using bean, pea, lentil, and seed sprouts are discussed later in this chapter.

Although iguanas have strong jaws and many teeth, they do not actually chew their food before swallowing it; rather, pieces of leafy vegetation are secured and bitten from a larger portion before swallowing them. If two or more iguanas are housed together, it is better to place the food in more than one plate, bowl, or pile because this will help avoid disputes over favored food items. Another option is to prepare a thoroughly combined mixture or salad of foods, which eliminates waste of vitamin supplements (if provided) and ensures that each "bite" is complete. This is advantageous and convenient if two or more iguanas, or a large group of iguanas varying in size, are being fed. After preparing several meals, the amount of food required becomes evident.

**Iguanas should be fed between 11:00 A.M. and 2:00 P.M. because they eat most heartily after being warmed up by basking in radiant energy. Also, they then have time in the afternoon to digest their meal.** The intestinal bacteria and protozoa responsible for digestion of fibrous plant matter prior to nutrient absorption operate optimally at temperatures of approximately 29–35 °C (approximately 84–95 °F). If you can only feed your iguana late in the day, make sure a warm area is available where it can bask for an hour or two after the meal.

Now we know why green iguanas are adapted to a diet consisting mainly of nutritive plant fiber. Like some children, some captive iguanas will accept—and may prefer or even become habituated to—aberrant, abnormal diets consisting of animal protein in the form of insects, arachnids and other small invertebrates, small eggs, and rodents such as mice and small rats. I have examined adult iguanas whose owners fed them crickets and other insects when they were hatchlings, and then mice and rats as they grew to maturity. Obviously, when you consider how the gastrointestinal organs of the iguana have adapted to process a folivorous diet, none of these food items is suitable for an iguana's alimentary tract. Although most of these iguanas were healthy and showed no outward signs of clinical disease because of their unnatural diets, I still do not recommend such diets.

In their native habitats, green iguanas generally confine their diet to vegetable matter in the form of leaves, blossoms, and soft fruits. **Although young common green iguanas often eagerly eat insects and arachnids, they are adapted morphologically to a diet composed mainly of plant material (Troyer, 1984b). There is a greater need for protein while young iguanas grow and develop rapidly during the first 2-3 years of their life; so, although invertebrates or other small animals can augment protein intake, plant sources alone can provide sufficient nutrition for orderly growth and development to proceed. When iguanas become adults, their nutritional needs are mainly directed toward maintenance, and a diet composed of high calcium:low phosphorus leafy vegetables fulfills this requirement.**

Many iguana owners give their pets soft fruits such as kiwi, strawberries, melons, pitted stone fruits (apricots, peaches, nectarines, and plums), and figs. These items add variety and flavor to the diet and are acceptable in small quantities as *treats* or special "goodies." However, most fruits contain more phosphorus than calcium, and some have so much readily fermentable sugar that they promote excessive gas production which can cause bloat and distress to iguanas unaccustomed to eating them.

Some owners feed their iguanas commercial dog, cat, or primate chow. In my opinion, this is unwise from several standpoints:

- These products were formulated for canines, felines, and primates—not for iguanas which anatomically are different from dogs, cats, and monkeys.
- Many, if not most, of these commercial diets contain substantially more **preformed** vitamins A and $D_3$ than are required by iguanas. (An appropriate diet composed of green leafy vegetables contains adequate beta carotene from which vitamin A can be converted biologically, and, with appropriate ultraviolet radiation, iguanas can synthesize their own vitamin $D_3$.)

**If dog, cat, or primate chow is included in the diet, it should not exceed 5% of the total ration.**

**It has now been proven that green iguanas thrive, grow to maturity, and reproduce without developing metabolic bone disease, abnormal mineralization of soft tissues, or visceral gout when fed a diet in which the only source of protein is nutritious, fibrous plant protein.**

My recommendation is to feed iguanas a diet consisting of nutritious leafy vegetation, particularly cruciferous vegetables selected from the family Brassicaceae which includes collard, mustard, and turnip greens; cabbage; bok choy; broccoli leaves; dandelion leaves and blossoms; and mulberry and hibiscus leaves. Without an exception, the leaves of these plants are excellent sources of calcium and nutrient fiber without containing high levels of phosphorus or oxalic acid. Other sources of vegetation that are highly palatable and well balanced with respect to their calcium:phosphorus ratio are nasturtium leaves and flowers, okra, endive, and escarole. Some commonly grown houseplants, especially *Hibiscus*, *Nasturtium*, *Eugenia*, and the ubiquitous wandering jew, *Zebrina pendula*, are avidly eaten and are nutritious for green iguanas.

When fed a proper leafy diet, supplementation with vitamin-mineral products is, in my opinion, usually unnecessary. Also, feeding a more "natural" diet results in steady growth and development without metabolic bone disease, soft-tissue mineralization, and some of the secondary dietary upsets such as constipation, diarrhea, and intestinal gas. Some diets rich in less complex carbohydrate sources often promote these upsets, particularly for the first few days or weeks after they are introduced into the iguanas' ration.

FIGURE 3.6

SEE PLATE 3

Many of these preferred food items can be obtained free of cost as slightly wilted vegetables from your grocer, and others can be grown (see Growing "Organic" Vegetables Hydroponically later in this chapter) or collected in your neighborhood. Bean, pea, lentil, and seed sprouts can be easily and economically produced in your kitchen (see Bean, Pea, Lentil, and Seed Sprouts, also later in this chapter). Figure 3.6 illustrates a variety of attractive and nutritious food items that are ideal for iguanas. Most are readily available year-round in grocery stores, particularly in neighborhoods with substantial Asian communities.

Iguanas can discern the colors red, yellow, orange, and green; therefore, this information should be used to prepare diets that are visually attractive.

As a guideline, deep colors are usually indicative of superior nutrient and flavor content in produce. Avoid "using up" fading, yellowed greens on your pet. Wilted greens are satisfactory, however, and can be freshened by soaking in cool water for 5 or 10 minutes. To help greens stay fresh longer, remove ties or rubber bands and fading leaves, rinse them well, then roll them up jelly-roll style in a dry dishcloth or paper towels. Store them in a plastic bag in the refrigerator.

During the past three to four years, several artificial diets have been marketed for the common green iguana. Most of these products claim that they are "complete"—nothing but them and water need be offered. Many contain far more protein and preformed vitamins A and $D_3$ than are necessary for proper nutrition of the green iguana. In an attempt to assess the value of four of these commercial diets, one of my students and I conducted a feeding trial in which groups of juvenile green iguanas were fed nothing but the test diets and fresh water to ascertain how they would grow and develop. Two of the diets appeared to provide the growing iguanas with sufficient nutrients; one did not provide sufficient nutrients and, on humane considerations, had to be discontinued rather than watching test iguanas starve to death; and the last diet in the group appeared to be formulated with sufficient nutrients, but was of such low palatability that the iguanas refused to eat it. The two that were palatable and were proven to provide adequate nutrient value to support normal growth were Nutri'Guana® and Pretty Pets Iguana Diet®. While several other products are currently available, some just did not pass the taste test by our "panel of independent experts"—young, healthy iguanas given the opportunity to select an artificial diet to their liking! (See "Commercial Iguana Diets" listed in Sources For Reptile-Related Products at the end of this book.)

## BRASSICA PLANTS

The greatest sources of calcium that also contain only modest amounts of phosphorus belong to the *Brassica* genus of plants. This sin-

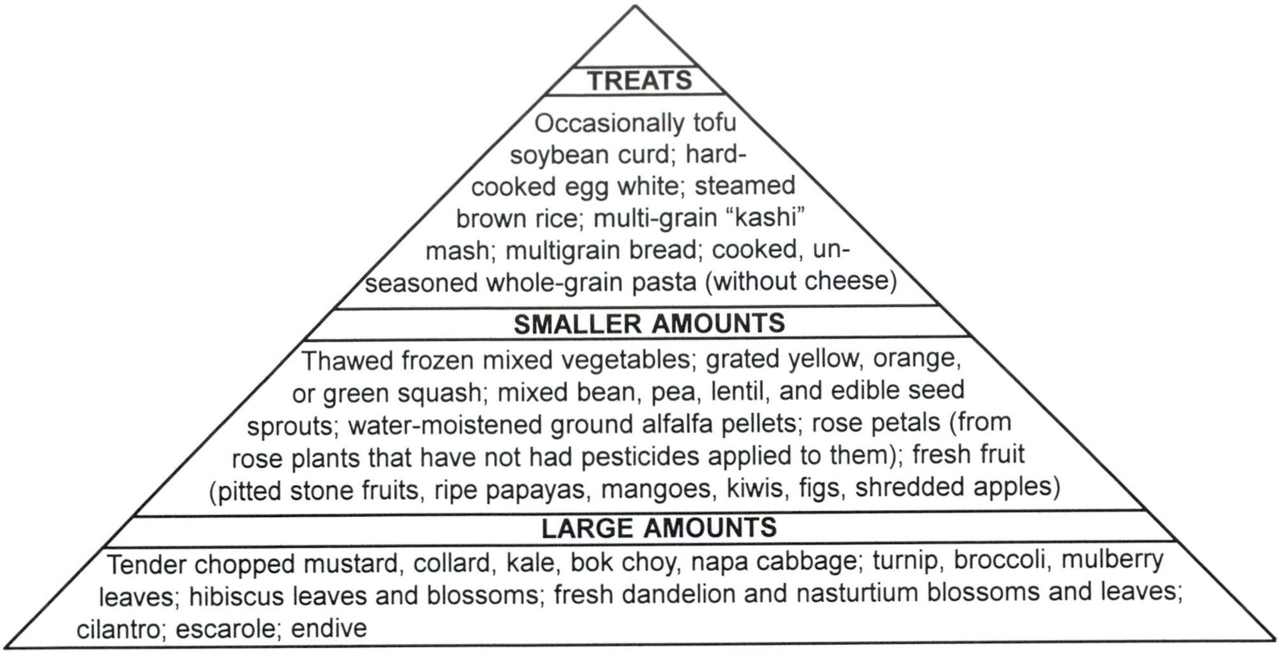

**TREATS**

Occasionally tofu soybean curd; hard-cooked egg white; steamed brown rice; multi-grain "kashi" mash; multigrain bread; cooked, unseasoned whole-grain pasta (without cheese)

**SMALLER AMOUNTS**

Thawed frozen mixed vegetables; grated yellow, orange, or green squash; mixed bean, pea, lentil, and edible seed sprouts; water-moistened ground alfalfa pellets; rose petals (from rose plants that have not had pesticides applied to them); fresh fruit (pitted stone fruits, ripe papayas, mangoes, kiwis, figs, shredded apples)

**LARGE AMOUNTS**

Tender chopped mustard, collard, kale, bok choy, napa cabbage; turnip, broccoli, mulberry leaves; hibiscus leaves and blossoms; fresh dandelion and nasturtium blossoms and leaves; cilantro; escarole; endive

**AN IDEAL DIET**

gular group of vegetables is remarkable because its numbers are so dissimilar in their appearance: cabbage, kale, broccoli, mustard greens, rutabaga, and kohlrabi are all members of this nutritious genus. See Table 3.5.

**Whenever possible, the food fed to green iguanas should contain a calcium:phosphorus ratio of at least 2:1. As long as too much supplemental *preformed* vitamin $D_3$ is not fed, any mild excess of calcium will be excreted in the iguanas' feces.**

The calcium content of vegetables comprising the family Brassicaceae varies widely, not only *between* plants within the genus, but also *within* the same plants depending on which part of the edible plant is analyzed. For example: broccoli leaves are substantially richer in calcium than both the stems and flowerets even though the parts may be separated from each other on the same stalk by only a few centimeters or less; and turnip greens are one of the richest leafy sources of calcium, but the bulbous turnip roots contain only a very modest amount of this essential mineral.

Because the stiff stemlike leaf veins of some of these leafy varieties are fibrous, they should be eliminated by either trimming the leaves or cut into short bite-size lengths before feeding to iguanas.

**Although eating excessive amounts of some members of the family Brassicaceae could predispose or even induce a thyroid-hormone deficiency because they contain isothiocyanate compounds (which are natural goitrogens and are capable of inhibiting the production of thyroid hormone by the thyroid gland), in practice, it is a problem only when they**

are eaten excessively while simultaneously excluding other nutritious foods. If there is doubt about excessive consumption, occasionally adding a partial or full tablet of dried kelp is beneficial and is harmless (unless massive numbers of tablets are given to an iguana).

## ANOREXIA (LOSS OF APPETITE/REFUSAL TO EAT)

There are many reasons why iguanas exhibit anorexia (the proper term to describe a loss of appetite or refusal to eat):

- Inadequate or incorrect diet
- Improper environmental temperature
- Infectious or metabolic disease
- Failure of the animal to adapt to the conditions of captivity
- Too frequent handling
- Parasitism
- Reproductive activity
- Prior to or during periodic skin shedding

Although the most common reason for anorexia is an inadequate or incorrect diet, environmental temperature also plays a major role. An environmental temperature which is too low to allow for normal activity of digestive enzymes will prevent even the well-adapted iguana from displaying an appetite or from digesting or assimilating its food. **Most iguanas exhibit active eating when the environmental temperatures are approximately 25–35 °C (77–95 °F).** (Of course, exceptions exist.)

Iguanas are functionally "ectothermic" (their body temperature is mainly dependent upon the environmental temperature). Because of this, their basal metabolic rate usually is much lower than that of a similar size bird or mammal. Due to their lower rate of metabolism, iguanas can usually survive prolonged periods of fasting, but once they have crossed a poorly defined threshold, their condition and health decline very rapidly. At first, the affected animal lives off its stored fat, but soon this source of readily available energy is exhausted and other tissues, especially muscle, are sacrificed to sustain life. The iguana slowly becomes gaunt and wasted and is more prone to infectious diseases and the stress of captivity.

Often a brief exposure to natural *unfiltered* sunlight (not through a window pane) outdoors together with a "shower" will induce many previously anorectic iguanas to eat voluntarily. A word of caution: Iguanas that have never exhibited overt aggression toward their keeper may display marked changes in behavior after even brief exposure to natural sunlight outdoors. This aggressiveness usually subsides as soon as the iguana is taken back to its enclosure. Many previously docile animals actually have bitten owners who have been unwary enough to casually pick them up after they have been permitted to sunbathe. Nevertheless, sunbathing is highly therapeutic for iguanas, and when given a choice between artificial basking lights and a splash of unfiltered sunlight, iguanas consistently opt for the sunshine.

Sometimes iguanas will refuse to feed just prior to or during their periodic skin shedding, but this behavior is highly individual. Some shedding iguanas consume pieces of their own skin (this is normal behavior; in essence, they are recycling nutrients that skin contains).

**Some female iguanas cease eating coincident with copulation (Rodda, 1992). Even those females who continue to eat following copulation refuse food during the latter stages of egg development**; consequently, they lose considerable weight and are in poor condition. Generally, this is because the actual mass of the eggs occupies most of the available intracoelomic space, leaving little or no room for ingested food. Shortly after such a female deposits her clutch of eggs, she will regain her appetite and eat avidly. Eggs contain substantial amounts of fat, protein, and calcium and, thus, require considerable energy and other resources for their formation. Similarly, male iguanas expend much energy during their courtship rituals and while producing sperm. Therefore, it is important that breeding iguanas be fed a nutritious diet and be in fit condition before being placed together.

Some iguanas are often intolerant of handling after capture, physical restraint, or having their cages changed. In the latter instance, familiar scent and visual cues may have been lost, and it may take a period of time before a resident iguana will become accustomed to its altered quarters. Such an iguana should be left undisturbed as soon as it has been moved to new quarters. A well-placed stout branch to climb and a hiding box or other refuge often prove useful in aiding a poorly adapting iguana to accept its captive or altered cage conditions and encourage it to commence eating again. Some iguana keepers have found that providing a visual barrier in the form of a black or otherwise opaque nonreflective cage surface in exchange for clear glass or plastic walls gives their iguanas some privacy and encourages previously nonfeeding iguanas to accept food. Usually, these changes in eating behavior are transient. Most iguanas eventually become accustomed to having their cages cleaned (and even renovated) and they no longer become stressed by these activities because their hearty appetites and robustness help them to overcome such minor psychic disturbances as cage cleaning.

**As a rule, if an iguana refuses to eat for a period of a week or more, its general health and the conditions under which it is being kept should be evaluated.** The iguana may be entirely normal; perhaps it is entering a cycle of reproductive activity. However, it may be infected with a disease-causing organism; it may be parasitized by worms or protozoa; or it could be affected by a metabolic disorder such as diabetes. If no physical evidence of disease is found, one or more forced hand-feedings should be given so that nutritional intake is maintained.

For captive iguanas, good health and development are especially dependent upon being fed a well-balanced diet. Many illnesses and even injuries result from nutritional deficiencies. Early signs of malnutrition include the following:

- Slow, if any, growth
- Lackluster skin
- Brittle bones that often lead to spontaneous limb fractures
- Thinness
- Lack of appetite
- Overall apathetic behavior and lethargy

It can take either a few months or even a year for an iguana to die of severe malnutrition. Iguanas with milder deficiencies can live for several years, but many suffer from ailments that often go unnoticed. Once understood, proper nutrition is easy to provide.

## TECHNIQUE FOR HAND FEEDING

- Restrain the iguana so that its head and body are supported. If necessary, hold the limbs closely against its body to prevent it from scratching the handler. Wrapping the iguana in a towel is also useful in helping restrict its activity.
- Gently pull the dewlap downward as the head is supported, thus causing the lower jaw to descend. Alternatively, open the mouth gently with a clean, soft rubber or plastic kitchen spatula. In very small iguanas, a round wooden stick, such as those used for cotton-tipped swabs, can be rolled toward the back of the mouth, thus causing the jaws to open. If the dewlap is pulled downward, it must be done without great force to avoid tearing the soft tissue or fracturing the jaw.
- Place the food item (dandelion blossom, rolled tender leaves, rose petals, softened alfalfa pellets, tofu, etc.) into the mouth.
- Advance the food gradually and *gently* into the back of the mouth and thence into the throat and down the esophagus. A clean rubber-eraser-tipped pencil can be used as a push-rod to aid in moving the food down through the esophagus and into the iguana's body.

## GROWING "ORGANIC" VEGETABLES HYDROPONICALLY

With currently available hydroponic technology, high-quality vegetables can be grown in a limited space, without regard for climatic conditions and without the need for soil. Using this technique, the quality

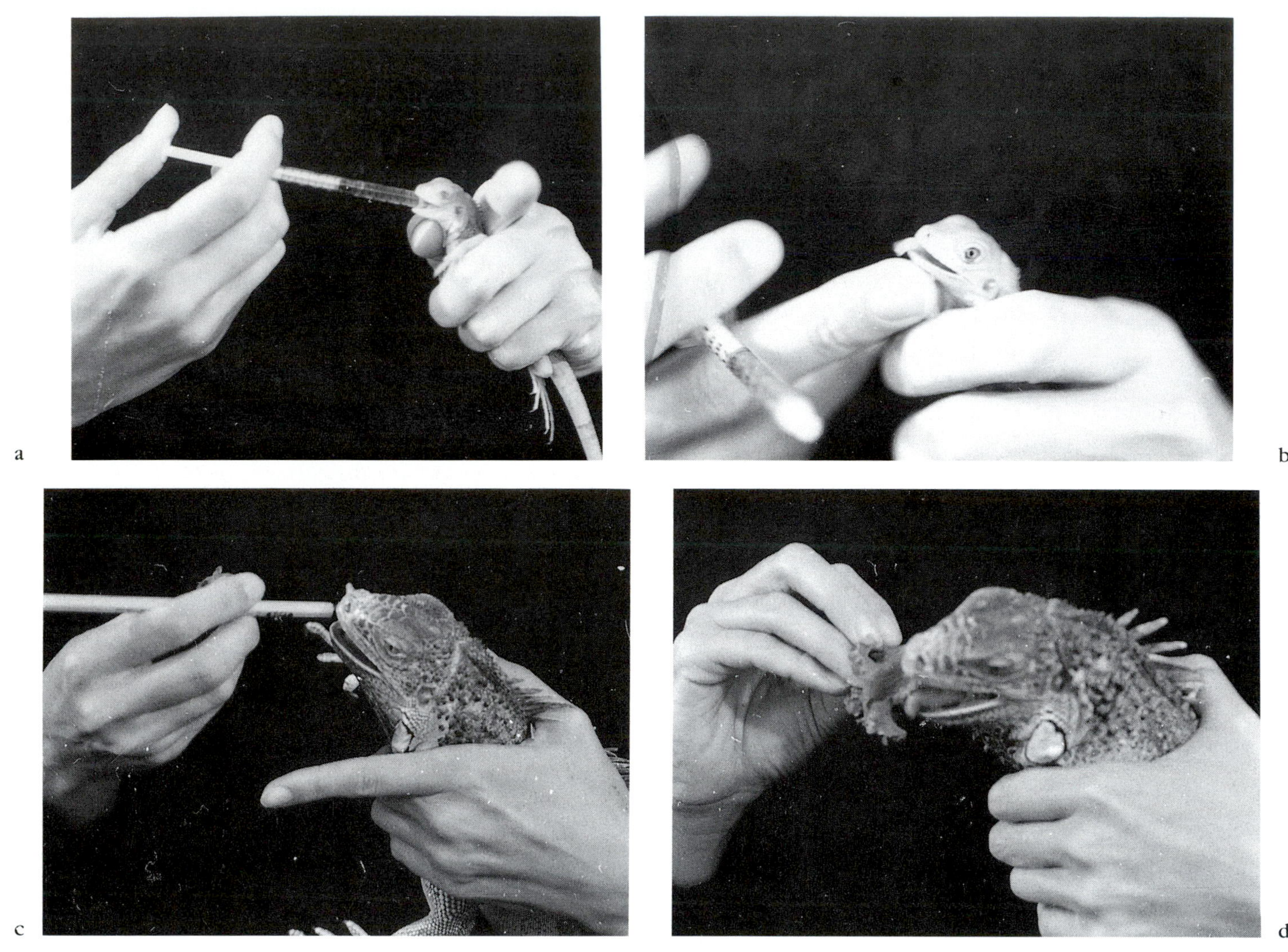

**Figure 3.7a–d.** Forced-feeding and/or hand-feeding may be necessary to assure ingestion of nutrients. Liquid gruels are delivered with a small syringe. Solid food items are placed into the mouth and, if necessary, are directed into the throat with a smooth round-ended object. Photo credit: Wendy Townsend.

of the vegetables can be easily monitored and controlled; the quantity of the vegetables can be increased or decreased, as required; and, most importantly, the vegetables are pesticide- and parasite-free.

The growing trays are sewn with seeds of plants that are selected for their nutritive value. Some of the plants that can be grown efficiently in these trays are alfalfa; clover; nasturtium; broccoli; kale; and collard, mustard, turnip, and dandelion greens. Many grains, such as hard wheat and barley, yield tender edible grasses a few days after they sprout and develop their green chlorophyll.

Small hydroponic units for home use are, apparently, not being manufactured commercially at present, but it is possible to construct suitable units from off-the-shelf materials available at most building construction suppliers. An excellent source of information, plans, and growing supplies is Hydro-Fresh Farm. See "Sources For Reptile-Related Products." The balanced growth-solution is available from this firm. In addition, you can consult your local college, county, state, and federal agricultural extension offices.

### How to Make a Hydroponic Growing Unit

The following are required:

- A relatively closed environment in which the humidity and temperature can be controlled.
- An automatic illumination system employing fluorescent lighting of an appropriate wave length (examples are Sylvania GroLux F20T-12/GRO, 20 watt, 61 cm; Sylvania Gro-Lux F40/GRO, 40 watt, 122 cm; Westinghouse Agrolite F20T12/AGRO, 20 watt, 61 cm; and Westinghouse Econ-O-Watt F40CW/RS/EW-II, 34 watt). Note that these sources of artificial illumination are balanced for plant growth and are *not* suitable for use in iguanas' cages.
- Large-diameter polyvinylchloride (PVC) irrigation pipes, split lengthwise, which are used as growing trays. These split pipes are then closed with end-caps placed on each end and secured with PVC cement. The full-circle end-caps help maintain the split pipes' rigidity, thus keeping them from becoming distorted.
- Pea gravel-sized tumbled volcanic pumice (used instead of soil) which is placed in the split PVC irrigation pipes.
- A rack arrangement for suspending the growing trays.
- A 19-liter (5-gallon) plastic bucket (which will serve as a sump container).
- A submersible pump.
- Flexible plastic tubing to distribute the dilute nutrient growth-solution which moistens the pumice growth-medium.
- An electric time-clock control to which the submersible pump is connected.
- Another time-clock control to which the fluorescent lights are connected to ensure an appropriate 16-hour light cycle:8-hour dark cycle photoperiod for the young growing plants.

Two or three times a day, the pump distributes the nutrient growth-solution to the growing trays for 30-minute cycles. The growing trays are self-emptying through overflow standpipes that return the nutritive growth-solution to the sump that holds the submersible pump; therefore, the trays cannot overflow. After the pump is turned off, any surplus growth-solution is returned to the sump.

Most plant varieties grown in these units can be harvested as fresh green leafy fodder about 10 to 14 days after the germinated seeds emerge from the surface of the growth-medium.

## BEAN, PEA, LENTIL, AND SEED SPROUTS

Home-sprouted legumes (beans, peas, lentils, etc.) and seeds are excellent sources for macro- and micronutrients in diets for iguanas. The ease of producing these sprouts in varying quantities and the low cost of equipment and seed stock make the culture of these nutritious and desirable items appealing. (Furthermore, these sprouts are entirely appropriate and beneficial for humans to consume.)

The following legumes are particularly appropriate for sprouting: small mung beans, adzuki beans, garbanzo beans (chickpeas), whole green or yellow peas, and lentils.

The following seeds are well suited for sprouting: soft wheat "berries," triticale, maize, whole unsalted sunflower seeds, millet, rapeseed, alfalfa, and barley. Small quantities of radish seeds may be added to mixtures to augment the excellent flavor of the resulting young sprouts. Radish sprouts impart a tangy flavor and are readily accepted by iguanas; however, too many make the entire sprout crop excessively spicy for most iguanas (and some humans).

The nutrition of a crop of freshly sprouted seeds can be enhanced by mixing several different kinds in each batch because any specific deficiency in one is then offset by the benefits of another. Also, the overall palatability of sprouted legumes and seeds tends to be improved when several kinds are mixed.

All beans, peas, lentils, and sprouting seeds must be obtained from sources intended for human consumption, such as health food stores. **Sprouted seeds and legumes sold for garden or farm use must not be fed to iguanas because they are often treated with fungicides and insecticides that are highly toxic.**

### Equipment Required for Growing Sprouts

- 1-quart or larger size glass canning jars fitted with open-type outer rings.
- Disks of fiberglass or stainless steel screening mesh fitted into the lids' tops.

### Technique for Growing Sprouts

- Place 22–60 ml (1½ to 2 tablespoons) of dry mixed seeds and/or legumes into each container.

- Add sufficient slightly tepid water to cover the seeds and/or legumes to a depth of 10 cm (4 inches).
- Allow the seeds and/or legumes to soak overnight. As they soak, they absorb water and swell to approximately twice their original size.
- After approximately 12 hours of soaking, pour the water off through the screened lid.
- Allow the now-softened mixture of seeds and/or legumes to germinate in a dark area.
- After approximately 36 hours, the first tiny sprouts appear.
- Each day, rinse the jars of sprouting seeds and/or legumes in cold water, and thoroughly drain them through the screened lid.
- After three to five days, the sprouts are ready to harvest.
- At that time, rinse the sprouts in cold water, drain them thoroughly through the screened lid, remove them from the jars, and use them immediately or store them in a refrigerator.

As the sprouts mature, they develop chlorophyll which imparts a mildly bitter flavor. Although this flavor may be objectionable to humans, it does not appear to affect the palatability to iguanas and, in fact, actually improves the nutritional value of the sprouts. Culturing the sprouts in total darkness is particularly important if some of them are to be consumed by humans because this mildly bitter flavor will be minimized.

Depending upon the varieties and quantities grown, a few cents worth of dry seeds and legumes provide over a liter of fresh sprouts in as few as four or five days, and they may be produced every month of the year.

Sprouts from legumes (including alfalfa) are excellent sources of high-quality vegetable protein, vitamins, minerals (including calcium), and useful energy in the form of cellulose and other complex carbohydrates.

Fresh sprouts are especially valuable for treating iguanas which have become accustomed to eating only iceberg lettuce, grapes, or other nutritionally deficient items. Sprinkle the sprouts as a "top dressing" over the iguana's preferred leafy or fruit items so that it must eat its way through the sprouts in order to reach the lettuce or grapes. Thus, it will ingest both its preferred item and those more nutritionally sound items placed in its gustatorial pathway. At each daily feeding, increase the proportion of sprouts and other high-quality leafy vegetables in relation to that of the lettuce or grapes. Colorful dandelions, nasturtiums, rose petals, and/or mulberry leaves can also be placed in the iguana's field of vision. Rolling them gently between your thumb and a finger will release volatile plant chemicals that serve as taste cues and, therefore, make the newly proffered item attractive to a naive iguana. Within two weeks or less, an iguana usually will be sufficiently retrained so that it will accept a far more nutritious and varied leafy vegetable diet.

**TABLE 3.1 Examples of Plant Materials That are Safe, Nutritious, and Palatable**
(Please note that some of these food items may not possess the desirable calcium: phosphorus ratio of at least 2:1; however, they possess other important nutrients)

Alfalfa: fresh, dried leaves, pellets, meal
Apple: fresh, with peel, sliced or grated (discard core and seeds)
Barley: freshly sprouted seeds, freshly grown leaves
Beans (several edible varieties): fresh leaves and stems, fruit
Bean spouts (azuki, black-eyed, garbanzo, lentil, mung, pea, etc.): fresh leaves, stems, blossoms, fruit
Beet: tops, stems, flowers grated roots
Berseem (Egyptian clover): leaves, sun-cured hay
Blackberry: tender leaves, berries
Buffalo grass (*Bulbilis dactyloides*): hay
Cabbage family (also see collards, crucifers, mustard, turnip)
Cactus (especially *Opuntia*): flowers, prickly pears, tender young cactus pads
Carrot: leaves, grated root
Clover (Ladino, Alsike, etc.): fresh, sun-cured hay
Collards*: fresh green leaves, flowers
Cotton: leaves, dried or fresh
Cowpea: sun-cured hay, leaves
Crucifers*: bok choy, broccoli (especially broccoli *leaves*), kale, napa (DO NOT FEED TO EXCESS)
Dandelion: leaves and stems, flowers, fresh or dried
Dicondra: fresh or sun-cured hay
Eugenia: fresh leaves, fruits
Figs: fresh fruit
Grass clippings: freshly mowed or sun-cured
Hibiscus: leaves, flowers, fresh pods
Kudzu: sun-cured hay
Lespedeza: sun-cured hay, leaves
Millet: leaves, sun-cured hay
Mint: sun-cured hay
Mixed vegetables: frozen, then thawed before serving
Mulberry: freshly picked tender leaves, fruit
Mustard*: fresh green leaves, flowers
Nasturtium: leaves, stems, flowers
Okra: freshly chopped, tender leaves and blossoms
Pea: fresh pods, sun-cured hay
Pear: fresh, cut or grated (discard core and seeds)
Peavine: sun-cured hay
Peanut: sun-cured hay with or without nuts
Rape*: fresh leaves, sun-cured hay
Rutabaga*: freshly grated root
Saltbush (winter range): sun-cured hay
Soybean: fresh leaves or sun-cured hay
Squash: freshly grated flesh, bloosoms, tender leaves
Stone fruits: peach, nectarine, apricot, plum, etc.
Sunflower: seeds (unsalted)
Timothy: sun-cured hay
Tofu soybean cake
Triticale: freshly sprouted seeds, sun-cured hay
Turnip*: fresh leaves, grated root
Vetch: sun-cured hay
Watercress: leaves, stems, blossoms
Wheat (soft wheat berries): freshly sprouted, hydroponically grown

*Although each of these plants is a member of the family Brassicaceae, they appear to be less likely to induce goitrogenic effects than head-type cabbage, brussel sprouts, etc.
Adapted from Frye and Townsend, 1993.

**TABLE 3.2 Vegetables with a Desirable Calcium:Phosphorus Ratio**
(all figures refer to mg/240ml (mg/8oz)

| Vegetable | Calcium mg | Phosphorus mg | $Ca:PO_4$ ratio |
|---|---|---|---|
| Beet greens | 188 | 80 | 2.35:1 |
| Broccoli leaves | 349 | 89 | 3.92:1 |
| Broccoli stems | 111 | 47 | 2.36:1 |
| Cabbage (green outer leaves) | 429 | 72 | 5.95:1 |
| Cabbage, chinese | 400 | 72 | 5.56:1 |
| Chard | 300 | 100 | 3.00:1 |
| Collard greens | 414 | 150 | 2.76:1 |
| Dandelion greens | 168 | 70 | 2.40:1 |
| Endive | 104 | 39 | 2.66:1 |
| Kale | 390 | 134 | 2.91:1 |
| Kohlrabi | 390 | 120 | 3.25:1 |
| Mustard greens | 582 | 168 | 3.46:1 |
| Turnip greens | 694 | 98 | 7.08:1 |
| Watercress | 53 | 15 | 3.53:1 |

For comparison purposes:

- Broccoli flowerets contain 85 mg of calcium and 140 mg of phosphorus, yielding a $Ca:PO_4$ ratio of 0.41:1.
- Broccoli leaves contain 349 mg of calcium and 89 mg of phosphorus, yielding a $Ca:PO_4$ ratio of 3.92:1.
- Thus, parts of the same plant can be widely diverse with respect to their nutritional content.

Ca = calcium
$PO_4$ = phosphorus (as phosphate ion)

**TABLE 3.3 Vegetables and Fruits with an Undesirable Calcium:Phosphorus Ratio**
(all figures refer to mg/240ml (mg/8 oz)

| Vegetable | Calcium mg | Phosphorus mg | $Ca:PO_4$ ratio |
|---|---|---|---|
| Bananas | 7 | 22 | 1:3.10 |
| Broccoli flowerets | 85 | 140 | 1:1.65 |
| Brussels sprouts | 36 | 161 | 1:4.48 |
| Corn (maize) | 16 | 206 | 1:12.90 |
| Cucumber | 10 | 21 | 1:2.10 |
| Grapes | 19 | 35 | 1:1.80 |
| Lettuce (iceberg) | 17 | 40 | 1:2.40 |
| Mushrooms | 19 | 131 | 1:6.90 |
| Tomatoes | 11 | 29 | 1:2.60 |

Ca = calcium
$PO_4$ = phosphorus (as phosphate ion)

**TABLE 3.4 Food Values**

| | | Vitamins | | | | Minerals | | Other | |
|---|---|---|---|---|---|---|---|---|---|
| Food | Measure | A units | B-1 (mg) | B-2 (mg) | C (mg) | Calc. (mg) | Phos. (mg) | Iron (mg) | Prot. (gm) |
| Apple | 1 small | 90 | 0.360 | 0.050 | 6 | 7 | 12 | 0.3 | 0 |
| Apricot # | 3 medium | 7,500 | 0.033 | 0.100 | 4 | 13 | 24 | 0.6 | 1 |
| Asparagus | 8 stalks | 1,100 | 0.360 | 0.065 | 20 | 21 | 40 | 1.0 | 2 |
| Avocado | 1/2 medium | 500 | 0.120 | 0.137 | 9 | 44 | 42 | 6.3 | 2 |
| Banana | 1 medium | 300 | 0.045 | 0.087 | 10 | 8 | 28 | 0.6 | 1 |
| Beans, green* | 3/4 cup | 950 | 0.060 | 0.100 | 8 | 55 | 50 | 1.1 | 2 |
| Beet greens* | 1/2 cup | 22,000 | 0.100 | 0.500 | 50 | 94 | 40 | 3.2 | 2 |
| Beets | 1/2 cup | 50 | 0.041 | 0.037 | 8 | 28 | 42 | 2.8 | 2 |
| Blackberries | 3/4 cup | 300 | 0.025 | 0.030 | 3 | 32 | 32 | 0.9 | 0 |
| Blueberries | 3/4 cup | 35 | 0.045 | 0.031 | 11 | 25 | 20 | 0.9 | 0 |
| Broccoli flowers | 3/4 cup | 6,500 | 0.120 | 0.350 | 65 | 64 | 105 | 1.3 | 2 |
| Broccoli leaf | 3/4 cup | 30,000 | 0.120 | 0.687 | 90 | 262 | 67 | 2.3 | 3 |
| Broccoli stem | 3/4 cup | 2,000 | — | 0.187 | — | 83 | 35 | 1.1 | 2 |
| Brussels sprouts | 3/4 cup | 400 | 0.180 | 0.090 | 130 | 27 | 121 | 2.1 | 4 |
| Cabbage (1) | 1 cup | — | 0.780 | 0.075 | 50 | 46 | 34 | 2.0 | 2 |
| Cabbage (2) | 1 cup | 160 | 0.090 | 0.150 | 50 | 429 | 72 | 2.8 | 2 |
| Cabbage (3) | 1 cup | 5,000 | 0.036 | 0.462 | 50 | 400 | 72 | 2.5 | 2 |
| Cantaloupe | 1/2 small | 900 | 0.090 | 0.100 | 50 | 32 | 30 | 0.5 | 1 |
| Carrots (4) | 1/2 cup | 4,500 | 0.070 | 0.075 | 5 | 45 | 41 | 0.6 | 1 |
| Cauliflower | 3/4 cup | 10 | 0.085 | 0.090 | 75 | 122 | 60 | 0.9 | 2 |
| Celery (5) | 4 stalks | 20 | 0.030 | 0.015 | 5 | 78 | 46 | 0.5 | 1 |
| Celery, green | 4 stlk | 640 | 0.030 | 0.045 | 7 | 98 | 46 | 0.8 | 1 |
| Celery root | 1/2 cup | — | — | — | 2 | 47 | 71 | 0.8 | 3 |
| Chard, leaves* | 1/2 cup | 15,000 | 0.450 | 0.165 | 37 | 150 | 50 | 3.1 | 2 |
| Cherries # | 12 large | 259 | 0.051 | — | 12 | 19 | 30 | 0.4 | 1 |
| Collards* | 1/2 cup | 6,300 | 0.130 | — | 70 | 207 | 75 | 3.4 | 3 |
| Corn on cob | 1 medium | 860 | 0.209 | 0.055 | 8 | 8 | 103 | 0.4 | 3 |
| Cucumber | 1 medium | 35 | 0.060 | 0.054 | 12 | 10 | 21 | 0.3 | 1 |
| Dandelion greens* | 1/2 cup | 20,000 | 0.190 | 0.270 | 100 | 84 | 35 | 0.6 | 3 |
| Eggplant | 1/2 cup | 70 | 0.042 | 0.036 | 10 | 11 | 31 | 0.5 | 1 |
| Endive | 10 stalks | 15,000 | 0.058 | 0.072 | 20 | 104 | 39 | 1.2 | 1 |
| Grapefruit | 1/2 medium | 20 | 0.070 | 0.060 | 45 | 21 | 20 | 0.2 | 0 |
| Grapes | 1 small bunch | 25 | 0.030 | 0.024 | 3 | 19 | 35 | 0.7 | 1 |
| Guava | 1 | 200 | 0.156 | 0.105 | 125 | 15 | 16 | 3.0 | 1 |
| Honeydew melon | 1/4 med | 100 | — | — | 90 | — | — | — | 0 |
| Huckleberries | 1/2 cup | 100 | 0.045 | 0.021 | 8 | 25 | 20 | 0.2 | 1 |
| Kale* | 1/2 cup | 20,000 | 0.189 | 0.570 | 96 | 195 | 67 | 2.5 | 4 |
| Kohlrabi | 1/2 cup | — | 0.030 | 0.120 | 50 | 195 | 60 | 0.7 | 2 |
| Leeks | 1/2 cup | 20 | 0.150 | — | 24 | 58 | 56 | 0.6 | 2 |
| Lettuce, green | 10 leaves | 2,000 | 0.075 | 0.150 | 7 | 49 | 28 | 1.5 | 1 |
| Lettuce, white | 1/4 head | 125 | 0.051 | 0.062 | 5 | 17 | 40 | 0.5 | 1 |
| Mushrooms (6) | 3/4 cup | — | 0.160 | 0.070 | 2 | 14 | 98 | 0.7 | 4 |
| Mustard greens | 1/2 cup | 11,000 | 0.138 | 0.450 | 126 | 291 | 84 | 9.1 | 2 |
| Okra | 1/2 cup | 440 | 0.126 | — | 17 | 72 | 62 | 2.1 | 2 |
| Onions, fresh | 4 medium | 60 | 0.042 | 0.125 | 7 | 41 | 47 | 0.4 | 1 |
| Orange | 1 medium | 190 | 0.090 | 0.075 | 50 | 44 | 18 | 0.4 | 0 |
| Parsley | 1/2 cup | 8,000 | 0.057 | — | 70 | 23 | 15 | 9.6 | 20 |

Recommended Food

(Continued)

**TABLE 3.4 Food Values (Continued)**

| | | Vitamins | | | | Minerals | | Other | |
|---|---|---|---|---|---|---|---|---|---|
| Food | Measure | A units | B-1 (mg) | B-2 (mg) | C (mg) | Calc. (mg) | Phos. (mg) | Iron (mg) | Prot. (gm) |
| Parsnips (6) | 1/2 cup | 100 | 0.120 | — | 40 | 60 | 76 | 1.7 | 2 |
| Peaches, white | 3 halves# | 100 | 0.025 | 0.065 | 6 | 10 | 19 | 0.2 | 1 |
| Peaches, yellow | 1 lrg# | 1,000 | 0.025 | 0.065 | 9 | 10 | 19 | 0.3 | 1 |
| Pear | 1 medium | 17 | 0.030 | 0.060 | 4 | 15 | 18 | 0.3 | 0 |
| Peas, fresh* | 1/2 cup | 1,500 | 0.390 | 0.250 | 20 | 28 | 127 | 0.2 | 7 |
| Persimmon (7) | 1 lrg | 1,600 | — | — | 40 | 22 | 21 | 0.2 | 2 |
| Pineapple @ | 2/3 cup | 30 | 0.100 | 0.025 | 38 | 8 | 26 | 0.2 | 0 |
| Plums | 3 medium | 130 | 0.120 | 0.056 | 5 | 20 | 27 | 0.5 | 1 |
| Potato, sweet | 1 medium | 3,600 | 0.155 | 0.150 | 25 | 19 | 45 | 0.9 | 3 |
| Potato, white | 1 medium | — | 0.220 | 0.075 | 33 | 13 | 53 | 1.5 | 3 |
| Potato, yam | 1 medium | 5,000 | 0.180 | 0.360 | 6 | 44 | 50 | 1.1 | 2 |
| Pumpkin | 1/2 cup | 2,500 | 0.056 | 0.057 | 8 | 23 | 50 | 0.9 | 1 |
| Radishes | 15 large | — | 0.030 | 0.054 | 25 | 21 | 29 | 0.9 | 1 |
| Raspberries | 1/2 cup | 260 | 0.021 | — | 30 | 41 | 38 | 0.8 | 1 |
| Rutabaga | 3/4 cup | 25 | 0.075 | 0.120 | 26 | 74 | 56 | 0.7 | 1 |
| Spinach* | 1/2 cup | 11,000 | 0.090 | 0.312 | 30 | 78 | 46 | 2.5 | 2 |
| Squash, hubbard | 1/2 cup | 4,000 | 0.050 | 0.075 | 3 | 19 | 15 | 0.5 | 1 |
| Squash, summer | 1/2 cup | 1,000 | 0.040 | 0.050 | 3 | 18 | 15 | 0.3 | 1 |
| Strawberries | 1/2 cup | 100 | 0.025 | — | 50 | 34 | 28 | 0.6 | 1 |
| Tangerine | 2 medium | 300 | 0.120 | 0.054 | 48 | 42 | 17 | 0.2 | 1 |
| Tofu bean cake | 120 grams | — | 0.070 | 0.010 | — | 150 | 150 | 2.3 | 86 |
| Tomato | 1 medium | 1,500 | 0.100 | 0.050 | 25 | 11 | 29 | 0.4 | 1 |
| Turnips* | 1/2 cup | — | 0.062 | 0.062 | 22 | 56 | 47 | 0.5 | 1 |
| Turnip greens | 1/2 cup | 11,000 | 0.060 | 0.045 | 130 | 347 | 49 | 3.4 | 2 |
| Watercress | 3/4 cup | 1,250 | 0.030 | 0.090 | 15 | 40 | 11 | 0.8 | 0 |
| Watermelon | 1 medium slice | 450 | 0.180 | 0.084 | 22 | 33 | 9 | 0.6 | 0 |

Recommended Food

(1) inside white leaves; (2) outside green leaves; (3) Chinese; (4) diced; (5) bleached; (6) domestic; (7) Japanese.

# pitted; * cooked; @ fresh.

Calc = calcium; Phos = phosphorus; Prot = protein.

Modified from *International Turtle and Tortoise Society Journal*, August/September/October, 1970, and Composition of Foods, U.S. Department of Agriculture Handbook Number 8, Washington, DC, 1963.

**TABLE 3.5 Some Nutritious Members of the Brassica Family of Plants**

| Common name | Latin name | $Ca:PO_4$ ratio |
|---|---|---|
| Broccoli, cauliflower, broccoflower | *B. o. var. botrytis* | 1.49:1 |
| flowerets | | 0.61:1 |
| leaves | | 3.91:1 |
| Cabbage varieties: | | |
| Chinese (pe-tsai; napa) | *B. o. var. pekinensis* | 5.55:1 |
| Head, green leaves | *B. o. var. capitata* | 5.96:1 |
| Head, white leaves | | 1.35:1 |
| Kale, borecole | *B. o. var. acephala* | 2.90:1 |
| Kohlrabi | *B. o. var. gonggylodes* | 3.25:1 |
| Mustard varieties: | | |
| Abyssinian | *B. carinata* | 3.65:1 |
| Black | *B. nigra* | 3.54:1 |
| Chinese (pak-choi) | *B. c. ssp. chinensis* | 3.62:1 |
| Field | *B. campestris* | 3.48:1 |
| Indian (brown) | *B. juncea* | 3.48:1 |
| White | *B. alba (B. hirta)* | 3.54:1 |
| Wild (charlock) | *B. kaber (B. arvensis)* | 3.78:1 |
| Rutabaga | *B. rapa* | 1.32:1 |
| Turnip greens | *B. c. ssp. rapifera* | 4.24:1 |

Ca = calcium
$PO_4$ = phosphorus (as phosphate ion)
Modified from *IPM Practitioner*, *25*(7):5, 1993

# CHAPTER 4

## TOXIC-PLANT POISONING

There are many species of mildly irritating to profoundly toxic wild and cultivated plants that could be ingested by captive iguanas. Table 4.1 is a partial list of the more common species that have been implicated in plant intoxications.

Note: Although pothos and philodendron-like plants are listed as being noxious or toxic when ingested by most animals, actual intoxication of iguanas has not been observed when these plants have been used to enhance their enclosures. This is probably because iguanas possess an acute sense of taste and, after biting a small piece of a noxious leaf, they soon learn to avoid the plant.

**TABLE 4.1 Toxic Plants**

| Plant Name | Toxic portion(s) | Plant Name | Toxic portion(s) |
|---|---|---|---|
| *Acokanthera* | Flowers, fruit | Creeping Charlie (*Glecoma*) (not the indoor plant with the same common name) | Foliage |
| Aconite (Monk's Hood) (*Aconitum*) | Roots, flowers, leaves, seeds | Crocus | Bulbs |
| African Lily (*Agapanthus*) | Foliage, bulbs | Croton | Foliage, shoots |
| Algae, Blue-Green (*Mycrocystis*) | All parts | Cyclamen | Foliage, stems, flowers |
| *Aloe* | Succulent foliage | Daffodil (*Narsissus*) | Bulbs, foliage, flowers, pods |
| *Amaryllis* | Bulbs, stem, flower parts | Daphne (*Laurus*) | Berries |
| *Amsinckia* (Tarweed) | Foliage, seeds | Deadly Nightshade (*Solanum*) | Foliage, unripe fruit, sprouts |
| *Anemone* | Leaves, flowers | Death Camus (*Zygadensus*) | All parts—especially roots |
| Apple (*Malus*) | Seeds (only if crushed) | Delphinium | Bulbs, foliage, flowers, seeds |
| Apricot (*Prunus*) | Foliage, inner-pit seeds | Destroying Angel (Death Cap) (*Amanita; many other fungi*) | All parts |
| Arrowhead Vine (*Syngonium*) | Foliage, fruits | Dianthus | Foliage, fruit |
| Autumn Crocus (*Colchicum*) | Bulbs | Dogwood (*Cornus; Cyboxylon*) | Fruit (mildly toxic) |
| Avocado (*Persea*) | Foliage, fruit (in some circumstances) | Dumb Cane (*Dieffenbachia*) | Foliage |
| Azalea (*Rhododendron*) | Foliage, flowers | Eggplant (*Solanum*) | Foliage |
| Baneberry (*Actaea*) | Foliage, fruits | Elderberry (*Sambucus*; *Alnus*) | Leaves, bark, shoots |
| Begonia | Tubers, foliage, blossoms | Elephant Ear (Taro) (*Caladium*) | Foliage |
| Belladonna (*Digitalis*) | Berries and other parts | English Ivy (*Hedera*) | Especially berries |
| Betal Nut Palm (*Areca catachu*) | All parts | Euphorbia (Spurges) | Foliage, flowers, latex-like sap |
| Bird of Paradise (*Strelitzia*) | Foliage, flowers, seed pods | Fiddle Leaf Fig (*Ficus lyrata*) | Foliage, latex |
| Bittersweet Nightshade (*Solanum*) | Berries | Fig (*Ficus benjamina*) | Foliage, latex |
| Black Locust (*Robinia*) | Bark, sprouts, foliage | Fiddle Neck (*Senecio*) | All parts |
| Bleeding Heart (*Dicentra*) | Foliage, flowers, roots | Fly Agaric Deathcap (*Amanita*) | All parts |
| Bloodroot (*Sanguinaria*) | All parts | Four O'Clock (*Mirabilis*) | All parts |
| Bluebonnet (*Centaurea*) | Foliage, flowers | Foxglove (*Digitalis*) | Foliage, flowers |
| Blue-Green Algae (*Mycrocystis*) | All parts | Gelsemium | All parts |
| Boston Ivy (*Hedera*) | All parts | Golden Chain (*Laburnum*) | Seeds and pods |
| Bottlebrush (*Equisetum*) | Flowers | Grape Ivy (*Cissus*) | All parts |
| Boxwood (*Boxus*) | Foliage, twigs | Heart Ivy (*Hedera helix*) | All parts |
| Buckeye Horse Chestnut (*Aesculus*) | Sprouts, nuts | Heavenly Bamboo (*Nandina*) | All parts |
| Buttercup (*Ranunculus*) | All parts | Hemlock Roots (Water & Poison) (*Comium*; *Cicuta*) | All parts |
| Caladium | All parts | Henbane (*Hyoscyamus*) | All parts |
| Calla Lily (*Zantedeschia*) | All parts | Holly, English and American (*Ilex*) | Foliage, berries |
| Cardinal Flower (*Lobelia*) | All parts | Horse Chestnut (*Aesculus*) | All parts |
| Carolina Jessamine (*Gelsemium*) | Foliage, flowers, sap | Horsetail Reed (*Equisetum*) | All parts |
| Casava | Roots | Hyacinth (*Hyacinthus*) | Bulbs, foliage, flowers |
| Castor Bean (*Ricinus*) | Uncooked beans | Hydrangea | All parts |
| Celandine (*Chelidonium*) | All parts | Impatiens (*Touch-Me-Not*) | All parts |
| Chalice; Trumpet vine (*Nicotiana*) | All parts | Iris (Flags) | Bulbs, roots, foliage, flowers |
| Cherry (*Prunus*) | Inner-pit seeds | Ivy (all forms) (*Hedera*) | Foliage, fruit |
| China Berry Tree (*Melia*) | Berries | Jack-in-the-Pulpit (*Arisaema*) | Roots (mildly toxic) |
| Chinese Evergreen (*Aglaonema*) | Foliage | Jasmine (*Jasminum*; *Gardinia*) | Foliage, flowers, (especially nectar) |
| Chinese Lantern (*Physalis*) | All parts | Jasmine, Star (*Jasminum*) | Foliage, flowers |
| Christmas Cactus (*Euphorbia*) | Entire plant | Jerusalem Cherry (*Solanum*) | Foliage, fruits |
| Columbine (*Aquilegia*) | Foliage, flowers, seeds | Jessamine | Berries |
| Common Privet (*Ligustrum*) | Foliage, berries | Jimson Weed (Thorn Apple) (*Datura*) | Foliage, flowers, pods |
| Coral Plant (*Euphorbium*) | All parts | | |

**TABLE 4.1 Toxic Plants (continued)**

| Plant Name | Toxic portion(s) |
|---|---|
| Johnson Grass, Wilted (*Sorgum*) | All parts |
| Lambkill (Sheep Laurel) (*Kalmia*) | Foliage |
| Lantana | Foliage, flowers, especially berries |
| Larkspur (*Delphinium*) | Entire young plant; seeds & pods |
| Laurel (*Laurus*) | All parts |
| Lily of the Nile (*Agapanthus*) | All parts |
| Lily of the Valley (*Convallaria*) | Foliage, flowers |
| Lobelia | All parts |
| Locoweed (*Astragalus*; *Oxytropis*) | All parts |
| Locust(s) (*Robinia*) | All parts |
| Lupine (*Lupinus*) | Foliage, pods, especially seeds |
| Marijuana (*Canibis*) | All parts |
| May Apple (*Podophyllum*) | Fruit |
| Mescal (*Lophophora*) | All parts may be toxic |
| Milk Weed (*Asclepsias*) | Foliage |
| Mistletoe (*Viscum*; Phorodendron) | Foliage, berries |
| Moccasin Flower (*Cypripedium*) | Foliage, flowers |
| Monkshood (*Aconitum*) | Entire plant, including roots |
| Moonseed (*Menispermum*) | Berries |
| Morning Glory (*Ipomoea*) | Foliage, flowers, seeds |
| Mountain Laurel (*Kalmia*) | Young leaves and shoots |
| Mushrooms (some wild forms) | Entire cap and stem |
| *Narcissus* | Bulb, flowers |
| Nectarine | Foliage, inner-pit seeds |
| Nephthytis (*Syngonium*) | Foliage |
| Nicotine, (Tree, Bush) (*Nicotiana*) | Foliage, flowers |
| Nightshades (*Solanum*) | All parts, especially unripe fruits |
| Oak trees (*Quercus*) | Leaves, acorns |
| Oleander (*Nerium*) | Foliage, stems, flowers |
| Pansy (*Viola*) | All parts |
| Peach (*Prunus*) | Foliage, inner-pit seeds |
| Pear (*Pyrus*) | Seeds (only if crushed) |
| Pennyroyal (*Hedeoma*; *Mentha*) | Foliage, flowers |
| Peony (*Paeonia*) | Foliage, flowers |
| Pepper (*Piper*; *Capsicums*) | Foliage |
| Periwinkle (*Vinca*) | All parts |
| Philodendron, (some species) | All parts |
| Pinks (*Dianthus*) | All parts |
| Plum (*Prunus*) | Foliage, inner-pit seeds |
| Poinsettia (*Euphorbia*) | Foliage, flowers, latex sap |
| Poison Hemlock (*Comium*) | Foliage, seeds |
| Poison Ivy (*Tocicodendon*) | Foliage, fruit |
| Poison Oak (*Rhus*) | Foliage, fruit |
| Poison Sumac (*Tocicodendon*) | Foliage, fruit |
| Juniper (*Juniperus*) | All parts |
| Pokewood or Pokeberry (*Phytolacca*) | Roots, fruit |
| Poppy (except California) (*Papaver*) | All parts |
| Potato (*Solanum*) | Raw foliage, sprouts ("eyes") |
| Pothos (*Epipremnum*) | All parts |
| Privet (*Ligustrum*) | Berries |
| Pyracantha | Foliage; fruit under some circumstances |
| Ranunculus | All parts |
| Redwood (*Sequoia*) | Resinoids leached when wood is wet |
| Rhododendron | Foliage, flowers |
| Rhubarb (*Rheum*) | Uncooked foliage, stems |
| Rosary Bean (*Abrus*) | Foliage, flowers, pods |
| Rosemary (*Rosmarinus*) | Foliage in some species |
| Rubber Tree (*Ficus*) | Foliage, latex |
| Russian Thistle (*Carduus*; *Silybum*) | Foliage, flowering parts |
| Sage (*Salvia*) | Foliage in some species |
| Salmonberry (*Rubus*) | Foliage, fruit |
| Scarlet Pimpernel (*Anagallis*) | Foliage, flowers, fruit |
| Scotch Broom (*Cytisus*) | Foliage, flowers, seeds |
| Senecio ("Fiddle Neck") | All parts |
| Shasta Daisy (*Chrysanthemum*) | Foliage, flowers |
| Skunk Cabbage (*Symplocarpus*) | Roots |
| Snapdragon (*Antirrhinum*) | Foliage, flowers |
| Spanish Bayonet (*Yucca*) | Foliage, flowers |
| Split Leaf Philodendron (*Monstera*) | All parts |
| Squirrel Corn (*Dicentra*) | Foliage, flowers, seeds |
| Star of Bethlehem (*Ornithogalum*) | Foliage, flowers |
| Star Thistle (*Centaurea*) | All parts |
| String of Pearls (*Seneciao*) | All parts |
| Sudan Grass, Wilted (*Sorgum*) | All parts |
| Sundew (*Drosera*) | Foliage |
| Sweetpea (*Lathyrus*) | Stems, seeds |
| Tansy (*Tanacetum*) | Foliage, flowers |
| Taro (Elephant Ears) (*Colocasia*) | Foliage, uncooked tubers |
| Tarweed (*Eriodictyon*) | Foliage, seeds |
| Tiger Lily (*Lilium*) | Foliage, flowers, seed pods |
| Toad Flax (*Linaria*) | Foliage |
| Tobacco (*Nicotiana*) | Foliage, flowers |
| Tomato Plant (*Lycopersicon*) | Foliage, vines |
| Toyon Berry (*Heteromeles*) | Berries |
| Tree of Heaven (*Ailanthus*) | Foliage, flowers |
| Trillium | Foliage |
| Trumpet Vine (*Campsis*) | All parts |
| Tulip (*Liriodendron*) | Bulb, foliage, flowers |

**TABLE 4.1 Toxic Plants (continued)**

| Plant Name | Toxic portion(s) | Plant Name | Toxic portion(s) |
|---|---|---|---|
| Umbrella Tree (*Schefflera*) | All parts | Water Hemlock (*Cicuta*) | Roots, foliage |
| Venus Flytrap (*Dionaea*) | Foliage, funnel flowers | Wild Parsnip (*Pastinaca*) | Underground roots, foliage |
| Verbena | Foliage, flowers | Wistaria (*Wisteria*) | Foliage, seeds, pods |
| Vetch (several forms) (*Vicia*) | Seeds, pods | Yellow Star Thistle (*Centaurea*) | Foliage, flowers |
| Virginia Creeper (*Parthenocissus*) | Foliage, seed pods | Yerba Santa (*Eriodictyon*) | Foliage, seeds |
| | | Yew (*Taxus*) | Foliage |

Modified from a list compiled by the *International Turtle and Tortoise Journal* May–June, 1969; a compilation by the San Diego Turtle and Tortoise Society published in the *Tortuga Gazette* January, 1982; the San Diego Poison Information Center, University of California, San Diego; *Poisonous Plants in the Garden*, University of California Agricultural Extension Division; Davis, California; and *Magic and Medicine of Plants*, Reader's Digest Association, Inc., Pleasantville, New York, 1986. Also see: Fowler, M.E., 1975; Garner, 1961; Hulbert & Oehme, 1961; Tucker & Kimball, 1961; and U.S. Dept. of Agriculture, Farmer's Bulletin #2106, 1958.

# CHAPTER 5

## DISORDERS RELATED TO NUTRITION

Although iguanas are usually hardy in captivity (some have lived for nearly twenty years or more), they are prone to several infectious and parasitic diseases and metabolic disorders if their environmental conditions and care are not appropriate. **Most illnesses that occur in all species of captive iguanas are related to nutrition. These illnesses may reflect gross malnutrition originating from the insufficient quantity or the deficient quality of the foodstuffs they are fed; generally, it is the latter condition that induces disease.**

Growing iguanas require a well-balanced diet that contains adequate calcium without concomitant excessive phosphorus (the reasons for this are complex), but simply stated, calcium is essential for the following physiological processes:

- Growth and maintenance of the skeleton and teeth
- Skeletal, and smooth- and heart-muscle contractions
- Nerve-impulse conduction to and from the brain and spinal cord
- Blood coagulation
- Cellular movements

### METABOLIC BONE DISEASE CAUSED BY EXCESSIVE PHOSPHORUS: INADEQUATE CALCIUM

When a diet contains too much phosphorus in relation to calcium, the body makes every effort to reestablish a normal calcium:phosphorus ratio by removing calcium from existing calcified tissues such as bone. Unless calcium is replaced, the tissue stores from which the calcium is extracted soon become markedly altered.

Earlier called "fibrous osteodystrophy," this important disorder of calcium, phosphorus, and magnesium metabolism has long been recognized as a major medical problem in zoo animals in general, and green iguanas specifically (Wallach and Hoessle, 1968). For instance, monkeys fed a diet unbalanced in its mineral content soon develop skeletal deformities. Owners of monkeys and some zoo personnel used to call this condition "cage paralysis" and "rubber jaw." Similarly, carnivores, especially felines, fed diets consisting mostly or entirely of muscle meat, rapidly lose bone mass and, as a result, suffer multiple skeletal fractures.

This nutrition-related disease was once erroneously called "osteogenesis imperfecta," which is a heritable disorder observed in many species (including humans).

Fortunately, much has been learned about nutrition in the last 30 years. As a consequence of experience gained through observation and experimentation, the diets fed to a diverse number of species have improved immensely and, as a result, many mineral- and vitamin-related disorders are seldom seen today. Sadly, this is not necessarily true with the diets fed to captive green iguanas. Mainly, this is because of ignorance—albeit innocent in intent. One of the more common sources for husbandry information regarding iguanas is the petshop salesperson. If that petshop salesperson is well-trained, experienced, and reads pertinent resource materials, then the customer is likely to be given factual and accurate information. However, if the clerk is inexperienced and told only to sell whatever is over-represented in the shop's inventory, the likely result is misinformation that can foster one or more nutritional disorders occurring in the purchased pet.

Once a significant imbalance in calcium and phosphorus occurs, tiny glands in the iguana's neck are stimulated to secrete a hormone that causes calcium stored in the bones to be removed. The calcium then becomes incorporated in the blood plasma and tissue fluids, and finally calcium is lost in urine. **If this loss of calcium is not controlled and the calcium that was lost is not replaced, the result is a condition called *metabolic bone disease*. The early signs of this disorder are limbs which gradually swell and, particularly, jaw bones that become markedly shortened and markedly bowed (Figures 5.1 to 5.5).** What at first may appear to be chubby limbs really are severely softened bones and wasted muscle tissue. When the limb bones are thus affected, there may be additional swelling and lameness. In extreme cases, fine muscular twitching, spasms, and, eventually, paralysis and death can occur. If the affected bones are subjected to stressful forces (that otherwise would be of no consequence to a normal skeleton), they may fracture or collapse. When the vertebrae that comprise the spine are affected, they may collapse and, in doing so, compress the delicate spinal cord. If the mandibles (lower jaw bones) are affected, they tend to become not only diffusely swollen, but they also become bowed outward. This is because the tongue is attached to the inner aspect of the centermost portion of the lower jawbone and the force of the muscular tongue's backward pull causes the lower jaw to assume a bowed shape. This is not to suggest that the upper jaw and skull are not equally soft: it does not tend to become as deformed as the lower jaw only because there is nothing exerting tension on the upper jaw.

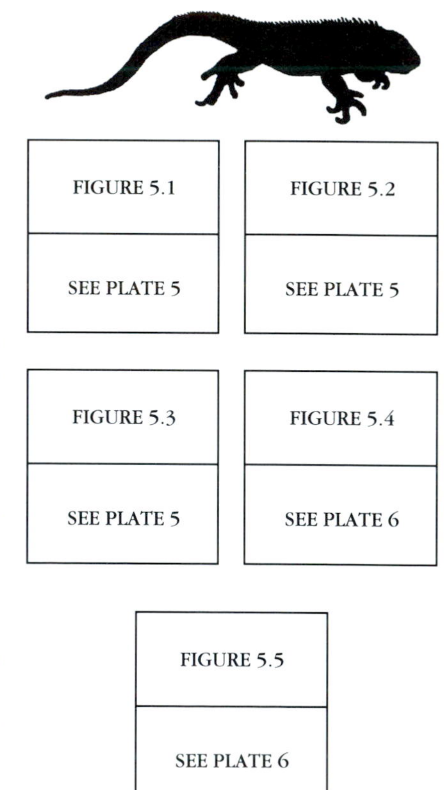


Metabolic bone disease usually can be linked to diets consisting primarily of head lettuce, carrots, squash, and cucumbers; melons, grapes, bananas and other fruit; some greens such as spinach (which, although containing an adequate Ca:$PO_4$ ratio, also contains oxalic acid which reacts with calcium to form calcium oxalate, a relatively insoluble salt); and invertebrates such as mealworms and crickets. Each of these items is rich in available phosphorus, but very deficient in gross or **available** calcium. Not only will calcium be lost to an iguana's bones if it eats spinach frequently, but excessive calcium-oxalate crystals can damage the kidneys sufficiently to cause uremia and death from renal failure.

## METABOLIC BONE DISEASE CAUSED BY INSUFFICIENT VITAMIN $D_3$ ("RICKETS")

In rickets (which is another form of metabolic bone disease characterized by softening of the bones), the available dietary calcium may or may not be sufficient, but there is a dietary or environmental (lack of sunlight or source of suitable ultraviolet light) deficiency of vitamin $D_3$. Either preformed vitamin $D_3$ is not present in the food, or the iguana is not exposed to ultraviolet irradiation of suitable wavelength. (The end result is the same as when calcium is not absorbed from the intestine.)

Bone is a dynamic tissue; it is in almost constant "turnover." Small amounts are removed every day, and small amounts are formed and added every day. Under conditions of inadequate calcium absorption from the large intestine—which requires vitamin $D_3$—the bones may be affected, and eventually they become thinner and weaker. Once a threshold is reached, these weakened bones may actually become grossly thicker—but not necessarily stronger.

Rather than forming bone substance by the orderly mineralization of cartilage "templates" at the ends of growing bones, the bones of individuals who are suffering from rickets tend to undergo a variable degree of cartilage overgrowth called *hypertrophy* (abnormally large cell size) and *hyperplasia* (abnormally large numbers of cells). Such bones remain very poorly mineralized and, thus, are soft. One characteristic of rickets is the formation of swellings termed "rachitic rosettes" at the junctions where the bony ribs join the cartilaginous ribs (Figure 5.6). These structures are rounded swellings that can be seen as the iguana's ribcage expands during each breath. In addition, the ends of the limb bones may be greatly thickened or buttressed, and the bone next to adjacent joints may become broadly flared. Both of these anatomical (and pathological) alterations are examples of the body's attempt to strengthen grossly weakened bony tissue. Radiographs (X-ray photographs) of affected bones reveal soft-tissue swellings that constitute the rachitic rosettes (Figure 5.7). These radiographs exhibit little or no evidence of mineralization. The outer layers of bone also exhibit marked thinning. Fractures also occur frequently in weight-bearing limb bones, as well as in ribs and vertebrae.

**Figure 5.6.** This juvenile iguana has rickets. Note the swellings along its rib cage.

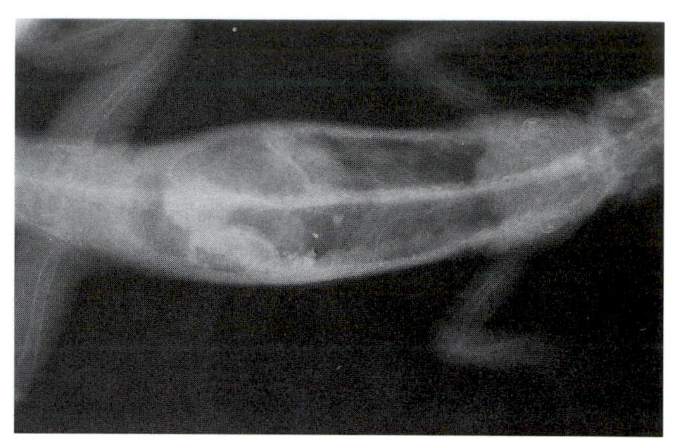

**Figure 5.7.** X-ray photograph of the iguana in Figure 5.6. Note the bilateral opaque swellings on the inside of the ribcage.

### The Role of Vitamin $D_3$

The lack of sufficient vitamin $D_3$ is an important factor in inducing rickets. Iguanas are heliothermic reptiles—in order to thermoregulate and increase their body temperature, they bask in sunlight. Sunlight's ultraviolet light helps synthesize (form) vitamin $D_3$. Unfortunately, not all cages housing captive iguanas are furnished with artificial illumination which possesses the ultraviolet spectrum necessary to facilitate the biosynthesis of this vitally important vitamin. This can be remedied because a variety of **full-spectrum** (with at least a chromatic index of 90 or better) lighting devices that promote conversion of the intermediate metabolite previtamin D molecule to the active vitamin $D_3$ are now available (see Sources For Reptile-Related Products at the end of this book).

Fortunately, most forms of metabolic bone disease are treatable. Even if the bony deformities at first appear to be profound, many affected iguanas return to normal over a period of several months following effective treatment.

## PATHOLOGICAL MINERALIZATION CAUSED BY EXCESSIVE VITAMIN $D_3$ COMBINED WITH EXCESSIVE DIETARY CALCIUM

Vitamin $D_3$ is required by iguanas (and many other animals) to aid in the absorption of soluble calcium salts from the digested food in the large intestine.

A diet containing too much vitamin $D_3$ and too much calcium can initiate changes in an iguana's skeleton and soft tissues.

**The problem is that with ingestion of too much vitamin $D_3$, there is absorption of too much calcium. This results in an abnormally high blood-calcium level which promotes the deposition of calcium salts into tissues in which calcium is not normally found.** You can easily imagine how normally soft and pliant tissues would be impaired in their important functions if they became severely mineralized. Thus, the clinical signs of hypervitaminosis $D_3$ are referable to which organs are involved: the heart muscle, aorta and other large muscular arteries, pulmonary airways (the trachea and lungs), stomach and intestines, kidneys and urinary bladder, genital tract (particularly the oviducts), skin, spleen, brain, and spinal cord and the thin vascular membranes that envelope them can be affected.

**Almost invariably, this disorder of soft-tissue mineralization is induced by the feeding of artificial dietary items that contain supplementary forms of vitamin $D_3$.** One of the first descriptions of hypervitaminosis D in a reptile was of an iguana that had severe arteriosclerosis resulting from the feeding of an improper diet excessively high in preformed vitamin $D_3$ (Schuchman and Taylor, 1970).

Some reference books and articles advise feeding dog or cat food or monkey biscuits to iguanas. There is no arguing that many iguanas find these commercial diets that have been formulated for dogs, cats and primates highly palatable and prefer to eat them rather than leafy green vegetables (which are a more natural diet for them). However, these items have **not** been formulated for iguanas and, in my opinion, should not be fed to them because they contain too much preformed vitamin $D_3$.

The simple ingestion of too much calcium without a concomitant increase in vitamin $D_3$ usually does not cause a problem, and only results in excessive calcium being passed in the feces with little absorption taking place.

As noted when discussing egg formation and egg resorption (see Chapter 10), a female iguana's blood may contain enormously high levels of calcium during this time. However, these instances are transient and tend to be self-limiting; as soon as the eggs are either fully formed and shelled, or resorbed completely, the female iguana's blood-calcium concentration returns to normal levels **without** remedial treatment.

**When the cause for hypercalcemia (too much blood calcium) is due to nutritional overload, the affected iguana should be treated.** Fortunately, an effective treatment for too much calcium in the blood plasma and soft tissues has been developed (Frye, 1991b; Frye, Centofanti, and Harris, 1991) and the deleterious effects of this condition can be reversed. It requires special treatment in a veterinary hospital for approximately two weeks in addition to removal of all food and vitamin-mineral supplements which contain excessive vitamin $D_3$. Since this is an entirely **preventable** disorder, pay attention to what you feed your iguana.

## VITAMIN DEFICIENCIES AND EXCESSES

### Vitamin A Deficiency

Vitamin A deficiency is unusual in iguanas fed a natural vegetarian diet because such a diet consists of leafy green vegetables which contain ample amounts of beta carotene (the metabolic precursor of vitamin A). Beta carotene is present in green leafy plants; green, yellow, and orange vegetables; and some fruits. It is converted in the digestive process to one or more forms of vitamin A, called *retinyl (and/or retinol) esters*. If diets high in animal protein are fed for a few months or longer, stores of vitamin A in an iguana's liver will be depleted.

The clinical signs of vitamin A deficiency are the following:

- Swollen or reddened eyelids and their associated mucous membranes
- Nasal discharges and/or wheezing or other respiratory distress
- Skin changes such as chronic difficulties in shedding, misshapen claws, or à thickened epidermis
- Unusually dry mouth
- Endocrine glandular dysfunction, the signs of which depend on which glands are involved

### Vitamin A Overdosage

**Vitamin A overdosage can occur when excessive amounts of injectable or oral preformed vitamin A are administered in the hope of stimulating a flagging appetite.** However, there is no evidence that vitamin A has a salutory effect on a poor appetite, and its use for this purpose should be discontinued. Since vitamin A deficiency in an herbivorous iguana is rare, injectable or even oral vitamin A supplements usually are not necessary.

### Vitamin $B_1$ (Thiamin) Deficiency

**Thiamin (Vitamin $B_1$) deficiency is not caused by feeding a thiamin-deficient diet but, rather, by feeding a diet which contains a natural source of *thiaminase*—an enzyme that destroys thiamin already in the iguana's body tissues.** Some plants, particularly certain ferns and other ornamental house plants, contain this enzyme.

The signs of thiamin deficiency are related to nerve disorders such as the following:

- Inability to use certain muscle groups
- Twitching
- Muscular spasms

Similar muscular abnormalities can be seen in vitamin E and/or selenium deficiency; muscle twitching and spasms are also seen in low blood calcium. Therefore, an iguana exhibiting these clinical signs should be evaluated by a veterinarian. Discovered early and treated with oral or injectable thiamin hydrochloride, thiamin deficiency almost always can be treated effectively. Again, prevention is preferable to treatment.

### Vitamin B Complex

Deficiencies in the other B-complex vitamins are unusual in iguanas because they are synthesized in the intestinal tract by the normal intestinal flora composed of beneficial bacteria and protozoa that reside in the alimentary tracts of these animals. Under some circumstances, these microorganisms are killed off by antibiotics; then the entire digestive process becomes impaired and vitamin deficiencies can occur.

### Vitamin C (Ascorbic Acid)

Vitamin C is produced by specialized cells within the kidney and gastrointestinal tract. A deficiency of vitamin C is highly unusual in iguanas and might suggest a disorder involving the kidneys and/or alimentary tract.

Signs of vitamin C deficiency would include the following:

- Bleeding gums, particularly after the normal shedding of teeth which occurs sporadically throughout the iguana's life
- Bruising or other evidence of spontaneous bleeding

When a deficiency of vitamin C is suspected, an affected iguana can be given supplementary vitamin C via injectable water-soluble ascorbic acid or by the oral administration of ascorbic acid in tablet form. The dosage for this drug has not been determined for iguanas. Because of its minimal toxicity, an overdosage of vitamin C is unlikely.

### Vitamin $D_3$

See the sections of vitamin $D_3$ and rickets earlier in this chapter.

### Vitamin $D_3$ and Its Relationship to Vitamin A

There is mounting evidence that **too much vitamin $D_3$ may mimic a deficiency in vitamin A, and too much vitamin A may induce the physiological signs of vitamin $D_3$ deficiency.**

### Vitamin E

**Vitamin E deficiency can occur, but generally this is only as a result of eating food which is rancid or has high levels of saturated fatty acids.** Since green iguanas are herbivorous, such an abnormal diet is most unusual.

However, when stale (dry, not canned) dog, cat, or primate chow is fed, vitamin E deficiency can occur.

Vitamin E (alpha and other tocopherols) is relatively nontoxic. An overdosage of vitamin E as a clinical entity has not been reported.

## MINERAL DEFICIENCIES OR IMBALANCES

### Selenium

**The micronutrient selenium is essential for both growth and maintenance of normal tissues, but, when present in more than small trace amounts, it can be toxic.** Selenium shares an important role as an antioxidant as do vitamins A, C, and E. Physiologically, selenium and vitamin E are linked in their effects on muscle, nerve, skin, cartilage, bone, heart, liver, thyroid, lungs, immune system function, and vascular tissues (Combs, 1994; Combs and Combs, 1986).

| FIGURE 5.8 |
| --- |
| SEE PLATE 12 |

In some geographic locations throughout the world, the soils in which edible plants are grown are deficient in selenium. A specific degenerative disorder of muscle tissue, called "White Muscle Disease" (Figure 5.8), is related to a deficiency of selenium (and/or Vitamin E). Conversely, in some areas with intense agriculture and irrigation systems which rely on subsurface water pumps, the levels of selenium salts in plants may be excessive or even toxic. If the vegetables you feed your iguana were grown in selenium-deficient soil, a small amount of supplemental selenium can be added to the ration. The amount necessary to maintain health is minuscule. A veterinarian can aid you in deciding whether and/or how much supplement should be given.

The clinical signs of selenium deficiency are variable, but usually include:

- Some form of muscular dystrophy, including effects on the heart muscle
- Muscle tremors
- Fatigue
- Possible inflammation and gross dystrophic alteration of muscle and hardening of body fat
- Easily elicited pain when the subcutaneous fatty tissues are palpated
- Sudden death

### Iodine

Micronutritional deficiencies can occur as a result of feeding abnormal or unbalanced diets. **If an iguana's diet is composed mostly of plants of the cabbage family (especially head cabbage, brussels sprouts, etc.), a** deficiency of thyroid hormone may be induced because there are substances in these vegetables that inhibit the absorption of iodine—which is essential for the synthesis of thyroid hormone (see Brassica Plants in Chapter 3). A chronic deficiency in available iodine usually results in a change in the thyroid gland. The gland becomes enlarged and is called a "goiter." Interestingly, there are geographical locations in North America, particularly in the vicinity of the Great Lakes, and in the Midlands area of the United Kingdom, known as "goiter zones" where many people develop enlarged thyroid glands unless they are supplemented with iodine in one form or another. Not surprisingly, some animals raised in these areas also display an increased incidence of goitrous thyroid disease.

In iguanas, the thyroid is located immediately in front of the heart and lies between the large blood vessels that enter and leave the heart. If the goitrous thyroid gland becomes sufficiently large, it may impair the flow of low-pressure blood returning to the heart and (less often) the flow of blood leaving at higher pressure from the heart.

Clinical signs of an enlarged thyroid gland include the following:

- As the gland enlarges, it displaces other organs such as the heart, major blood vessels, and/or lungs leading to cardiovascular and pulmonary dysfunction.
- The esophagus may be compressed causing difficulty in swallowing.
- Occasionally, there is a noticeable swelling in the anterior (front) portion of the chest cavity.
- Lethargy.

When this condition is diagnosed by a veterinarian (most often with the assistance of thyroid-function laboratory tests), the treatment is aimed at altering the diet so that fewer cabbage-like plants are fed and an additional source of iodine is included in the diet. This supplemental iodine can be added easily by feeding ground kelp tablets sprinkled as a top dressing on favored food items; 1⁄16 to ½ tablet/day, depending upon the size of the iguana, given over a period of several weeks will treat this deficiency. Because kelp is not particularly toxic, even a small overdosage is harmless.

### Electrolytes, Especially Sodium

Because all living animal tissues require sodium as a major electrolyte for their cellular maintenance and nerve conduction and since sodium is so ubiquitous in most plants, it seldom is necessary to add sodium chloride (table salt) to the captive iguana's diet.

Iguanas possess an interesting and highly efficient means for handling the problem of excreting excess salt without having to lose precious water from their bodies. Specialized glandular structures which secrete sodium, potassium, and chloride are located just beneath the surface of the tissue lining the nasal passages; these secretions empty into the nasal cavities. It is for this reason that iguanas sneeze frequently. This sneezing does not mean that your iguana has a "cold"—it is entirely normal behavior.

FIGURE 3.1

SEE PLATE 3

You might notice that the fluid that iguanas sneeze out tends to form crusts around the nostrils and, if dried on clear glass or plastic surfaces, it forms crystal-like white spots. These dried deposits consist of chloride salts of sodium and potassium. As the iguana burrows beneath the surface of its cage litter or rubs its nose against an item of cage "furniture," these nasal deposits are scraped off and lost. However, if the iguana is not active, the salt crystals will accumulate (shown previously in Figure 3.1).

# CHAPTER 6

# DISORDERS RELATED TO THE DIGESTIVE SYSTEM

## CONSTIPATION/OBSTIPATION, BLOATING, AND GASTROINTESTINAL BLOCKAGES

The feces of captive iguanas vary widely in their consistency, content, and frequency. There are no specific guidelines with which to judge whether a particular animal is constipated. The digestive process depends substantially upon the kind of food consumed; amount of water imbibed; environmental temperature and, consequently, body temperature; and length of time since the iguana's last meal. The very nature of the food that is ingested plays a major role. Many small particles possess a greater surface area upon which digestive enzymes, gut microfloral bacteria and protozoa, and other digestive agents can act on than does an identical weight which is composed of larger pieces. If water is not readily available to the iguana, its stool masses may become dry, thus impeding their passage through the intestines where the majority of moisture absorption occurs.

Pet iguanas can suffer from constipation because, in captivity, exercise may be severely curtailed; diets may lack sufficient fiber; and large amounts of cage litter, such as sand, gravel, ground corncob, or wood chips, may have been ingested. Even long human, dog, or cat hairs can be accidentally ingested by an iguana. If they are not digested as they traverse an iguana's relatively short gastrointestinal tract, hairs can become enmeshed in the stool boluses and cause physical obstruction of the bowel. Obesity can directly or indirectly lead to difficulty in passing feces through the caudal alimentary tract, especially through the sacculated colon and into the rectum and coprodeum. In my experience, most instances of true constipation and/or obstipation have involved the much-expanded colon that serves as a fermentation vessel for most of the dietary fiber upon which green iguanas subsist.

Constipation and obstipation can be caused by the following:

- The diet itself, specifically the amount of moisture present either as a component of the food or as readily available drinking water
- Ingestion of substances or foreign bodies that can serve as physical obstructions to stool passage
- Presence of excessive fat that can impinge on the large intestine, thereby impeding the progress of stool boluses
- Intestinal intussusception

- Presence of large numbers of shelled eggs that can impose pressure on the female's large bowel
- Traumatic injuries, developmental malformations, or metabolic bone disease-related abnormalities of the pelvis that narrow the cross-sectional diameter and, therefore, impede stool passage

Treatment ranges from bathing the iguana in tepid water (which often is sufficient to induce defecation) to major surgery for physically removing masses of dried stool and foreign material from the intestine.

Many herpetoculturists employ pelleted alfalfa rabbit or guinea pig chow as cage litter. When this material is purposefully or accidentally ingested, it provides essential nutrients and safe fiber. When swallowed, it soon softens and is digested and processed just as any other nutritive fiber would be. The nonnutritive fiber contributes to the stool bulk and is passed in the feces without inducing blockages. However, when pelleted alfalfa becomes dampened with water or soiled with feces, it ferments rapidly and soon becomes moldy, so it must be changed frequently. One good way (that can be managed easily) for providing both a toileting area and a food supply of pelleted alfalfa is to place a pan or tray of the material into the cage and change it as it becomes moistened with water or urinary wastes or soiled with feces.

With the retention of fecal material in the large bowel, there is a progressive absorption of fluid from the stools. Soon, the fecal boluses become abnormally dry and hard, making it difficult for the normal peristaltic waves that propel the stools toward the rectum and anus to advance them into the terminal alimentary tract (the coprodeum) and thence out through the anal vent. Radiography at this point may reveal a physiological blockage called an *ileus*, usually characterized by gas-filled loops of intestine just in front of the obstruction. This is a severe condition and must be treated aggressively by a veterinarian.

Medical management of constipation can be achieved by using any of the following: petroleum jelly; magnesium oxide (milk of magnesia) suspension; stool-softening agents such as *dilute* dioctyl sodium sulfosuccinate (DSS); phenolpthalein, and/or stool-bulk augmenters such as hemicellulose. Siblin (Park-Davis) is an effective medication available at most pharmacies. Also, several proprietary laxative products formulated for cats are highly effective in relieving constipation and obstipation in iguanas, and they are available from veterinarians and pet shops. **Place a *small* volume of any of the above products into the mouth of the affected iguana. Solid laxatives are less likely to be inhaled than liquid mineral oil is; therefore solid laxatives are preferred by most veterinarians who treat iguanas.** When the blockage is caused by a mass of firm, dry feces in the rectum or coprodeum, an infant-size glycerine suppository inserted into the cloaca may aid a constipated iguana to pass its stools.

### Are Enemas Safe?

| FIGURE 6.1 | FIGURE 6.2 |
|---|---|
| SEE PLATE 12 | SEE PLATE 12 |

In the past, I have been extremely conservative in recommending whether or not to administer enemas to reptiles in general, and to iguanas specifically. However, when given carefully and correctly, enemas are safe and definitely bring immediate relief. The alimentary tract of iguanas, like other reptiles, terminates in the coprodeum portion of the common cloacal vault. Into this common tubular structure also exit the urodeum (into which the urinary wastes empty) and the proctodeum (in which the genital tract terminates). **Thus, unless an enema tube or catheter is placed carefully and the enema fluid is administered at low pressure, bacteria- and protozoa-contaminated fluid can be forced into the caudal genitourinary tract(s), and serious infections may then ensue.**

Figures 6.1 & 6.2 illustrate an immature green iguana before and immediately after the administration of a warm-water (32–34 °C; 90–93 °F) enema delivered through a well-lubricated, soft rubber catheter. This small iguana had not responded to several attempts to treat its constipation by oral administration of different laxatives and warm-water soaking. The enema had to be performed one more time approximately one week after this photograph was made. Once the large sacculated colon was evacuated and the much-stretched organ was permitted to rest and regain its muscle tone and resiliency, the iguana was able to pass its feces without difficulty.

## VOMITING

The diagnoses of and causes of vomition in iguanas are essentially the same as those observed in higher vertebrates, but also include causes specific to reptiles. The following can cause vomiting:

- Improper environmental temperature
- Handling the iguana within a few hours after it has eaten
- Infectious and/or metabolic disease
- Parasitism
- Plant intoxications
- Putrefaction of ingested material
- Foreign bodies
- Ulcerative lesions within the gastrointestinal tract
- Abscesses
- Tumors either involving or impinging upon the walls of the gastrointestinal organs
- Mere gorging

A proper diagnosis requires obtaining a thorough history and evaluation of captive husbandry practices. Diagnostic radiography or other imaging techniques, microscopic examination of gastric-content specimens, and direct fiberoptic endoscopy (with or without simultaneous gastric biopsy) are diagnostic options which may reveal the cause of chronic vomiting. Analysis of the feces may disclose severe gastrointestinal parasitism.

**While not always leading to an invariably negative outcome, chronic vomiting usually is an unfavorable prognostic sign in iguanas.** The underlying causes can include many serious conditions such as the following:

- Gastric ulceration
- Obstructive bowel disease such as intestinal intussusception or torsion
- Benign and malignant tumors
- Severe pancreatic disease
- Plant and other organic and inorganic intoxications

Sometimes, other clinical signs may offer clues to the cause for vomiting:

- Blood-tinged mucus or parasitic worms may be present in the vomitus.
- Recognizable parts of a toxic plant might be present in the vomitus.
- The feces may be fatty (which is suggestive of pancreatic insufficiency).
- There may be a complete absence of stools (which suggests intestinal obstruction).

**An adequately warm ambient temperature must be provided when feeding captive reptiles because it permits and even enhances the proper digestion and assimilation of ingested food.** This digestive process is linked to several temperature-dependent digestive pancreatic, gastric and intestinal enzymes. Low environmental temperature does not permit the internal organs to reach temperatures sufficient to support digestion. When this occurs, the food simply putrifies and is soon vomited.

Handling an iguana too soon after it has eaten often results in the food being regurgitated. This behavior may be a defensive mechanism which has evolved to discourage predators. (It is often observed in a variety of lizards, especially monitors—but of course, the stench of a meat-eating monitor lizard's disgusting semi-digested meal may be far more effective in discouraging predators and handling than the less fetid smell of a vegetarian iguana's chlorophyll-scented stomach contents!)

Chronic regurgitation can lead to ulceration of the esophagus as a result of the hydrochloric acid present in stomach contents. Also, if any of the regurgitated ingesta is aspirated (inhaled), it can lead to inhalation pneumonia because the acidic ingesta can inflame and consequently damage the delicate lung tissues.

## DIARRHEA

Severe diarrhea is not a common problem in captive iguanas, but when loose stools are passed, they should be examined for the presence of disease-causing protozoa and worms. **Remember, it is entirely normal for iguanas to have some protozoa in their feces; these microorganisms are essential for normal digestive processes to occur. However, if diagnostic tests reveal disease-causing organisms, appropriate medication together with supportive therapy should be administered by a veterinarian.** Appropriate dosages of Kao-Pectate® (Upjohn), Kaopectate Concentrate® (Upjohn), Pectolin® (EVSCO), etc., can be administered to help relieve the condition. Dosages are directly related to the size and weight of the individual animal. Generally, give approximately 5–10 ml (1–2 teaspoons) of KaoPectate or Pectolin to a 2.5-kg (approximately 5-lb) iguana. Repeat at 12-hour intervals for 2–3 days. If Kao-Pectate Concentrate® is used, give approximately one third as much. If no improvement is seen within 36–48 hours, or if bloody stools are produced, take the iguana to a veterinarian.

Loose stools may be the result of the iguana's diet. For example, cucumbers, some squashes, and melons (because of their high water content and numerous seeds) often induce very soft feces. Merely changing the diet to include a less moisture-laden food may resolve the diarrhea. Adding pelleted ground alfalfa to the diet often firms the stools dramatically.

With continued diarrhea, the iguana may become dehydrated, and vital electrolyte imbalances can develop. A veterinarian must treat severe dehydration and resultant electrolyte imbalances by administering replacement fluid and electrolyte solutions that are appropriate. For example, an iguana that is dehydrated may also have an abnormally elevated potassium concentration in its blood plasma. If such an iguana is injected with Ringer's solution, the potassium level will be further elevated and could exceed a fatally toxic level. In this instance, the veterinarian should use either normal-strength or half-strength saline, depending on the laboratory analysis of the iguana's initial electrolyte profile. Conversely, if the iguana has been losing potassium and other vital electrolytes because of diarrhea, administration of Ringer's solution could be lifesaving. It is astonishing how rapidly some profoundly dehydrated iguanas can respond to proper rehydration after administration of intravenous fluid. I have seen more than one moribund iguana that was barely breathing regain its feistiness within minutes of receiving intravenous fluid and then try to bite its "benefactor" in appreciation!

Because the physiological effects of diarrhea and vomiting can be serious, every effort should be made to diagnose and treat these disturbances early, specifically, and aggressively. Moreover, because some particularly virulent disease-causing organisms can induce both of these disorders simultaneously, a definitive diagnosis is important in order to reduce the likelihood of horizontal (iguana-to-iguana) transmission within an animal collection or colony.

## BLOATING (TYMPANY)

The production of excessive intestinal gas is most often observed in herbivorous or omnivorous iguanas that have ingested food items containing readily fermentable fruit sugar (fructose) or other substances upon which gastrointestinal microflora subsist. This condition often follows a too-rapid change from a diet high in fiber to one containing a higher percentage of metabolizable carbohydrates.

Typical clinical signs of bloating are the following:

- A grossly observable swelling of the abdomen. This condition can prove fatal if the lungs are compressed by the expanded gastrointestinal organs.
- Open-mouth breathing and respiratory difficulties.
- Vomiting.

Treat bloating by doing the following:

- Administer a gas-dissolving agent such as simethicone. There are several nonprescription liquid products which contain this agent and each can easily be delivered via a stomach tube. Mylicon® (Stuart) or Riopan Plus II® have proven to be particularly efficacious when used in iguanas.
- Encourage the affected iguana to exercise, particularly to swim.
- Exclude any simple carbohydrate foods that are linked to bloating from the diet.

If the signs of excessive gas persist, consult a veterinarian. When deemed appropriate, a veterinarian can inject a modest dose of neostigmine or physostigmine to gently stimulate intestinal motility and, thus, help relieve the retention of gas (Frye, 1994a, 1994c).

## DISORDERS OF BLOOD SUGAR

### Diabetes Mellitus (High Blood Sugar)

Iguanas, like other animals, convert their food to more readily assimilated constituents. During this metabolic process, complex carbohydrates—particularly cellulose—are transformed into simple sugars which can be more easily utilized for energy conversion. Occasionally, metabolic defects, inborn or acquired, halt or impede these vital processes. Some plants contain substances that specifically attack and destroy the pancreatic cells that normally make insulin. When enough of these cells have been destroyed, the amount of glucose (sugar) in the blood rises to abnormal levels and diabetes ensues.

Although uncommon, diabetes mellitus occurs in iguanas (just as it does in human beings). Also, it is diagnosed by the same laboratory tests that are employed in human medicine and, once diagnosed, the treatment for diabetes is identical to that used in people: it consists of injections of insulin in appropriate amounts and given at specific times. **From the practical standpoint, treatment of diabetes mellitus in iguanas can be an exercise in futility because most diabetic iguanas do not feel well enough to eat voluntarily. Although insulin effectively lowers blood sugar, unless a sufficient amount of food is consumed, properly processed, and then assimilated by the iguana, its blood-sugar level can still become *too* low.** This abnormally diminished concentration of glucose can be fatal. In order to provide adequate nutrition, the iguana must be hand-fed. However, this can be stressful—and diabetic iguanas do not tolerate stress well.

Uncontrolled diabetes can lead to kidney, heart, and circulatory failure; blindness; and premature death. Thus, the successful management of diabetes in iguanas requires an enormous team effort by the owner(s) and their veterinarian.

### Hypoglycemia (Low Blood Sugar)

**Under conditions of severe stress, iguanas may suffer from hypoglycemia.** This occurs mainly because stressed animals usually do not eat, and the conditions of stress further sap energy as they try to cope with circumstances such as overcrowding, territorial disputes between dominant and lesser-ranking iguanas, restraint, handling, and shipping. Thus, the physiological processes (the ingestion, digestion, and assimilation of food) that are responsible for maintaining blood sugar within relatively narrow limits are not taking place, and, eventually, available sources from which blood glucose can be drawn are exhausted. Rarely, a low blood-sugar level occurs in iguanas due to a tumor of the pancreas, which arises from insulin-secreting cells whose abnormally high hormone production then results in profound hypoglycemia. In either case, the clinical signs of hypoglycemia are the following:

- "Fainting" or severe weakness, particularly after physical exertion
- Pupils that become and remain dilated even when the eyes are exposed to brilliant illumination

Hypoglycemia is diagnosed definitively by obtaining a small volume of blood and determining that its glucose concentration is abnormally low. If stress caused hypoglycemia, administering oral or intravenous glucose will increase the blood-sugar level to within its normal range (approximately 90–155 mg/dl). However the cause of the stress also must be removed. If a pancreatic tumor is responsible for hypoglycemia, surgery is required; but the prognosis for full recovery is guarded. The differential diagnosis of hypoglycemia requires the skills of a veterinarian experienced in treating reptiles in general, and iguanas in particular.

## EXCESSIVE BLOOD CHOLESTEROL

To date, I have encountered four cases of hypercholesterolemia (excessive blood cholesterol) in green iguanas: two of these iguanas had been on appropriate leafy green vegetable diets, supplemented with relatively large amounts of monkey chow, but both of them were diabetic; the other two iguanas had been fed grossly abnormal diets consisting almost entirely of canned dog food. The two diabetic iguanas did not exhibit cardiovascular or other disease that was related to their abnormally high blood-cholesterol levels. The two iguanas that had been fed dog food had severely diminished kidney function. Microscopic examination of their kidney tissues revealed massive deposits of cholesterol crystals in and around the portions of the kidneys that filter out and remove metabolic waste products (Figure 6.3). This evidence further strengthens the argument against feeding green iguanas commercially prepared foods that are formulated for dogs, cats, and primates. Also, cooked pasta and other dishes prepared for human consumption that contain cheese or other dairy products should not be fed to iguanas because they lack the enzymes necessary for properly digesting and assimilating dairy fats.

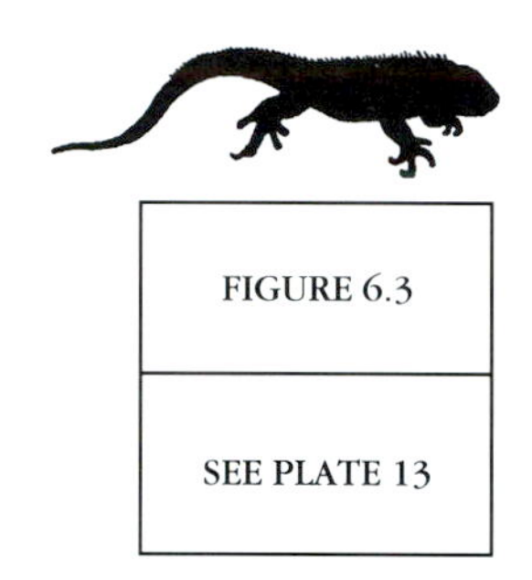

FIGURE 6.3

SEE PLATE 13

## VISCERAL AND ARTICULAR GOUT

Like most other terrestrial (land-dwelling) reptiles, green iguanas possess kidneys whose major excretory product are salts of uric acid, primarily sodium-, potassium-, and ammonium urate, all of which dissolve poorly in water. Iguanas must not become dehydrated because when their blood plasma becomes more concentrated as a result of dehydration, the accumulation of metabolic waste products—especially salts of uric acid—can reach toxic levels. Once blood uric acid exceeds a certain threshold, urates are deposited around the joints and in soft-tissue sites such as kidneys, liver, and the pericardial sac that surrounds the heart (Figure 6.4 & Figure 6.5). **These urate salts then initiate inflammation that can further impede the function of these tissues and organs.**

The major causes of gout in green iguanas are the following:

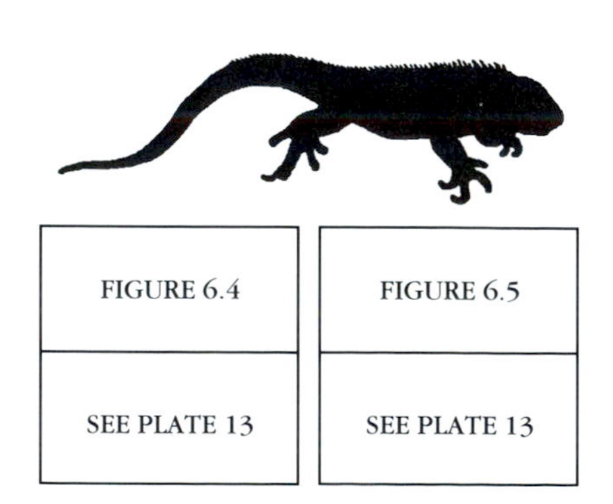

FIGURE 6.4 FIGURE 6.5

SEE PLATE 13 SEE PLATE 13

- Dehydration
- Using certain antibiotics without adequate fluid replacement

- Loss of kidney function from a variety of sources
- An incorrect diet, particularly one containing too much animal protein

Catfood, dogfood, and primate chow can induce visceral and periarticular gout in green iguanas because they are formulated from animal protein sources; they also contain amounts of some vitamins and fats that exceed the requirement for green iguanas.

Signs of visceral and periarticular gout are the following:

- An abnormally elevated blood uric acid concentration
- Joint swelling, involving one or more joints; lameness
- Clinical signs of kidney failure (lethargy, increased thirst, appetite loss)
- Sudden death from heart failure
- On postmortem examination, the finding of urate deposits in soft tissues and/or around joints

The treatment of visceral and periarticular gout is difficult because once the urate microcrystals are deposited in tissues, they resist removal due to their relative insolubility in blood plasma. Antigout therapy directed toward reducing the formation of urates (which is employed in humans and other mammals) has been only marginally effective in reptiles. Therefore, gout in green iguanas is a condition which is easier to prevent than to treat.

### Role of Some Antibiotics in Causing Gout

Another cause for the accumulation of urate salts and the failure to clear them from the kidney is the improper administration of some antibiotics, particularly those in the aminoglycoside class. While there is no argument that these potent agents are usually very effective, **the correct dosage must be used, and the patient must be sufficiently hydrated before, during, and immediately after their administration.** Most aminoglycoside drugs have the ability to damage those portions of the kidneys that are vitally involved with the filtration of blood and the removal of waste products of protein metabolism and other processes. If these kidney structures are damaged, urates can accumulate and when they do, the kidneys are further harmed and reduced in their ability to remove wastes. Therefore, urates continue to accumulate at an ever-increasing rate, to the point where the damage may become irreparable and eventually fatal.

That said, I advise the readers **not** to reject the use of these antibiotic drugs if an experienced veterinarian decides to employ them while treating your iguana. The calculated risk of using these efficient drugs must be weighed against the potential risk of not using these drugs. This is where clinical experience and judgement are important.

When using these drugs, the patient must be fed a bland, relatively low-protein diet to help lessen the amount of nitrogenous wastes that the liver and kidney must detoxify. However, some protein is necessary for normal cell and tissue maintenance; and, during healing, more protein is required for immunological processes such as antibody production. If the amount of protein intake is too low, the body will draw upon its own stores, such as skeletal muscle, to meet the requirement. The actual amount of net protein that is required is modest and can be provided by foods such as tofu beancake; small amounts of boiled eggwhite; collard, mustard, turnip, and dandelion greens; escarole; fresh, tender mulberry and/or hibiscus leaves and blossoms; and rose petals. All of these are visually attractive, readily digestible, and contain only a modest amount of protein.

# CHAPTER 7

## INFECTIONS AND INFECTIOUS DISEASES

Similar to all animals, green iguanas are susceptible to infection with fungal, bacterial, and viral disease agents. Many pathogens, such as *Salmonella*, can be transmitted from iguanas to humans. When iguanas are kept under hygienic conditions, are not overcrowded, lack stress induced by improper environmental temperature and territorial disputes, and are fed a nutritious diet, they tend to be hardy, long-lived creatures in captivity. However, when iguanas are kept in filthy enclosures, subjected to overcrowding, harried by dominant adult males, maintained at suboptimal temperatures, or fed a poor diet, their health can degenerate rapidly. The following information describes some of the most potentially serious pathological hazards to both iguanas and humans resulting from improper care.

### ABSCESSES

Cages soiled with feces and spoiled food are breeding grounds for a variety of disease-causing microorganisms. Overcrowding imposes severe physical and psychic stress on iguanas and, as they climb over each other, their filth-contaminated claws penetrate the skin of those upon whom they climb, which serves efficiently to inoculate bacteria and fungi into the soft tissues underneath the skin. Abscesses soon form. Given the opportunity to do so, bacteria from these localized infections can gain access to the circulatory system and become widely disseminated to internal organs such as the liver, spleen, lungs, and brain. **Abscesses, by their very nature, tend to be "walled-off" by inflammatory tissue which may effectively isolate the causative microorganisms from the beneficial effects of antibiotics and immune products. Thus, these infections are permitted to grow and extend to adjacent tissues unimpeded. It is for this reason that when multiple abscesses are found in an iguana, it is a cause for serious concern and aggressive veterinary medical intervention.**

The following are characteristic of abscesses:

- Usually, they are round "bulges" above the surrounding skin surface.
- They may be reddened or otherwise discolored.
- They feel firm when touched with a finger.
- They may evoke pain in the iguana when touched.

- Usually, they are found around the eyelids, ear openings, nose, limbs, digits, and trunk.
- Less often, they are found on the tail.

Any unusual lump, bump, swelling, discoloration, or "sore" (Figures 7.1 to 7.4) should be examined and evaluated by a veterinarian skilled in treating reptiles. Then, if the diagnosis is abscessation, it must be treated by a veterinarian because potent, efficacious antibiotics are required. The veterinarian would do the following:

| FIGURE 7.1 | FIGURE 7.2 |
|---|---|
| SEE PLATE 14 | SEE PLATE 14 |

| FIGURE 7.3 | FIGURE 7.4 |
|---|---|
| SEE PLATE 6 | SEE PLATE 7 |

- Incise and drain abscess contents.
- Remove the lining of the abscess cavity.
- Rinse the abscess cavity several times with an effective bacteriocidal wound-flushing antiseptic solution.
- Pack the cavity with a bacteriocidal antibiotic ointment or creme.
- Administer an effective injectable or oral bacteriocidal antibiotic (dosage depends on the iguana's body weight).

Fortunately, today there are many veterinarians who are interested in treating reptiles as patients and who have at their disposal an armamentarium of antibiotics and anesthetics that are remarkably safe and effective.

Veterinary care for abscesses should not be attempted by pet shop proprietors, zoo keepers, or biology teachers. This is because such persons not only do not have the specialized training, instruments, or drugs required for effective treatment, but, more importantly, many of the pathogens that infect iguanas can be equally pathogenic in people. Similar to medical care for dogs, horses, swine, goats, or wombats, medical care for iguanas should not be attempted by amateurs. Also, unlicensed veterinary medical treatment and surgery is illegal in most states and provinces. **Given the opportunity to extend to deeper tissues and structures (because ineffective treatment has been provided), abscesses can eventually cause the loss of limbs, eyes, ears, tail—or the life—of an inadequately treated iguana because the infection becomes widely disseminated (Figure 7.5).**

| FIGURE 7.5 |
|---|
| SEE PLATE 14 |

## RESPIRATORY INFECTIONS

**Respiratory infections are not particularly common in iguanas, but if they do occur, usually the iguana has been chilled or otherwise stressed.**

Signs of respiratory infection are the following:

- **Excessive** sneezing
- Obvious difficulty in breathing
- Abnormally rapid respiratory rate
- Bubbling or frothy secretions coming from the mouth or nostrils

- Lethargy
- Loss of appetite
- The nonspecific sign seen in green iguanas during many diseases: a change in skin color from normal brighter hues to darker, more somber colors

Some of these same clinical signs also are manifested when an iguana has anemia or internal parasites. Consult a veterinarian for a definitive diagnosis and effective treatment.

## SALMONELLOSIS

On 18 January 1994, the California Department of Health Services issued a press release and accompanying letter to local health officers, local communicable disease controllers, local directors of environmental health, local directors of public health laboratories, local public health veterinarians, and selected veterinarians with an interest in herpetological medicine (Frye, 1995b). These communications reflected an increase in the number of reports of human *Salmonella* infections associated with pet reptiles, especially iguanas, and listed serotypes that either have been isolated or strongly suspected as posing a public health hazard. These communications also mirrored the great interest people have in reptiles in general, and in large showy lizards specifically. Rather than living in single family homes as in years past, the majority of people are now sharing multifamily dwellings where barking dogs, yowling cats, or squawking parrots are not permitted as pets, and, consequently, there has been an increase in the ownership of animals more suited for confinement within aquaria and terraria.

Many of these reptile-associated infections were recorded in Southern California, particularly in Los Angeles County. In one small series of cases, *Salmonella* was isolated from all seven suspect reptiles that were tested.

The first report of reptile-associated salmonellosis was published by Hinshaw and McNeil in 1944. Within only 3 years, *Salmonella* sp. were isolated from lizards and rattlesnakes (Hinshaw and McNeil, 1946). During the late 1960s and throughout most of the 1970s, increasing interest was focused on reptiles, particularly chelonians (turtles and tortoises) (Altman, et al., 1972; Baker, et al., 1972; Boycott, et al., 1953; Duponte, et al., 1978; Jackson, et al., 1969; Kaufmann and Morrison, 1966; Lowenstein, et al., 1971; McCoy and Seidler, 1973; McInnes, 1971; Rosenstein, et al., 1965; Sieberling, et al., 1975; Wells, et al., 1974). As more cases of human illnesses associated with exposure to reptiles were recorded, several surveys of reptile collections were made to ascertain the extent of latent and overt infections (Boam, et al., 1970; Boever and Williams, 1975; Hinshaw and McNeil, 1944, 1946, 1947; Hoff and Hoff, 1984; Kennedy,

1973; Koopman and Janssen, 1973; McInnes, 1971; Otis and Behler, 1973; Schröder and Karasek, 1977; Tan, et al., 1978; Trust, et al., 1981; and Zwart, 1960). It was estimated that, in the early 1970s, the annual incidence of turtle-associated salmonellosis in humans was 300,000 cases.

Common green iguanas, currently one of the most popular reptiles being kept as a pet or study animal, often form astonishingly close bonds with their human keepers. Dining at their owners' tables, bathing or showering together, and even sharing their owners' sleeping quarters and bedding is not unusual behavior (Frye, et al., 1991). Thus, the opportunity for iguana:human (or human:iguana) cross-infection is readily afforded, if not actually encouraged. Many veterinarians whose clinical practices include iguanas are familiar with clients who lavish great affection (including lip contact) on their prized pets. It is not rare for iguana owners to permit their pets to range freely in an apartment or house; and, by doing so, the opportunity for fecal contamination of the owner's dwelling—particularly in food preparation and dining areas—is increased. Further opportunity for contamination of food preparation areas stems from the practice of disposing of fecal wastes and washing cage utensils and water containers in the kitchen sink.

It has been thought for many years that although *Salmonella* is frequently isolated from a variety of reptiles, these organisms represent nothing more than a usual constituent of the normal microflora of these animals and that only on rare occasions do these pathogenic microorganisms cause disease in their reptilian hosts. Recently, it has become obvious that rather than inducing relatively minor subclinical infections in reptiles, *Salmonella* commonly causes severe, often fatal, infections, especially in iguanas.

The question of how, when, and where iguanas (and other terrestrial reptiles) acquire their *Salmonella* must be addressed. It has been shown that newly hatched iguanas actively seek and ingest feces freshly deposited by older conspecifics (which is normal behavior). These hindgut fermenting iguanas require several species of bacterial and protozoal microorganisms (particularly *Nyctotherus* sp.) for the processing and digestion of complex carbohydrates, especially cellulose and 6-carbon sugars, which compose the major portion of their leafy and fruit-rich vegetable matter diet in the rainforest. **Although wild-caught iguanas may be harboring *Salmonella* sp., only rarely do they clinically display disease as a result of such microbial colonization; however, when these wild-caught iguanas are stressed sufficiently to lower their cell-mediated and humoral immunity, they may "break" with life-threatening salmonellosis.**

**It appears that most clinical salmonellosis in captive-bred iguanas stems from integumentary (skin) inoculation with a wide variety of Gram-negative and Gram-positive pathogenic microorganisms, of which *Salmonella* sp. form a significant population. Wounds inflicted with the feces-contaminated sharp claws of iguanas occur when they are over-**

**crowded. Then, these iguanas are stressed due to the overt territoriality and antagonistic behavior induced by lack of basking or resting sites, potential mates, adequate food, etc. Repeated competition between dominant iguanas and lower-ranked iguanas leads to severe psychological and physiological stress and all of the immunologically harmful sequelae that follow such stress.**

Depending upon the virulence of the serotype, the nature and chronicity of the lesions, and the innate immunity of the host iguana, a diversity of physical manifestations indicative of salmonellosis may be observed:

- Once the skin has been penetrated and inoculated with pathogens, subcuticular cellulitis, abscessation, and pyogranulomatosis may soon ensue.
- If periarticular tissues, particularly those covering the carpal (wrist) and tarsal (ankle) joints, are involved, septic arthritis often follows.
- In some instances, large areas of the scaly integument covering these inflammatory foci undergo necrosis. The progression from simple skin infection to more widely disseminated systemic disease can occur with alarming rapidity.
- The pathogenesis of this dissemination generally accompanies septicemia and infection of the atrioventricular and aortic heart valves (in a fashion analogous to that which marks the development of "rheumatic" vegetative endocarditis following a streptococcal pharyngitis in humans).
- Once established on the surface of the heart valves, small pieces of the infected clot detach and become thromboemboli which are carried in the bloodstream until they lodge in organs and tissues served by blood vessels which are too narrow to permit these infected thromboemboli to pass through.
- These end-organs then develop secondary abscessation; if the site of lodgement is the liver, kidney, lung, or brain, then hepatic, renal, pulmonary or brain abscessation results.

An otherwise healthy iguana who undergoes elective surgery occasionally develops severe disseminated abscessation or pyogranulomatous inflammation. One or more tiny, unrecognized abscesses become disseminated either as a result of the (limited) stress of anesthesia and surgery or activation and multifocal spread of infection from a preexisting, more-or-less quiescent (latent) infection.

**Young children who are still putting their fingers into their mouths should not be allowed to handle an iguana unless their hands are thoroughly washed immediately after touching the animal.** Another reason for limiting the intimate exposure of small children to pet iguanas is that often the children do not know how to restrain and handle the iguanas humanely and safely in order to avoid injury. Pet iguanas (and other lizards) often scratch their owners with their sharp (and usually feces-contaminated) claws. Without appropriate first aid, these abrasions and lacerations may become infected, and this may lead to septicemia (infection of the bloodstream).

Thus, clinical human salmonellosis that is associated with pet iguanas may be contracted through oral or nonoral contamination. The actual route of infection may depend upon the age of the human involved. Young children may be infected via either route and tend to have gastrointestinal involvement, and adults usually acquire their infections from scratches and bites and, therefore, develop abscesses. The end result of severe disseminated salmonellosis with soft-tissue (periarticular and articular) involvement can be equally severe and potentially life-threatening.

The methods used to diagnose salmonellosis in iguanas are similar to those employed in human medicine: microbiological culture and sensitivity testing, and routine clinical hematology, microbiology, biopsy/cytology, etc.

Doppler ultrasonography is particularly valuable when investigating and evaluating the acoustic characteristics of intracardiac and large-vessel blood flow in reptiles (Frye, 1994b); the equipment required for these studies is compact, ruggedly constructed, and affordable. In addition to being a clinical practitioner specializing in reptiles and amphibians, I am also a comparative pathologist; and, when the necropsy and histopathology results of each affected reptile were correlated with abnormal cardiovascular audio signals, I found that (in iguanas and some snakes) the incidence of endocarditis and endocardiosis was substantially more common in clinical salmonellosis than I had ever surmised.

**Iguana-associated salmonellosis constitutes a public health potential for zoonosis (a disease transmitted from an animal to a human). One treacherous feature of these infections is their resistance to numerous, usually very effective, drugs. This is serious considering how relatively easily drug-resistant pathogens (disease-causing agents) can be transmitted between several species of animals and humans.**

Iguana fanciers can still keep their much-favored pets and remain healthy by following a few guidelines:

- Provide adequate caging to prevent overcrowding.
- Use common-sense hygienic practices when servicing cages.
- Avoid contaminating any area used for preparation and consumption of food.
- Use paper plates or other disposable utensils when feeding iguanas.
- Provide prompt and effective first aid care for any persons scratched or bitten by an iguana.

People have been keeping animals in captivity for thousands of years—and are likely to continue doing so. It is not my raison d'etre to discourage the keeping of iguanas (or any other animals); however, I do urge that if creatures are taken from the wild, or bred and raised in captivity, they must be cared for in a fashion that promotes their health and that does not result in the spread of pathogens to either the keepers or the kept.

### Potential Risk to Humans with Compromised Immunity

In addition to salmonellosis, there are other infections that humans can acquire from being in close contact with iguanas. Many "inapparent" infections are self-limiting because a healthy person's immune response challenges them effectively. However, when even minor infections occur in persons with impaired immune systems, the outcome can be disastrous. Thus, whether people with Acquired Immunodeficiency Disease Syndrome (AIDS) or those infected with Human Immunodeficiency Virus (HIV) should or should not expose themselves to possible infection from iguanas is questionable.

Several factors must be considered. Does the quality of life, which may be enriched by keeping pets, necessarily transcend the potential risk to an immunocompromised iguana owner? That is something that can only be answered individually after weighing the risks and benefits. Health care professionals investigating this problem have concluded with decidedly mixed and divergent opinions (Chome, 1992; Glaser, Angulo, and Rooney, 1994). In the last analysis, if persons whose immunity has been severely diminished by immunosuppressant drug therapy or HIV infection wish to keep **any** pet animals, they **must** do the following:

- Practice strict hygiene.
- Avoid fecal contamination in food-preparation and food-consumption areas.
- Avoid claw scratches or bites. If injuries are sustained, treat them immediately and aggressively to prevent infection.

In a letter to the editor of *Notes from Noah*, Witmer (1994) wrote of his concern about petting zoos and bringing pet reptiles into close contact with young children and persons who might be immunocompromised. With the incidence of HIV infection increasing, these concerns are appropriate topics of discussion. There is no question that children and adults derive great educational benefit from exposure to reptiles and other animals. However, these experiences do not necessarily require "hands-on" contact in order to be enriching.

To lessen the opportunity for infection with *Salmonella*, do the following:

- Restrict physical contact with animals to children who are over 5 years of age—or until they understand the necessity for thorough handwashing and the importance of not putting their fingers into their mouths after handling animals.
- **Test all animals that will be handled. They must be found negative for *Salmonella* at least 3 times before they are permitted to be in contact with persons at risk.**
- Provide disposable germicidal handwipes when adequate handwashing facilities are not immediately available.

I do not wish to frighten readers who may not know that pet animals of most species are a **potential** source of infection. Just by using your common sense in avoiding contamination and by following the recommendations in this book, you can help **prevent** disease and its consequences. In the last analysis, the decision whether to keep any animal that could be a potential threat to one's health is a matter of personal choice. Whatever that decision is, it should be arrived at after considering all of the relevant facts.

## HERPES VIRUS

| FIGURE 7.6a | FIGURE 7.6b |
|---|---|
| SEE PLATE 15 | SEE PLATE 15 |

A herpes virus isolated from common green iguanas has been characterized (Clark and Karzon, 1972; Zeigel and Clark, 1969) and found to be associated with a form of lymphocytic leukemia in some infected iguanas. This disease is becoming better understood and is readily diagnosed through the microscopic examination of stained blood films which reveal multiple clear intraerythrocytic inclusions (Figures 7.6 a & b).

The clinical signs of iguana herpes viral infection (whether it involves leukemia or not) are the following:

- Loss of appetite
- Lethargy
- Anemia, usually reflected in a paleness of the tongue and oral mucous membranes
- Jaundice, observed as a yellow hue to the whites of the eyes, oral mucous membranes, and skin

**Herpes virus is infectious from iguana to iguana (but not from iguana to human), and all exposed animals should be isolated or euthanatized so that they do not pose a health threat to uninfected iguanas.**

The incubation period for herpes virus is unknown but appears to be prolonged. This may reflect the ability of herpes viruses to retreat to the central nervous system and become quiescent for variable periods of time before becoming active again. Some iguanas will respond to specific antiherpes therapy only to relapse months or years afterwards with a reactivation of their infection. This is also the pattern of herpetic infections in humans and other animals.

Successful treatment in several herpes-infected iguanas has been accomplished by administering the antiherpes drug, acyclovir (Zovirax® suspension—Burroughs Wellcome) at a daily oral dosage of 80 mg/kg. Treatment should continue for at least 4–6 weeks. During the first week of treatment, most iguanas display a reduced appetite. Therefore, try tempting the iguana with its favorite food items. If it still will not eat voluntarily, it should be hand-fed a bland diet consisting of moistened ground alfalfa pellets blended with tofu and fruit nectar. Generally, this anorexia dissipates within a few days, and the iguana's improved health is paralleled by a restored vigorous appetite. The efficacy of the treatment is judged by the clinical improvement and the reduction of the number of abnormal red blood cells found in stained blood films.

# COLOR SECTION

**Publisher's Note:**

The color section of *IGUANAS: A Guide to their Biology and Captive Care* has been preserved and reproduced as part of this updated volume. The new edition is dedicated exclusively to the green iguana; however, some of the prior volume's illustrations represent other species.

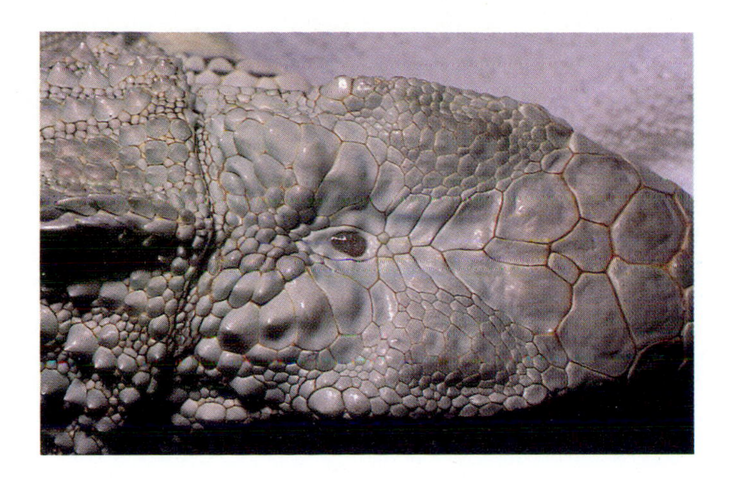

**Figure 1.1.** Between the two lateral eyes is the parietal eye, a photosensitive organ which helps regulate an iguana's basking activities.

**Figure 10.7a.** A hatchling green iguana emerging from its egg after slitting the eggshell with its caruncle or "egg-tooth." Once the iguana has begun to hatch, it may remain within the opened egg for as much as a day before emerging completely. Photo credit: Dr. Gunther Köhler.

**Figure 1.4.** Young green iguana displaying a fully extended dewlap.

**Figure 1.16b.** Many iguanas become accustomed to being hand fed. While it may appear to be appealing, this practice can result in lizards who may refuse to feed from a container. Photo credit: Wendy Townsend.

**PLATE 1**

**Figure 1.16c.** An iguana being hand fed. Photo credit: Wendy Townsend

**Figures 2.4a-b.** Photographs of the splendid outdoor iguana compound at the San Diego Zoological Park. The environment is surrounded by a low, smooth-sided concrete wall and is planted with mature mimosa and other trees which provide edible forage as well as vital shade and sites where individual lizards can exercise their territorial imperatives. Photo credit: Wendy Townsend.

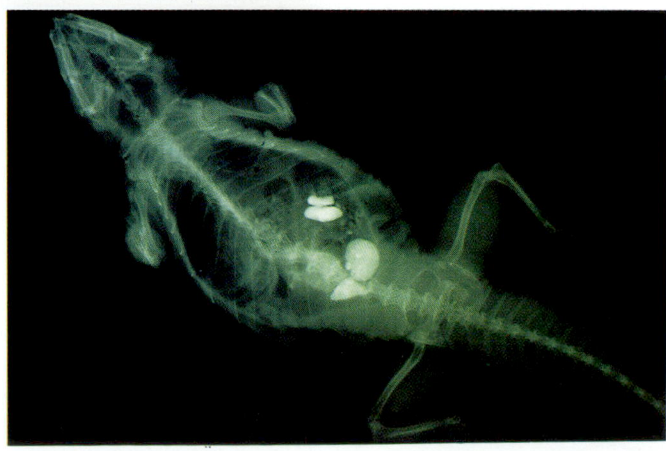

**Figure 3.2.** Radiograph of a chuckawalla whose stomach and intestines contain rocks and stones that it ingested from its cage environment.

**Figure 3.1.** Salt crystals have accumulated around the nostrils of this iguana.

**Figure 3.6.** An example of edible vegetables, blossoms, sprouts, and soybean cake that comprise a nutritious diet for captive green iguanas. Photo credit: Wendy Townsend.

**Figure 10.1.** Even small male iguanas attempt to mate with much larger female iguanas. The size disparity in this pair dooms their most ardent efforts to failure! Photo credit: Wendy Townsend.

**Figure 10.2b.** While maneuvering a compliant female iguana during courtship, the successful male iguana holds his mate with his teeth. Photo credit: Wendy Townsend.

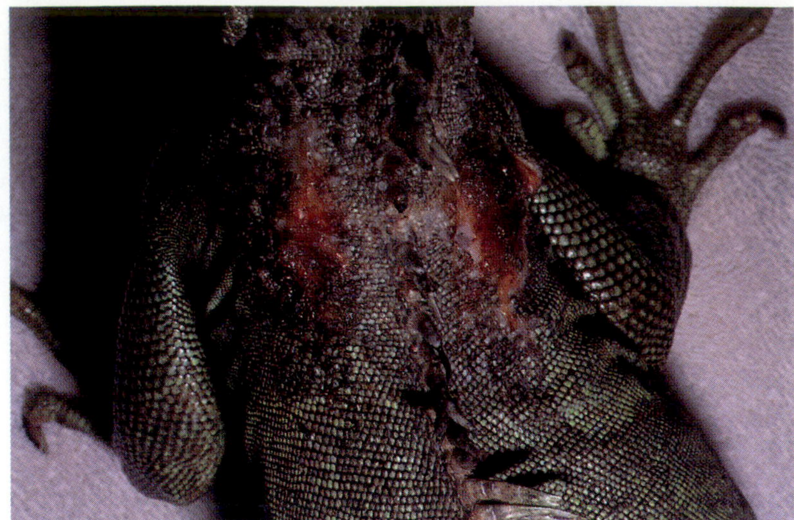

**Figures 10.2c-d.** Many captive female iguanas sustain severe abrasions and even lacerations to the skin covering their shoulders following courtship. This probably occurs only rarely in wild female iguanas because they can escape from males after they have mated.

**Figure 10.3a.** A gravid full-term female green iguana. Note how the eggs distend the body wall and how thin this female's legs and tailbase are.

**Figure 10.3b.** A female green iguana with a portion of her clutch of eggs. Photo credit: Wendy Townsend.

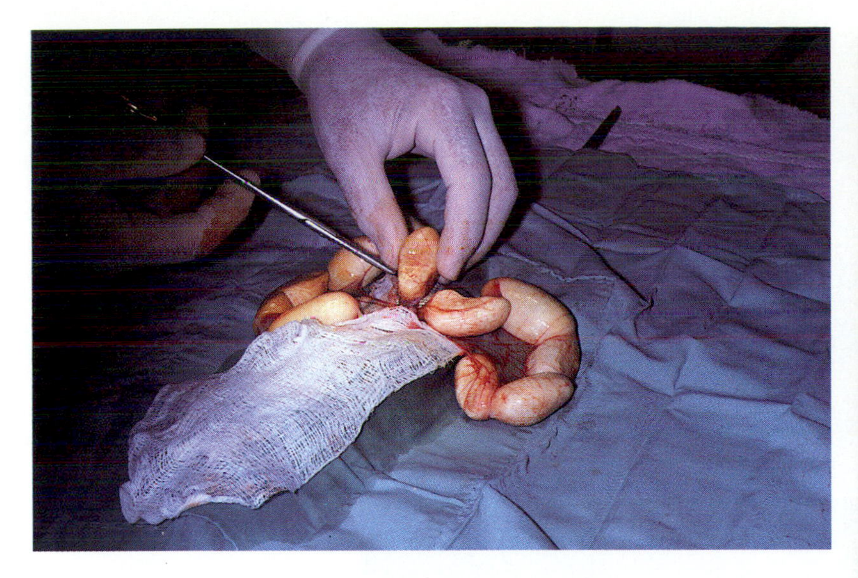

**Figure 10.8.** Intraoperative photograph of an ovariohysterectomy (spay) operation on an iguana. The two egg-filled oviducts have been brought to the exterior and are being ligated prior to being removed and the abdominal cavity being closed.

**Figures 5.1 & 5.2.** Severe nutrition-induced metabolic bone disease in a green iguana. Note the massive mandibular (lower jaw) swelling and bowing, and the iguana's inability to withdraw its tongue.

**Figure 5.3.** Green iguanas with metabolic bone disease usually exhibit multiple skeletal deformities of the limbs, trunk, spine, and head.

**Figure 5.4.** Note that limbs look "plump." These swollen and firm-to-the-touch limb bones are a hallmark of metabolic bone disease which is induced by a diet too high in phosphorus and too low in calcium.

**Figure 5.5.** As metabolic bone disease progresses, the lower jaw becomes so short that it no longer meets the upper jaw. This makes eating difficult.

**Figure 7.3a-b.** Examples of typical abcesses in iguanas. These inflammatory lesions must be treated effectively by a veterinarian to prevent widespread dissemination of infection to distant sites in the body.

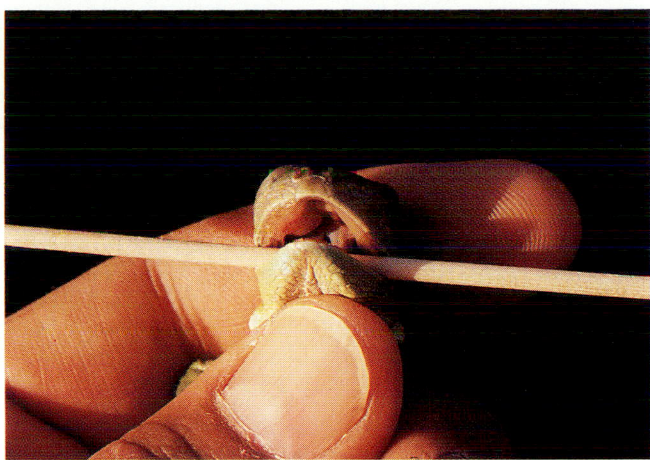

**Figures 7.4a-b.** Examples of typical abcesses in iguanas. These inflammatory lesions must be treated effectively by a veterinarian to prevent widespread dissemination of infection to distant sites in the body.

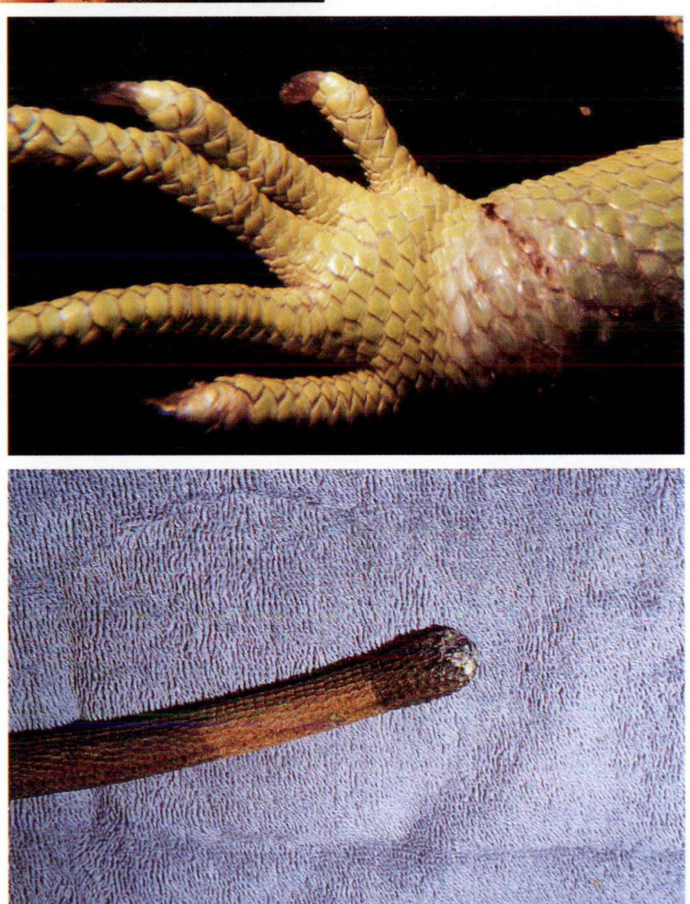

**Figures 9.9a-b.** Tail breakage in iguanas usually results in a somewhat shorter and less colorful regrown appendage. In some instances, the tail fails to regenerate and only heals as a scale-covered rounded stump.

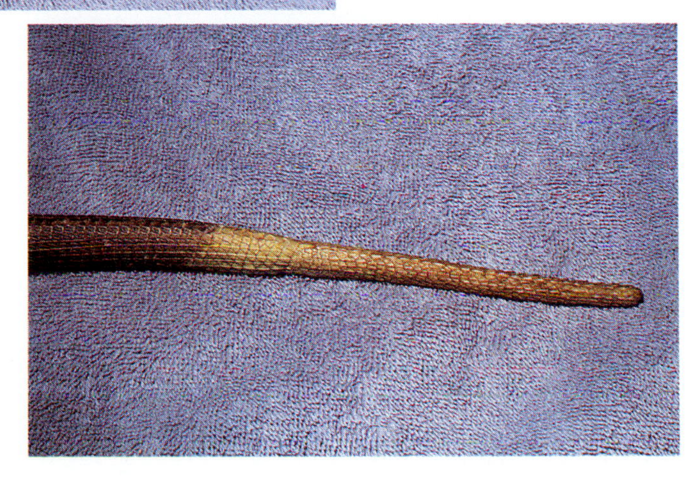

**Figures 9.9c-e.** The regenerated tail may grow in an opposite direction, or it may develop one or more branches or spurs. It sometimes fails to regenerate and only heals as a scale-covered rounded stump.

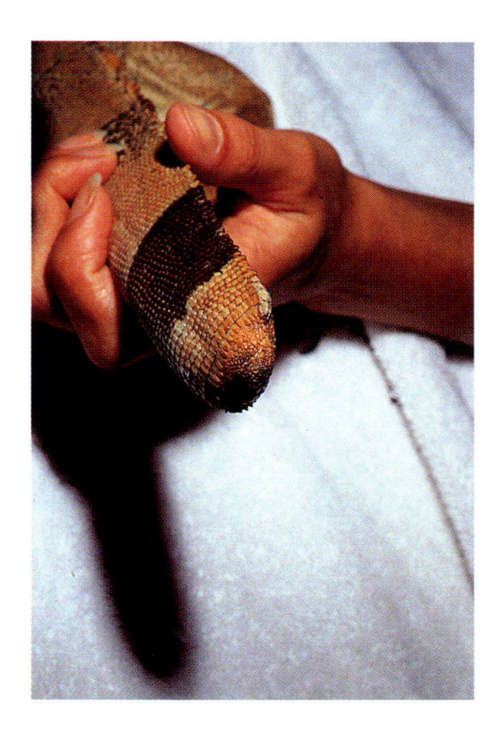

**Figure 9.7a.** This male iguana is grasping its owner's glove in a manner similar to that used to restrain a female during copulation. It is also masturbating on the inanimate object. Photo credit: Betty Jean Lifton.

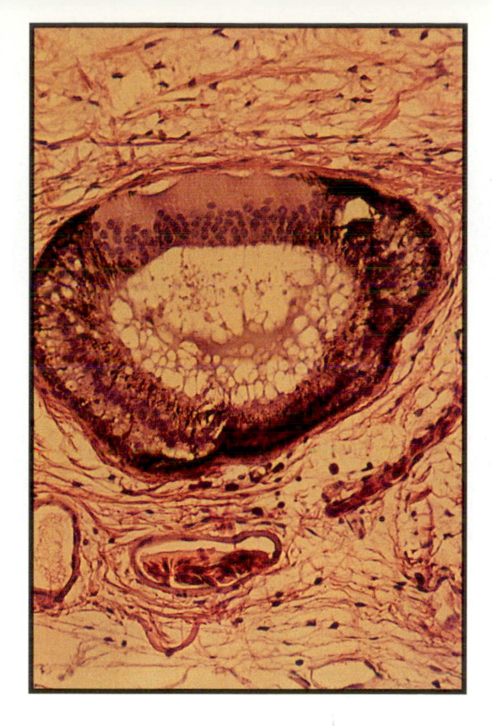

**Figure 1.2.** Histological section of an iguana's parietal eye. This photosensitive organ has a relatively clear cornea, cellular lens, fluid-filled chamber, and pigmented retina-like visual epithelium that receives light. Hematoxylin and eosin stain, X 27 original magnification.

**Figure 1.12.** Hatchling iguanas often cluster beneath a source of radiant heat. This is called "stacking" and it can be prevented by providing additional space for basking and resting. Photo credit: Max Peterson; courtesy of Chrystie Anderson.

**Figure 1.3.** A mature male green iguana basking in the sun. Note the prominent dorsal crest, which is composed of modified spinelike scales, and its slightly orange color. This iguana was just assuming his sexually mature breeding colors.

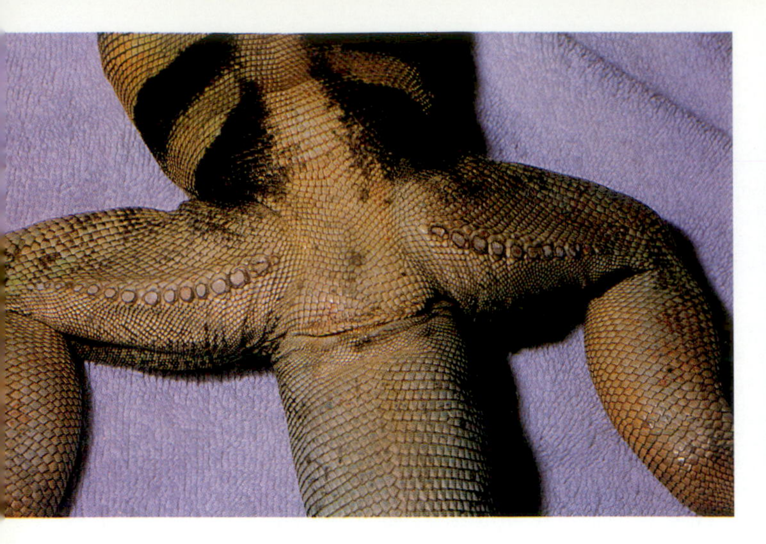

**Figure 1.5.** The underside of an adult male green iguana's thigh region. Note the line of large femoral pores and the distinctly orange skin color.

**Figure 1.6.** The underside of a mature female green iguana's thigh region. Note the very small femoral pores and the bright green skin color which many female iguanas retain throughout much of their lives.

**Figure 1.7.** Lateral view of the pelvic region and the tailbase of a young, mature male iguana. Note the hemipenial swelling that is located immediately behind the vent.

**Figure 1.8.** Ventral view of the iguana shown in Figure 1.7. Note the bilateral hemipenial bulges at the base of the tail and the prominent femoral pores. This young adult still retains his bright green skin color.

**Figure 1.13.** An immature green iguana just beginning to shed its skin. Note that, unlike a snake, this iguana's old epidermis has loosened and is being shed in numerous pieces rather than in just one piece.

**Figure 2.6.** If all of the skin surrounding the digits is not shed completely, the ringlike remnants of old skin can form the illustrated tourniquet-like bands which restrict the flow of blood to the digits. This young iguana has already lost several of its toes from this cause.

**Figure 1.16a.** An example of hand-feeding a juvenile green iguana. Here the iguana is eagerly eating a mixture of sliced bok choy, rose petals, and mashed butternut squash mixed with a very small amount of supplemental calcium.

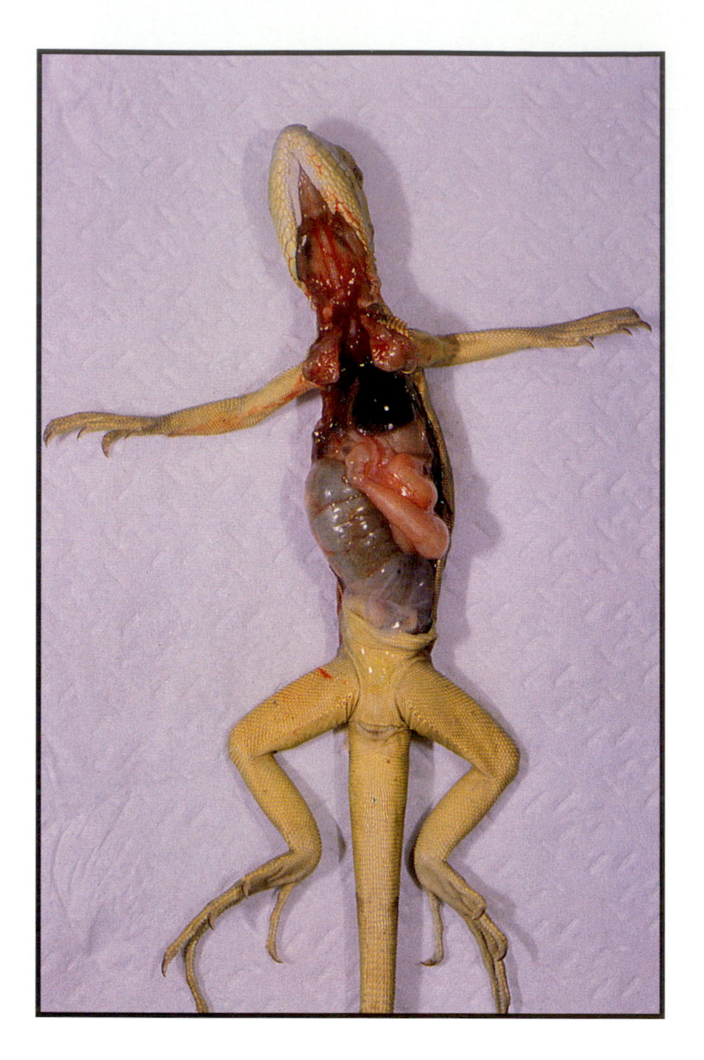

**Figure 3.3.** A postmortem dissection of a juvenile green iguana. Note the large grey object that fills the left side of the iguana's abdomen. This is the sacculated colon which functions as a fermentation vessel in this leaf-eating lizard.

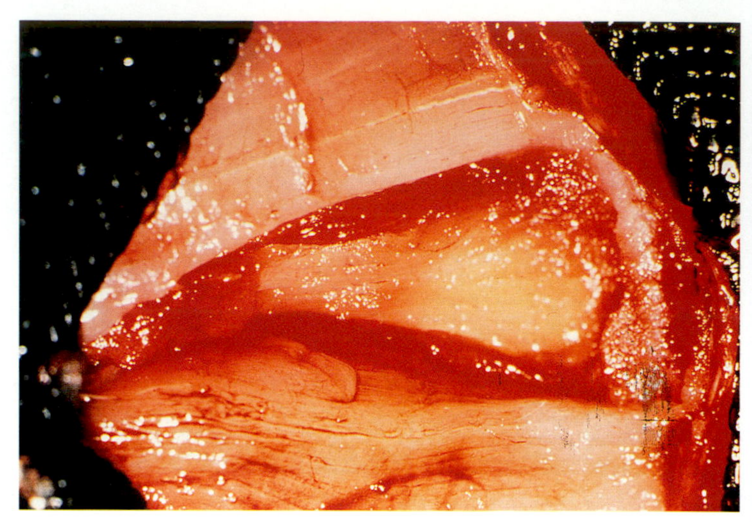

**Figure 5.8.** Postmortem specimen of an iguana that died from "white muscle" disease (a degenerative disorder of muscle). Note the white streaks that course in the direction of muscle fibers.

**Figure 6.1.** A juvenile iguana affected by severe bloat. This photograph was made immediately prior to administering an enema.

**Figure 6.2.** The iguana in Figure 6.1 moments after its intestinal blockage was relieved. The red object at the top of the photograph is the soft catheter through which the enema was delivered.

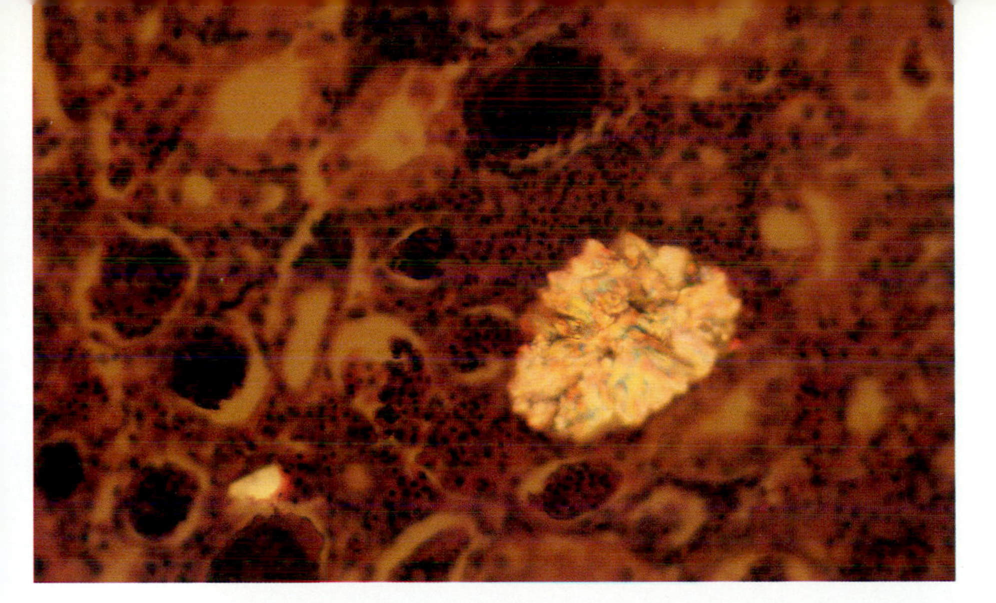

**Figure 6.3.** Photomicrograph of a stained histologic section of kidney tissue from a green iguana that had died as a result of massive deposits of cholesterol in its kidneys. The brightly colored substance is an accumulation of cholesterol crystals that had interfered with kidney function. Photographed with cross-polarized illumination. H & E stain, X 27 original magnification.

**Figure 6.4.** Postmortem specimen of the heart and liver of a green iguana that died of severe visceral gout. Note the chalky white deposits of urates on the surface of the heart and the abnormally pale liver that had enormous accumulations of urates within its tissues. The iguana had subsisted mainly on monkey chow and canned dog food.

**Figure 6.5.** Photograph of a grossly swollen and deformed toe of an iguana with articular gout. This iguana had been fed canned dog food for much of its life. Photo credit: Dr. Michael Murray

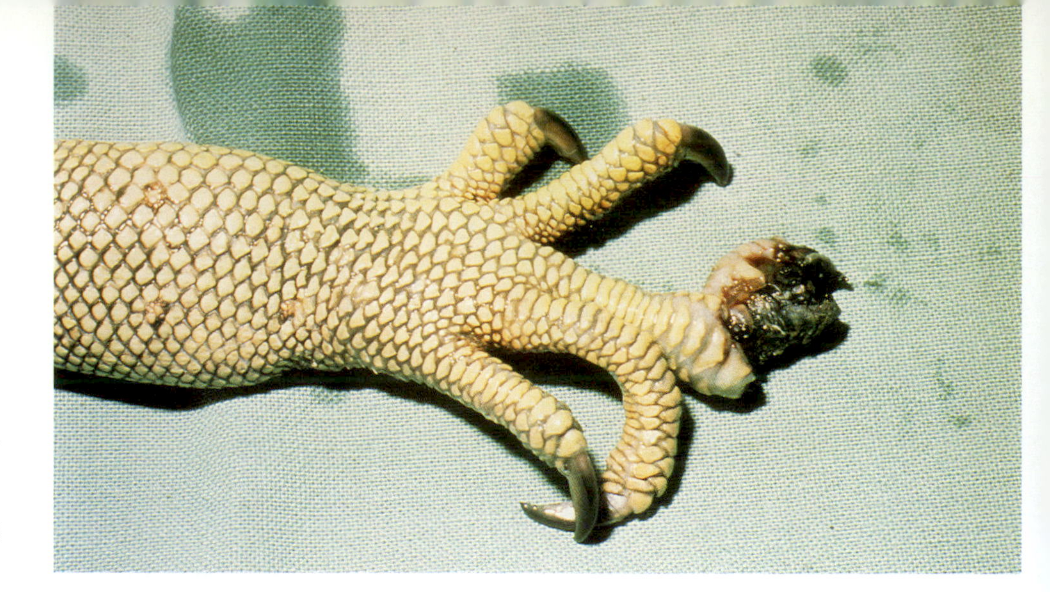

**Figure 7.1.** Abscessed toe and lower arm of an iguana. Because this infection was chronic and "walled-off," the entire limb was amputated at its junction with the foot.

**Figure 7.2.** Abscess on the chin of a half-grown green iguana.

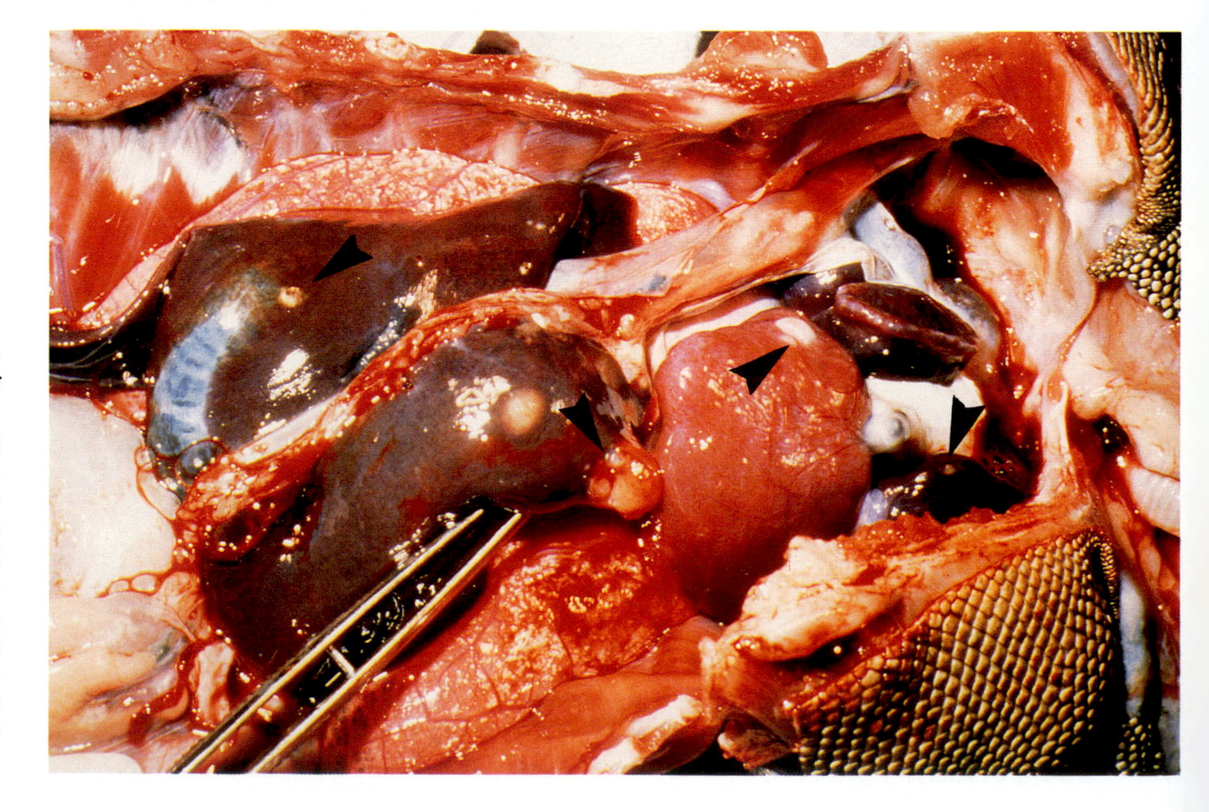

**Figure 7.5.** A postmortem specimen of an iguana cadaver illustrating widespread dissemination of infection from an abscess into the heart and liver. This iguana had a seemingly "insignificant bump" on its jaw, but, via its blood stream, that small lesion spread infective bacteria throughout its body.

**PLATE 14**

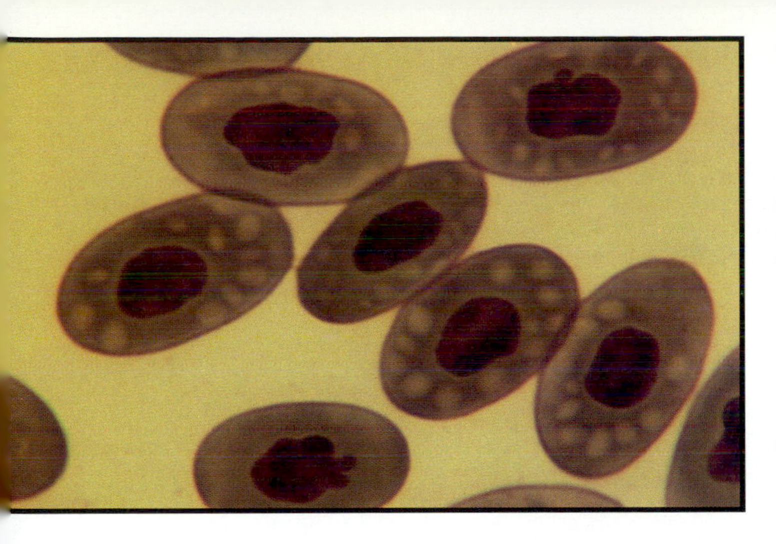

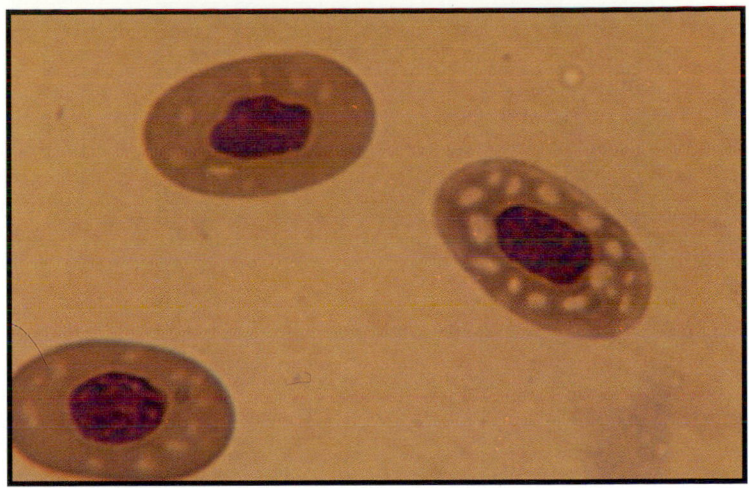

**Figures 7.6a & b.** Photomicrographs of red blood cells from green iguanas infected with herpes virus. Note the multiple "punched-out" clear spaces in the cells. Romanowsky stain, X 402 original magnification. This viral disease of iguanas is not infectious for humans.

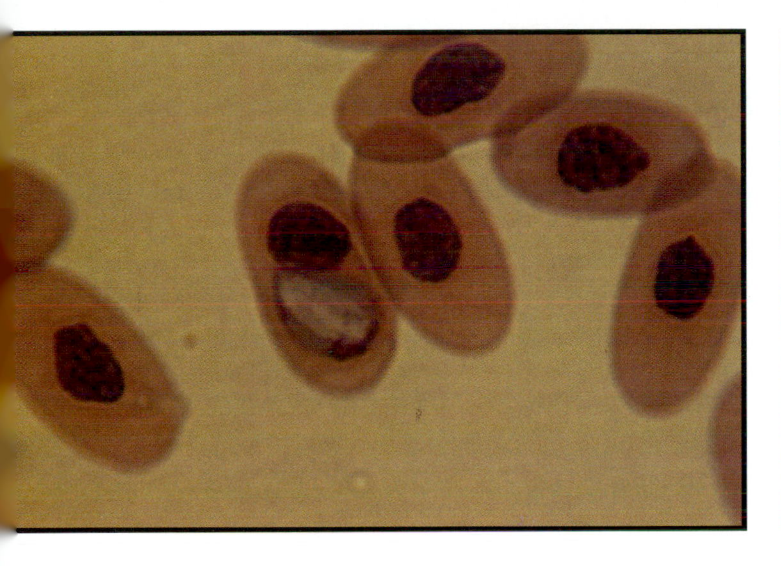

**gure 8.1.** Photomicrograph of iguana blood. The red blood cell (left nter) contains a *Schellackia* hemoprotozoan parasite. Jenner-Giemsa stain, 402 original magnification.

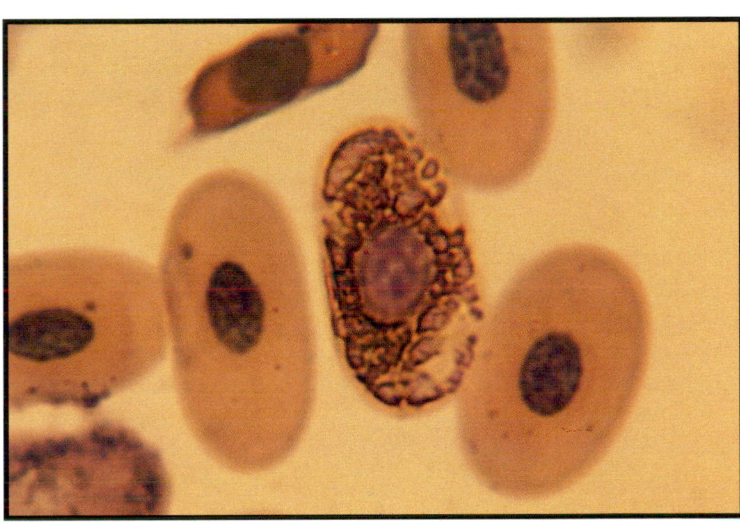

**Figure 8.2.** Photomicrograph of red blood cells from an iguana infected with the "malarial" protozoan parasite, *Plasmodium.* Jenner-Giemsa stain, X 402 original magnification.

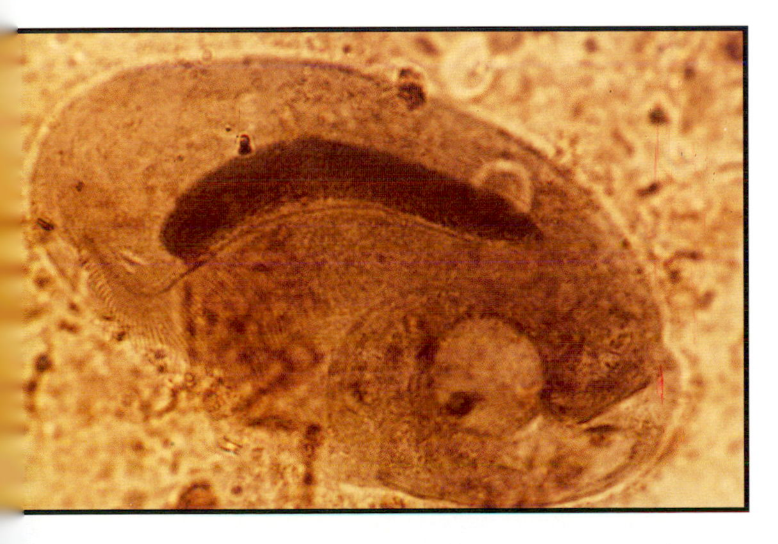

**gure 8.3.** Enlarged photomicrograph of the symbiotic cellulose-digesting otozoan *Nyctotherus kyphoides.* These *Paramecium*-like ciliated protozoa e essential for normal digestion in green iguanas. X 67 original magnifica- n. Photo credit: James Detterline, Ph. D.

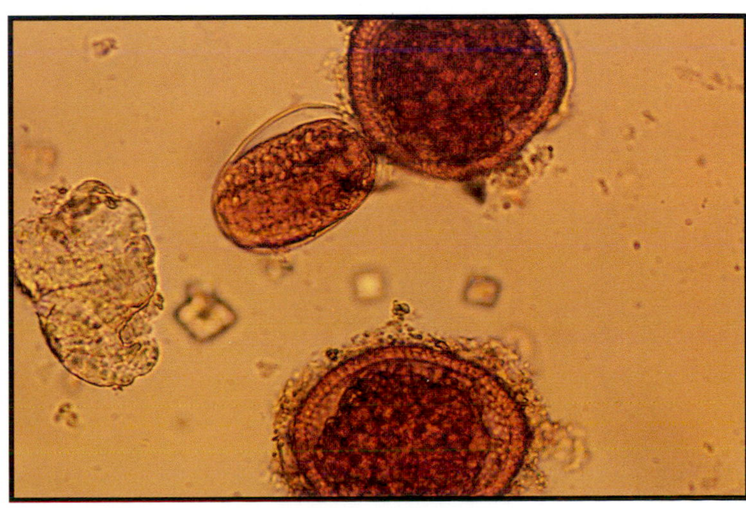

**Figure 8.4.** Photomicrograph of two ascaridoid nematode ova and a strongyle ovum from a wild-caught green iguana. Merthiolate stain, X 67 original magnification.

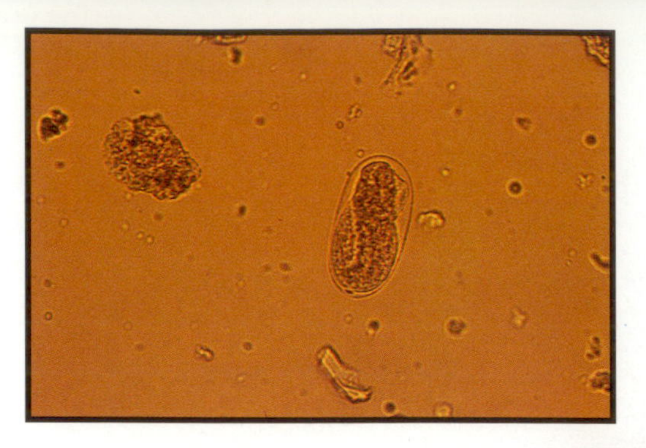

**Figure 8.5.** Photomicrograph of an embryonated rhabidiform ovum, probably *Entomelas* sp. or *Strongyloides* sp. from a wild-caught green iguana. Potassium dichromate solution, X 67 original power.

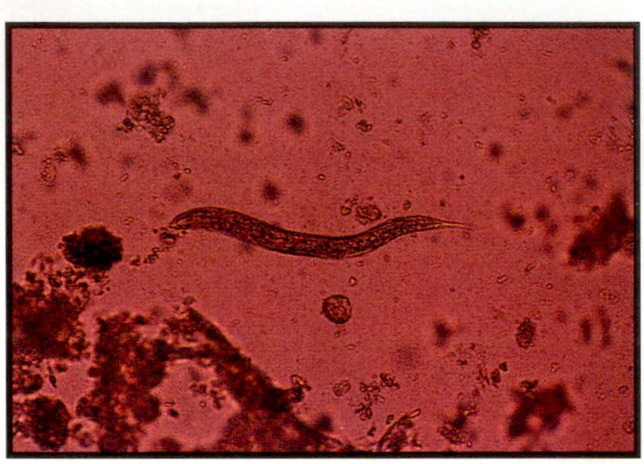

**Figure 8.6.** Photomicrograph of a rhabidiform larva found in the stool of a wild-caught green iguana. New Methylene blue stain, X 67 original magnification.

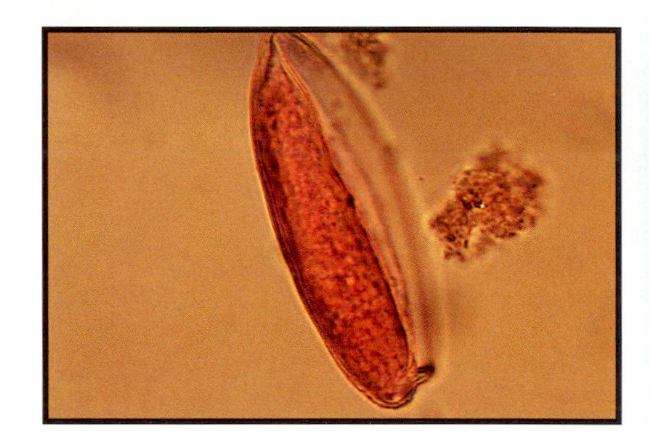

**Figure 8.7.** Photomicrograph of an oxyurid (pinworm) ovum from the feces of an iguana. Merthiolate stain, X 67 original magnification.

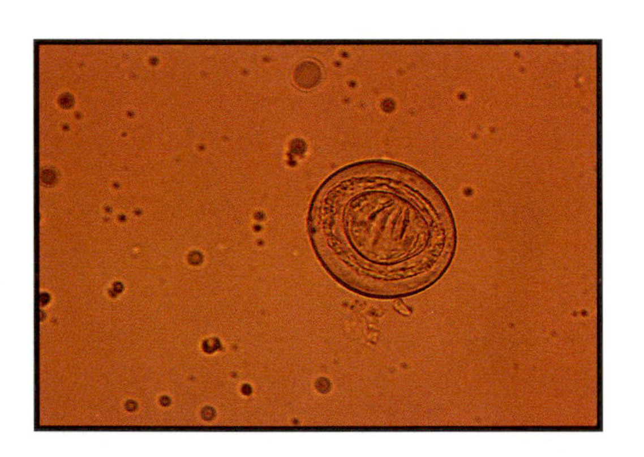

**Figure 8.8.** Photomicrograph of cestode (tapeworm) ovum. Note the tiny hooklets in the egg's interior. Potassium dichromate solution, X 67 original magnification.

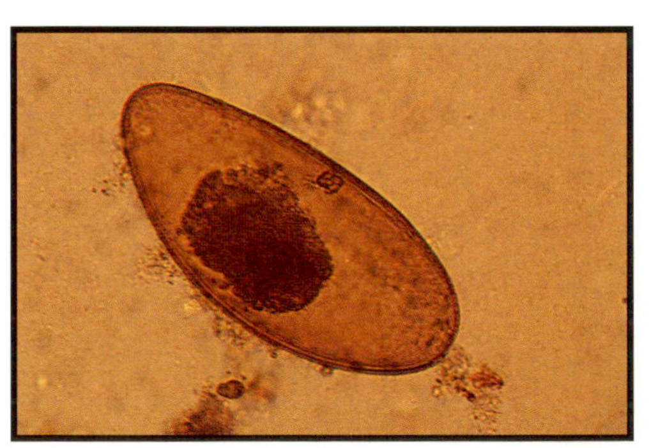

**Figure 8.9.** Photomicrograph of a large plant-mite ovum from the stool of a green iguana that had eaten homegrown broccoli leaves. These very large mite eggs are seen often in the feces of plant-eating reptiles. Unstained, X 27 original magnification.

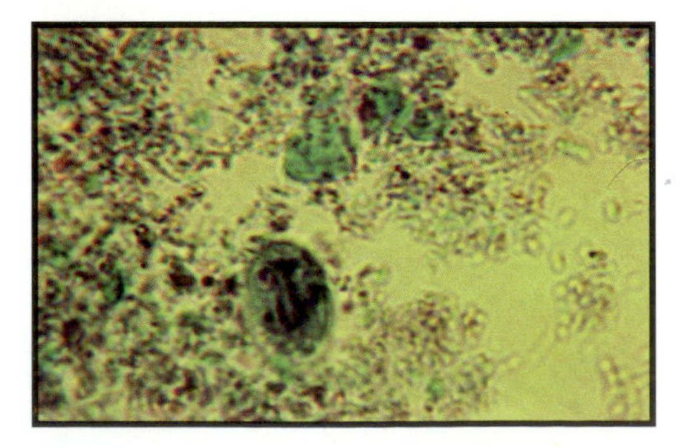

**Figure 8.10.** Photomicrograph of the intestinal protozoan parasite, *Giardia lamblia.* Trichrome stain, X 67 original magnification.

**PLATE 16**

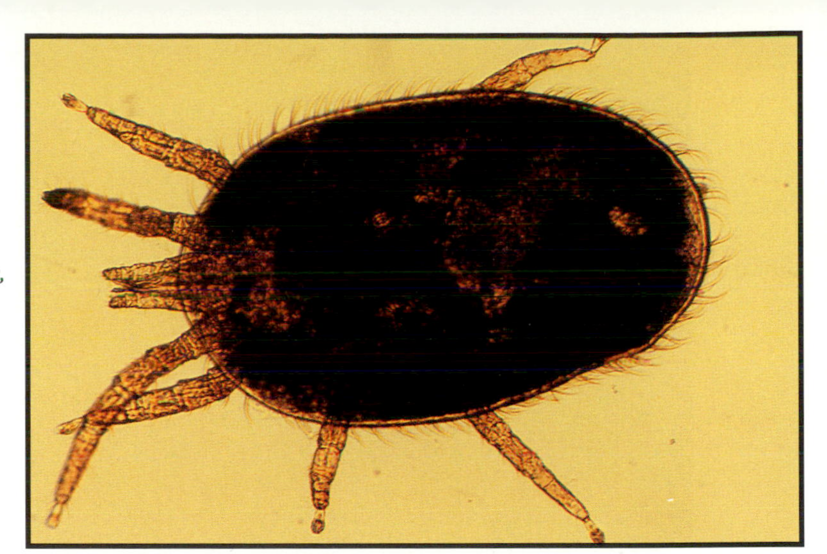

**Figure 8.11.** Photomacrograph of a snake mite, *Ophionyssus natricis,* an occasional ectoparasite of green iguanas. Unstained, partially cleared, X 8.7 original magnification.

**Figure 8.12.** Photomacrograph of a lizard mite, *Hirstiella trombiidiformis.* Note the pointed projection on the abdomen which is characteristic of this mite. Unstained, partially cleared, X 8.7 original magnificaton.

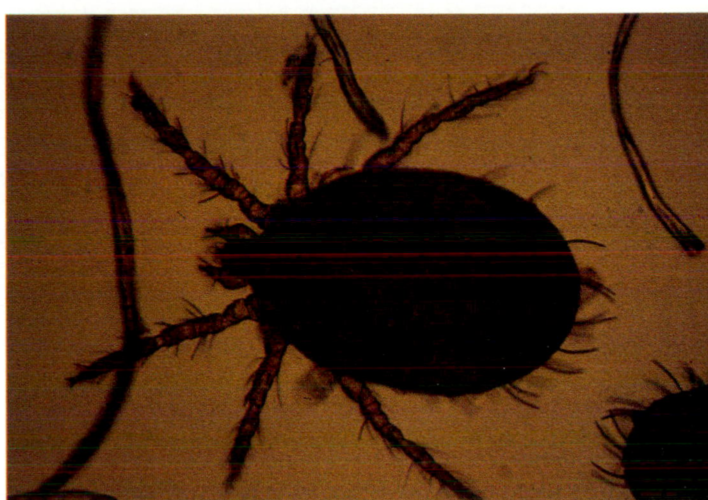

**Figure 8.13.** Photomacrograph of a nymphal trombiculid "chigger" mite. Note the three pairs of legs and the "hairlike" setae that help differentiate this parasitic nymphal mite from *Ophionyssus* and *Hirstiella,* which are parasitic in both their nymphal and adult stages and have smooth legs. Unstained, partially cleared, X 8.7 original magnification.

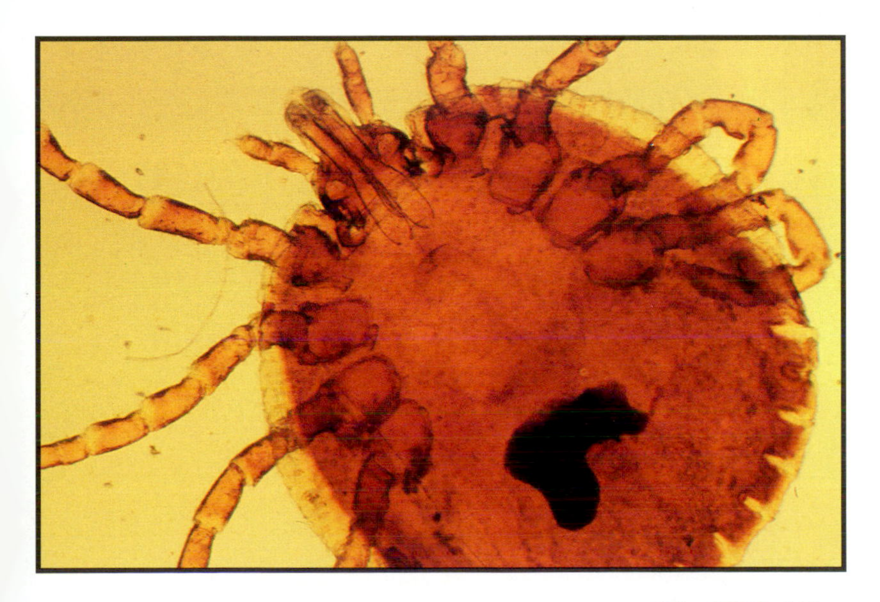

**Figure 8.14.** Photomacrograph of a partially cleared hard tick removed from a freshly imported wild-caught green iguana. Approximately 2.5 times original magnification.

a.

**Figures 9.1a - d.** Multiple bite wounds inflicted when two adult male green iguanas tried to share the same territory. Figure 9.1a illustrates that the victim's laceration exactly fits the outline of the attacking iguana's jaws. Figure 9.1c illustrates the massive skin and underlying soft-tissue trauma that resulted from this fight: the right quadriceps muscle was severed and had to be reconstructed surgically. Figure 9.1d illustrates the latex Penrose drain that was sutured into the wound to provide drainage after it was closed.

b.

c.

d.

**PLATE 18**

**Figures 9.2a & b.** Severe thermal burns which occurred while iguanas were resting on electrical in-cage heating devices.

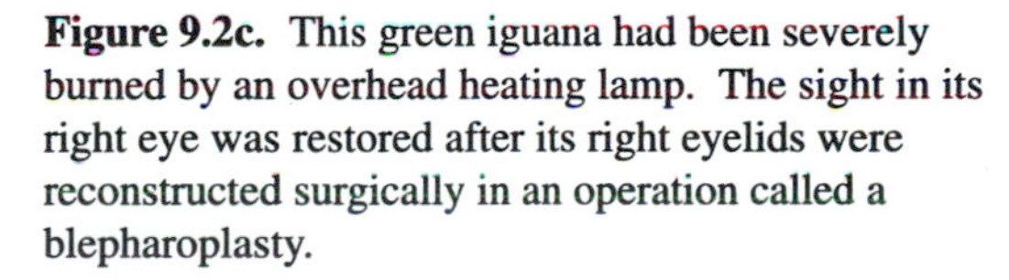

**Figure 9.2c.** This green iguana had been severely burned by an overhead heating lamp. The sight in its right eye was restored after its right eyelids were reconstructed surgically in an operation called a blepharoplasty.

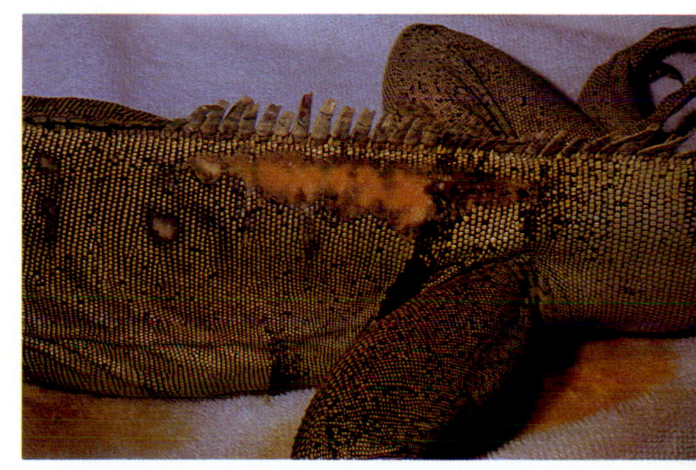

**Figure 9.2d.** A severely burned area often loses its pigment permanently.

a.

b.

**Figures 9.6a - c.** Scoliosis and kyphoscoliosis in three green iguanas. Sometimes only the tail is deformed; sometimes, the entire vertebral spine is severely deviated. Photo credit for Figure 9.6c: Matt Braunwalder.

c.

**Figure 9.7b.** After displaying sexual aggression which is directed toward its owner, this male iguana was "rewarded" by being permitted to bite and carry a child's pacifier. Whether this "reward" further encouraged this behavior is not known. Photo credit: Helen L. Benton.

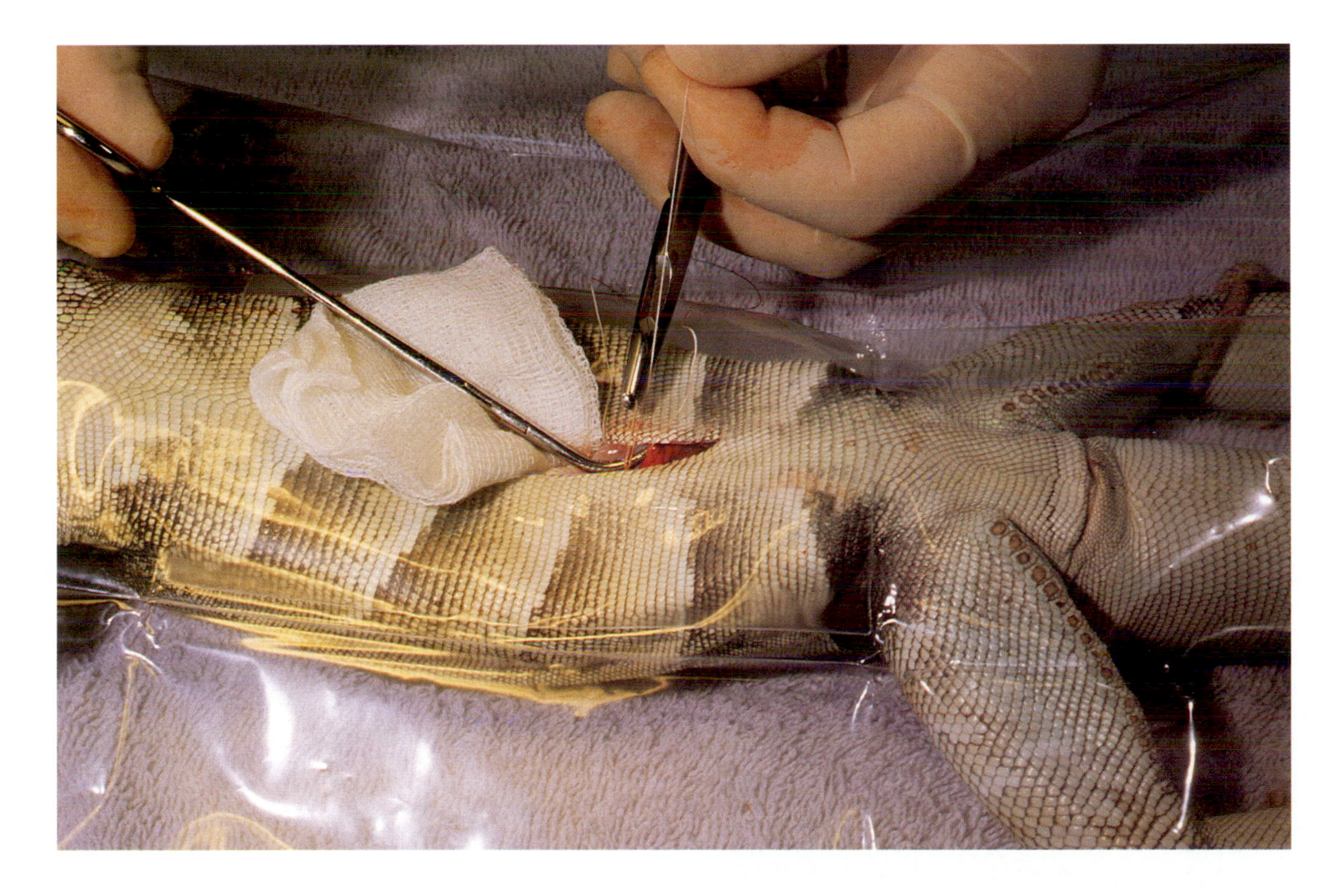

**Figure 9.7c.** Interoperative photograph illustrating the testis of an adult male iguana. The testis was held with a forceps and elevated slightly preparatory to being ligated and removed. The intimate relationship between the testes and the immediately adjacent major blood vessels (aorta and posterior vena cava) preclude their elevation fully from the coelomic cavity. Photo credit: Amro Hamdoon.

**Figures 9.8a & b.** Examples of dermatitis. Note the raised and discolored skin.

**Figure 9.8c.** Moist and necrotic skin covering part of this iguana's tail has already begun to slough.

**Figure 9.8d.** This lesion illustrates the tail of the iguana in Figure 9.8c after the devitalized skin had been removed. Note the blanched appearance of the tail muscles underlying this severely inflamed and infected lesion. Microbiological culture revealed *Salmonella* organisms in large numbers.

**Figure 10.2a.** The male everts one of his paired hemipenes and straddles the female. Photo credit: Chrystie Anderson.

**Figure 10.2e.** The male grasps the female's skin with his teeth and brings his cloacal vent into apposition with her cloacal vent; then he inserts his erect hemipenis into the female's cloaca. Photo credit: Chrystie Anderson.

**PLATE 23**

**Figure 10.3c.** Once the albumin and shells have been added to the eggs, the gravid female seeks out a site for excavating a nest in which she deposits her clutch. Note the great loss of muscle tissue that is displayed by this female; this is typical. Soon after she has deposited her eggs, the female commences eating again and usually gains weight and resumes fitness within a few weeks. Photo credit: Chrystie Anderson.

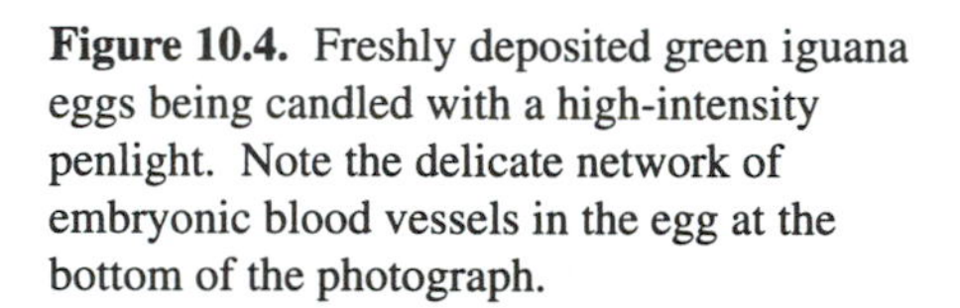

**Figure 10.4.** Freshly deposited green iguana eggs being candled with a high-intensity penlight. Note the delicate network of embryonic blood vessels in the egg at the bottom of the photograph.

**Figure 10.7b.** Hatchlings slit the leathery eggshells and remain in place for as long as a day before emerging. During this time they absorb the remaining yolk from their embryonic yolksac. They should not be extracted prematurely. Photo credit: Max Peterson; courtesy of Chrystie Anderson.

# CHAPTER 8

## PARASITES

### HEMOPARASITES (BLOOD PARASITES)

| FIGURE 8.1 | FIGURE 8.2 |
|---|---|
| SEE PLATE 15 | SEE PLATE 15 |

Some wild-caught iguanas possess a low level of hemoparasitism, but captive-bred iguanas should not have any unless they have been bitten by mosquitoes that have previously fed on an infected iguana. The most common blood parasites affecting iguanas are *Schallackia* (Figure 8.1) and *Plasmodium* (Figure 8.2). There are other hemoparasites as well, but they are less frequently encountered. **None of these parasites of iguanas' blood cells is transmissible to humans. Most iguanas appear to tolerate their blood parasites well; unless an infected iguana is severely stressed or becomes infected with one or more additional pathogens, it usually does not exhibit clinical signs of disease.** Iguanas with blood-cell parasites are diagnosed only after a stained blood specimen is examined microscopically. (These infections are "silent.")

#### Malaria

A low level of infection with malarial parasites does not necessarily require aggressive treatment because these organisms may not pose a significant health threat to the iguana, although this depends upon the type of parasites found, their number, and the iguana's overall response to the infection. However, when the iguana has severe anemia in addition to malaria, treatment with an antimalarial drug is necessary. In practice, the drug that has proven most effective is a proprietary mixture of chloroquine phosphate and primaquine phosphate (Aralen®—Sanofi). The treatment for iguana malaria is the following:

- Administer an initial "loading" dose of chloroquine phosphate/ primaquine phosphate mixture (based on the chloroquine phosphate content) of 5 mg/kg.
- Follow with weekly doses of 2.5 mg/kg. (This dosage schedule yields a dosage of primaquine phosphate of 0.5 mg/kg.)
- Usually, this drug combination is continued for at least 6 months, with the effect on the number of parasitized blood cells being monitored by twice-monthly microscopic examination of blood cells.

## ENDOPARASITES (INTERNAL PARASITES)

Although they are uncommonly seen in captive iguanas, a few protozoan parasites can utilize iguanas as hosts; these include a few coccidia and flagellates. Other protozoa, especially the cellulose-digesting *Nyctotherus* sp. (Figure 8.3), are symbiotic (mutually beneficial) organisms, and should not be exterminated.

**Roundworms, tapeworms, and pinworms are the most commonly encountered internal helminths (worms) in captive iguanas (Figures 8.4 to 8.8)**. Some of these worms possess direct life cycles—they are transmitted from one iguana to another, usually via fecal contamination; some utilize other creatures as intermediate hosts before developing in the iguana's body. Some worms inhabit the gastrointestinal tract; some infest other internal organs. Infestation with most of these parasitic worms is diagnosed by routine microscopic examination of the iguana's feces. Some mites (and their eggs) that are not actually iguana parasites are found in feces (Figure 8.9); they are plant parasites that are swallowed along with their vegetable hosts when iguanas eat them. It is not necessary to treat iguanas for these organisms. With the possible exception of *Giardia lamblia* (Figure 8.10), iguanas' gastrointestinal parasites are host-specific and are not pathogenic for immunologically competent humans.

Filarids are a group of worms that infest wild-caught iguanas. Adult filarid worms may live within specific organs or they may be found free within the iguana's body cavity where they mate and produce living young, called *microfilariae*, which gain access to the iguana's circulating blood. When a biting arthropod such as a mosquito bites an infected iguana, the tiny microfilariae are then transmitted to other susceptible iguanas. Fortunately, most iguanas entering the pet trade today are captive-hatched and are shipped before mosquitoes have an opportunity to feed on their blood; thus filariasis is relatively rare in pet iguanas. Filariasis is diagnosed by finding their characteristic microfilariae during the microscopic examination of stained-blood specimens.

A variety of effective parasiticides are available which can safely and efficiently treat most internal helminth parasites of iguanas. These drugs should be administered by a veterinarian skilled in herpetological medicine.

FIGURE 8.3

SEE PLATE 15

FIGURE 8.4

SEE PLATE 15

FIGURE 8.5

SEE PLATE 16

FIGURE 8.6

SEE PLATE 16

FIGURE 8.7

SEE PLATE 16

FIGURE 8.8

SEE PLATE 16

FIGURE 8.9

SEE PLATE 16

FIGURE 8.10

SEE PLATE 16

## ECTOPARASITES (EXTERNAL PARASITES)

The external parasites which occasionally are found on iguanas are mites (more often) and ticks (less often).

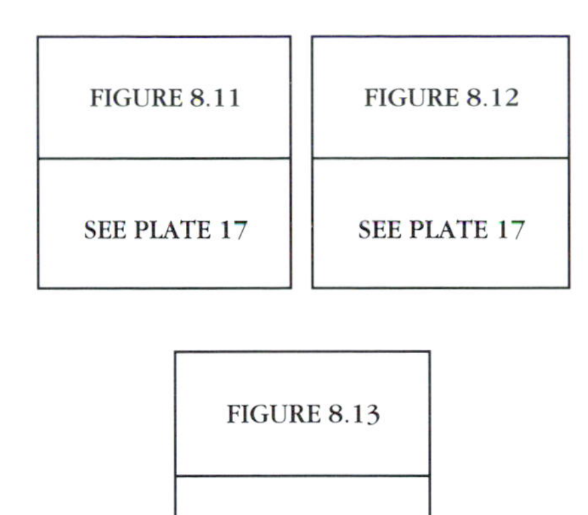

## Mites

Three kinds of mites generally infest iguanas: (1) the common snake mite, *Ophionyssus natricis*, which although usually found on snakes, can also parasitize iguanas (Figure 8.11); (2) the lizard mite, *Hirstiella trombidiiformis* (Figure 8.12), an ectoparasite of wild North American lizards; and (3) nymphal (immature) trombiculid grain mites (Figure 8.13), which are often brought into a reptile collection with contaminated bedding or cage-litter materials. Whereas both the 6-legged nymphs and 8-legged adults of the first two species of mites are parasitic on their iguanid hosts, only the 6-legged nymphs of grain mites are parasitic—adult grain mites are free-living and subsist on organic detritus they find within their environment.

Indicators of mite infestation are the following:

- Darkened or deep black scales
- Slightly raised scales which, when raised, have one or more mites underneath
- Dry patches of skin
- Individual mites crawling over the iguana's body, particularly around its cloacal vent, limb folds in the armpit or groin areas, or in its cage

Snake mites are dark brown or black and, when crushed, usually leave a blood-red smudge. *Hirstiella trombidiiformis* usually is found as individual or masses of bright orange mites clustered particularly on the integument covering the dorsal portions of the trunk, limbs (particularly in the skin folds next to the body), and tail (especially near the vent). A fine needle or broken applicator stick moistened with saliva can be used to tease one or more mites from their hiding place beneath the scale(s). Then the specimen is examined microscopically after mounting it beneath a cover slip with Hoyer's mounting and clearing medium (see Frye, 1994a).

Although three species of mites (and perhaps others) infest iguanas, the following treatment for all of them is identical:

- Place the infested iguana in a vessel containing tepid water just deep enough to cover its back and allow it to soak. A majority of the mites will be drowned after approximately 30 minutes.
- This soaking treatment may be repeated daily, but usually only two or three treatments are sufficient to accomplish eradication of most of the mites.
- After each soak, apply an **insecticide that is safe for kittens and puppies** (not adult cats and dogs) **indirectly**.

There are two methods for applying an insecticide.

1. Indirect. Spray a modest amount of a safe insecticide onto a clean cloth (or diaper or sanitary napkin); then apply this lightly saturated cloth to the iguana's skin.
2. Direct. Combine 1.0 ml ivermectin with 5.0 ml propylene glycol solution; add this mixture to 1.0 liter of distilled water in a spray bottle; then apply a light spray of this mixture directly on the iguana, but avoid saturating the skin, and be careful not to get the spray in the iguana's eyes.

The entire interior of the cage, including all cage "furniture" and litter, also must be either discarded or thoroughly cleansed in boiling water, and then sprayed with the dilute ivermectin/propylene glycol/water solution (see directions for solution above).

**DO NOT USE "PEST" STRIPS IN A CAGE OR SMALL ENCLOSURE BECAUSE THE INSECTICIDE THEY CONTAIN CAN BE LETHALLY TOXIC TO IGUANAS UNLESS ADEQUATE VENTILATION IS PROVIDED.**

## Ticks

FIGURE 8.14

SEE PLATE 17

**Infestation by ticks (Figure 8.14) is not commonly observed in captive-raised green iguanas because today most pet iguanas are obtained from iguana "farms" when they are hatchlings and are shipped almost immediately after they emerge from their eggshells. Thus, ticks have not had an opportunity to become established on these immature hosts.**

Contrary to popular folklore, ticks do not have mouthparts with righthand or lefthand "threads"; therefore they do not have to be twisted in one direction or another.

The following technique should be used for removing ticks:

- Remove individual ticks by applying a small volume of alcohol to them while they are still attached to the iguana's skin.
- After a few moments, grasp the tick(s) firmly with tweezers, **without crushing them, and detach them.**
- Alternatively, remove tick(s) by moving a stiff plastic credit card or dull knife blade between the iguana and the tick(s) in a scraping motion.

The following precautionary measures will prevent ticks from becoming established in an iguana's captive environment:

- Discard the litter.
- Clean the cage (including all of its furnishings) thoroughly with steaming hot water.
- Then spray with ivermectin/propylene glycol/water solution or a safe insecticide to eliminate any residual ticks and their eggs.

# CHAPTER 9

## MISCELLANEOUS CONDITIONS

### ABRASIONS AND LACERATIONS

Abrasions to the skin covering the front of the iguana's nose (*rostrum*), and miscellaneous lacerations elsewhere are relatively common. The former is the result of the iguana continually scraping its nose and chin against the surfaces of the cage or enclosure. Often, this behavior occurs because the animal fails to perceive the restraining walls of its glass or plastic cage, or screened walls of those which are covered with coarse hardware cloth. Transparent walls should be furnished with a wide strip of opaque plastic or dark paint so as to form a visual barrier for the iguana, thus inhibiting attempts to escape or habitually rub against the cage surfaces. Hardware cloth should be replaced either with a smooth surface or covered with a nonabrasive material.

FIGURE 9.1

SEE PLATE 18

Skin lacerations occur from contact with sharp edges, splinters, projecting nails in the cage, claw and bite wounds from cagemates (Figure 9.1), attacks by cats sharing the same household, etc.

To treat abrasions and lacerations, do the following:

- Gently cleanse the lesion with warm water or dilute hydrogen peroxide (1 part 3% hydrogen peroxide mixed with 2 parts water) until it is free of foreign matter. Alternatively, a 0.75% chlorhexidine acetate (Nolvasan®) solution can be used as a germicidal wound-flushing agent.
- Apply a soothing medication such as Neosporin® Cream or Polysporin® ointment.
- Continue applying medicated cream or ointment until the skin has healed completely.
- If the abrasion is more than superficial, apply NewSkin® liquid antiseptic bandage over the site to help protect it from further contamination or trauma while it heals.
- Deeper or more extensive lacerations may require suturing by a veterinarian. If the laceration has been contaminated or has been left open for several hours prior to veterinary medical treatment, the veterinarian may elect to insert a latex rubber Penrose drain (Figure 9.1d) to ensure that transudates and exudates will not accumulate in the injured site.

## ANEMIA

Severe anemia usually induces the following signs in affected iguanas:

- Rapid respiration
- Fatigue after even minor exertion
- Lethargy
- Inappetence
- Paler than normal oral mucous membranes
- Change in skin color from normal brighter hues to darker, more somber colors

The principal causes for anemia in iguanas are traumatic injuries, gastrointestinal parasitism, gastrointestinal foreign bodies, gastric ulcers, lizard malaria, and leukemia.

Because many iguanas sold through pet dealers today are captive-bred, the incidence of severe gastrointestinal parasitism and lizard malaria in them is substantially less than what is found in wild-caught iguanas that have been exposed to the natural vectors or reservoir hosts for these parasites.

Gastrointestinal parasites are diagnosed via the laboratory analysis of feces. Malarial parasitism is determined by the microscopic examination of stained specimens of blood; this test requires only a small volume of blood and it should not pose a threat to your iguana.

Some of these same clinical signs also are manifested when an iguana has a respiratory infection. Consult a veterinarian for a definitive diagnosis and effective treatment.

## BURNS

Because of the necessity to provide supplementary warmth for captive iguana cages or enclosures, there are ample opportunities for accidental burns to occur: undercage heating pads, resistance-heated electrical stones or blocks, heat tapes, thermal cables, overhead heat lamps, ceramic heat-emitting bulbs, and space heaters have all been implicated in causing thermal burns when they either produce too much heat or are located too close to an iguana's body (Figures 9.2a & b). Although iguanas are (relatively) intelligent creatures, they often do not react to intense heat. (You would be correct to think that once the pain of a burn was perceived, the iguana would move away from the source of that pain.) The reasons for this apparent insensitivity to pain—or a failure to move purposely away from it—are unclear.

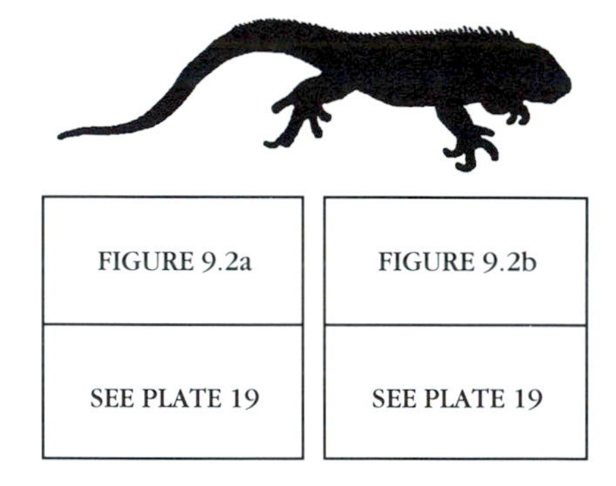

FIGURE 9.2a SEE PLATE 19

FIGURE 9.2b SEE PLATE 19

Do the following to avoid burns:

- Select substrate heating devices of appropriate thermal capacity (wattage rating) to furnish sufficient warmth, but not so much that overheating results.
- Elevate overhead heat lamps and ceramic heat bulbs to heights of at least 0.5 m (~19 inches) above the basking sites (depending upon the individual wattage of each device) so that they are not so close to basking sites that their beneficial effects are counteracted by thermal injuries.
- Position incandescent and ceramic bulbs in such a fashion that iguanas cannot come into close contact with the bulbs or their protective cages.
- Secure electric space heaters so that they cannot be upset, and place them so they cannot be approached too closely.

Signs of thermal burning are the following:

- Discoloration of the burned part, usually the belly or inner aspects of the limbs.
- Pain is elicited when the burn site is touched.
- Blistering may or may not be apparent.
- The dorsal spines and eyelids may be lost after they have been severely burned by excessively hot overhead infrared heating devices (Figure 9.2c).

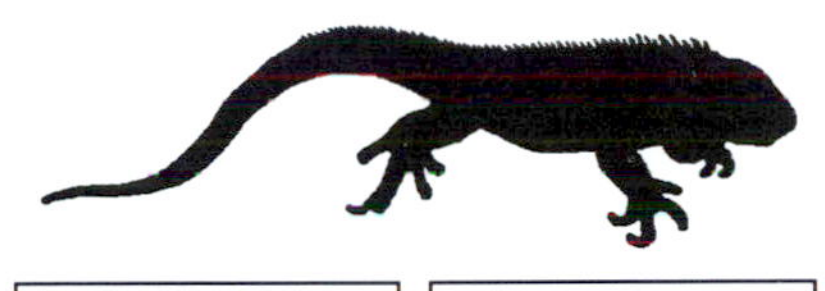

| FIGURE 9.2c | FIGURE 9.2d |
| --- | --- |
| SEE PLATE 19 | SEE PLATE 19 |

Severely burned skin may lose its normal pigmentation permanently; the healed site remains white or pale yellow (Figure 9.2d). If the muscles and ligaments underlying the burned area also are damaged by the excessive heat, they may become denatured and, after healing, result in deformities that are permanent.

To treat thermal burns, do the following:

- Apply a soothing medication such as Neosporin® Cream, Polysporin® ointment, or Silvadene® Creme.
- Continue applying medicated creme or ointment until the skin has healed completely.
- If the burned area is extensive (involves an area of more than 1.0 square cm (~0.5 square inch), it should be evaluated by a veterinarian. Prophylactic antibiotic treatment may be necessary to prevent infection.
- Do not house an iguana which has been burned in a cage containing particulate litter because the small pieces may adhere to the moist surface of the burned tissue.
- A burned iguana should be housed by itself because cagemates may further traumatize the injured area when they crawl over it.

## CARE OF CLAWS

Living in the rainforest, wild iguanas wear their claws down regularly as they walk and climb among the objects of their environment. However, captive iguanas living in cages or in household habitats furnished with soft carpeting tend to suffer from overgrowth of their claws. Overly long claws can catch in cloth curtains or drapery, and the iguana can be severely injured as it falls from a high perch. Severe overgrowth can lead to deformed toes. An abnormally long claw may become wedged into a crevice or cloth weave and, as the iguana struggles to free itself, the entire claw can be pulled out of the nail bed from which it grows. When more than a single iguana is kept in a cage, their sharp claws may puncture skin as they crawl over one another, thus allowing disease-causing bacteria and/or fungi to be introduced into the wound(s).

The claws of small iguanas can be easily trimmed with the same kind of nail clippers that we use to groom our own nails; for larger iguanas, the kind of nail clippers used in veterinary practice are best. Both of these devices are inexpensive and efficiently shorten overgrown claws without damaging the softer structures.

The following technique should be used:

- Trim back only the sharp tips of the claws (Figure 9.3).
- Trimming the claw back too far may cause a small amount of bleeding.
- Bleeding usually can be controlled by applying pressure to the claw with a dry cotton ball or cotton-tipped bud.
- When more severe bleeding occurs, apply a dry styptic pencil (usually employed for staunching the bleeding from minor shaving cuts) to help stop the blood flow.

An alternative to trimming the sharply pointed claws of iguanas which are handled frequently is covering them with soft plastic devices called Soft-Paws® (Rossi, 1994). These devices were designed to prevent cats from clawing upholstery and other objects. Before they are cemented in place, the claw is shortened with a clipper. Used on an iguana, they usually remain in place for 1–3 months and then must be replaced when they become dislodged as the claws grow. Iguanas whose claws are covered with these devices still are able to climb rough-barked tree limbs without difficulty. Because they come in several bright colors, I suggest that green, yellow, orange, or red not be used because iguanas are attracted to these colors and may be tempted to bite them, thus causing their premature detachment from the claws. Instead use blue or clear Soft-Paws® (see Appendix C). This product seems to be an ingenious solution to the problem of iguana scratches.

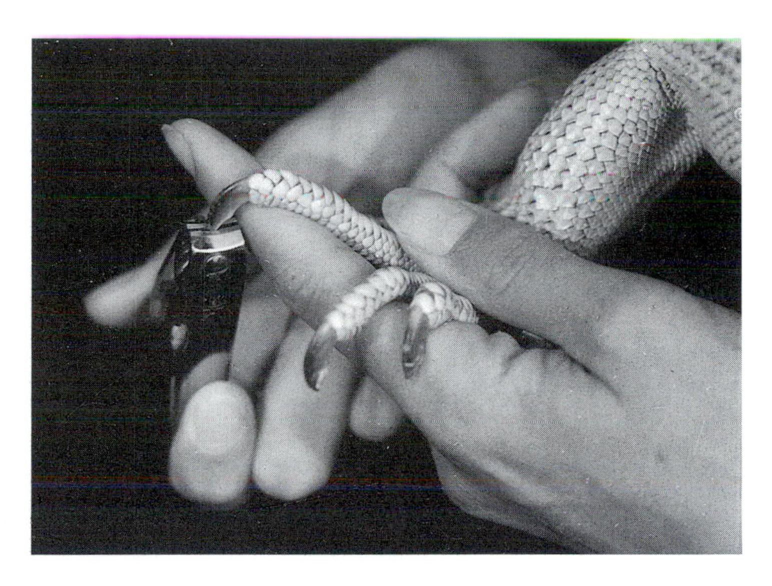

**Figure 9.3.** When clipping the claws, only the sharp tips should be removed. Photo credit: Wendy Townsend.

## LOSS OF DIGITS (FINGERS AND TOES)

Digits sometimes appear to spontaneously die, and then they drop off.

Loss of digits can be caused by the following:

FIGURE 2.6

SEE PLATE 11

- Trauma resulting from crushing injuries when an iguana's feet are caught beneath a falling branch or heavy stone, are trapped in a cage door, or are twisted as the iguana tries to free its claws from being entangled in fabric or screen.
- Tiny ringlets of retained shed skin that dry and form a constricting tourniquet (shown previously in Figure 2.6) which incarcerates the digits and stops normal blood flow to them.

Prevent trauma by making certain that cage furniture is installed so that falling branches, tree trunks, or stones cannot shift and crush the occupants; and before closing a cage door, be certain that the iguana's feet are free and clear of the door. Careful inspection of iguanas during and after periodic skin molts should become routine. Any retained pieces of skin should be soaked and softened, and then they can be easily removed before they cause inadvertent amputation.

## ELECTROCUTION AND ELECTRICAL INJURY

Fatal electrocution and sublethal electrical injuries occur when the iguana comes into contact with improperly functioning electrical heating and lighting devices installed in the cage enclosure. Sometimes, the insulation covering the electrical cord of a heating stone cracks and permits stray currents to injure cage inhabitants. **Check all electrical devices periodically for fraying cords, malfunctioning thermostats, etc.**

Signs of electrocution are the following:

- Sudden and profound collapse or paralysis.
- Skin color may darken.
- Charring or discoloration of skin which may be seen as discrete lesions.

**CAUTION: UNPLUG ALL ELECTRICAL DEVICES CONNECTED TO THE CAGE BEFORE TOUCHING THE VICTIM OF ANY SUSPECTED ELECTROCUTION!**

After the power has been disconnected, remove the iguana and seek veterinary care immediately. Although it might be limp and seem apparently dead, electrical shock injuries to iguanas are not invariably fatal.

## EYE DISORDERS

There are no eye diseases known to be specifically limited to green iguanas. They are subject to the same ophthalmic disorders that are encountered in other vertebrates, including most found in humans. **Abscessation of the eyelids and other superficial tissues that surround the eyes is probably the green iguana's most common eye problem.** These inflammatory lesions often are caused by claw wounds from iguanas when they are kept in overcrowded conditions. Periocular abscessation must be treated by a veterinarian.

A veterinarian would do the following to treat periocular abscessation:

- Incise and evacuate the purulent contents of these abscesses.
- Flush the resultant cavities.
- Instill a water-soluble antibiotic ointment into the wounds for a few days or until they heal completely.
- Depending on the severity of the infection, administer either topical antibiotic ointments, aqueous wound-flushing solutions, or injectable or oral broad-spectrum antibiotic drugs.

When oral antibiotics are employed, the potential benefit of the drug's positive effect on the pathogenic bacteria must be counterbalanced against its potential—and real—negative effect on the intestinal microflora that are so essential for the processing and digestion of the iguana's cellulose-rich leafy diet. Therefore, minor abscesses should be treated with effective topical ointments or aqueous solutions rather than with more aggressive systemic therapy.

Pieces of litter material can lodge beneath an iguana's eyelid and cause discomfort. If such foreign objects are suspected, flush the conjunctival space beneath each eyelid with a proprietary ophthalmic irrigating solution such as Dacriose®; gently squeeze the plastic bottle in which it is sold to deliver a stream of aqueous solution.

Corneal abrasions can result from contact with cage surfaces, eye rubbing, tail lashes from other iguanas, etc. Injuries to the cornea usually are accompanied by a great reluctance to open one or both eyes and, perhaps, reddening of the entire eyeball or conjunctival membranes that line the inner surface of the eyelids. When a corneal injury is suspected, the iguana should be examined and treated by a veterinarian.

Superficial conjunctivitis (inflammation) and other minor infections affect the eyelids and mucous membranes that surround the eye. When not treated, previous minor infections can disseminate and cause extensive damage in organs far distant from the eyes.

Cataracts and glaucoma do occur in iguanas, but they are not common because both conditions are usually (but not invariably) age-related, and most iguanas do not live long enough to be affected by these conditions.

I have diagnosed tumors of the glands that surround the eyeball, but they are rare. When surgical excision is required, the removal of these tumors can result in substantial bleeding because the iguana's periocular tissues are highly vascular and are supplied by a network of blood vessels that, when disturbed during surgery, can bleed profusely and are notoriously difficult to staunch.

As they age, the sclerae ("white" part of the eye that can be seen when the eyelids are wide open) of some elderly iguanas develop a brown pigmentation. This change appears to be only a mild age-related migration of melanin-containing cells into the sclerae and, thus, no diminution of visual acuity is caused by this alteration.

## FOREIGN-BODY INGESTION

Iguanas sometimes ingest foreign bodies that can cause intoxication, poisoning, or intestinal obstruction. Diagnostic radiography often reveals the nature of these objects. In some cases, they can be removed without surgery (Frye, 1994a); others require surgical intervention.

## FRACTURES

Limb, spinal, rib, and tail fractures occur principally from two causes: (1) underlying nutritional deficiencies that cause the iguana's bones to be soft and weak, and (2) the iguana falling or being caught beneath falling branches or tree trunks within the cage.

The signs of a fractured limb bone are the following:

- An obvious deviation from normal shape
- Inability to bear weight on the limb
- Sudden swelling of part of or the entire limb
- Pain induced when the affected limb is touched, even gently
- The sound of bone grating on bone if the limb is moved
- In cases of compound (open) fractures, a sharp-ended bone fragment perforating the skin, thus exposing the inner tissues to contamination and infection

Treatment for limb fractures is aimed at immobilizing the affected limbs so that the fractured bones can no longer move away from each other and stabilizing the ends of the fractured bones so that they are brought into close apposition to one another. Immobilization also reduces the pain because the fracture site cannot be further traumatized by movement of the sharp bone fragments. Fractured bones that are immobilized heal more quickly than bones that move freely. Moreover, immobilization reduces the opportunity for the fractured bones to further damage nerves and blood vessels in the vicinity of the fracture or to perforate intact skin and convert a closed fracture into an open one.

To treat minor fractures of the digits: (1) place the fingers or toes over a ball of clean cotton; and (2) wrap with soft, pliant cast-padding materials (Figure 9.4a–d). In some cases, limb fractures can be treated adequately with external splintage, using bulky, soft cast-padding. More serious limb fractures should be evaluated by a veterinarian because they may require surgical correction and the implantation of internal fixation devices (Figure 9.5a & b).

Spinal fractures are usually serious and often result in quadriplegia or paraplegia, depending on which part of the spine is damaged. If a vertebral fracture is suspected, place the injured iguana in a box large enough to contain it **without bending its body**, and transport it to a veterinarian immediately. The prognosis depends on how much damage the delicate spinal cord has sustained during the fracture of the vertebral bone.

Skull fractures are unusual and are almost always the result of attacks by household cats that have bitten iguanas on the head.

Rib fractures usually heal spontaneously without splintage. However, an iguana with one or more fractured ribs should not be handled, except when absolutely necessary and then only with gentleness, to avoid causing lung damage from the fractured rib ends.

Some tail fractures, if they are not complete, can be splinted so that the damaged tissues will reunite.

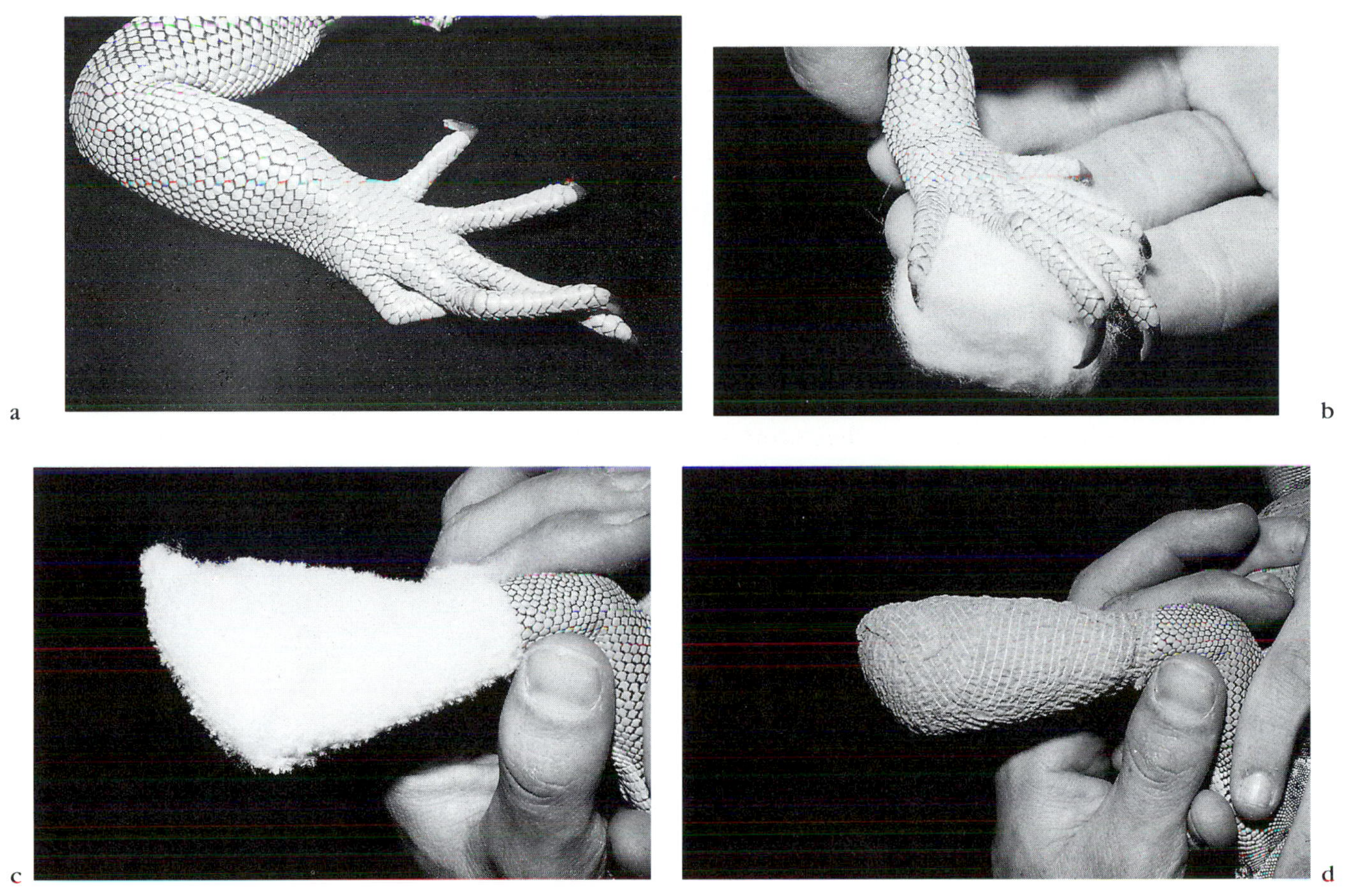

**Figure 9.4a–d.** Sequence for applying a soft padded splint to fractured digits.

## HOMOSEXUAL BEHAVIOR

Captive green iguanas sometimes display what can only be described as homosexual behavior. **Although both males and females have been observed in transient pseudocopulation with members of the same sex, this is not considered to be abnormal behavior by these animals and may only represent one form of a display of social dominance** (see Köhler, 1991 a & b). It is also likely that this same-sex mounting, however transitory, is an aberrant behavior conditioned by one or more factors of captivity, since it has only rarely been observed in wild iguanas (Dugan, 1982; Rodda, 1992). This behavior should not cause concern for iguana owners who witness it in their pets.

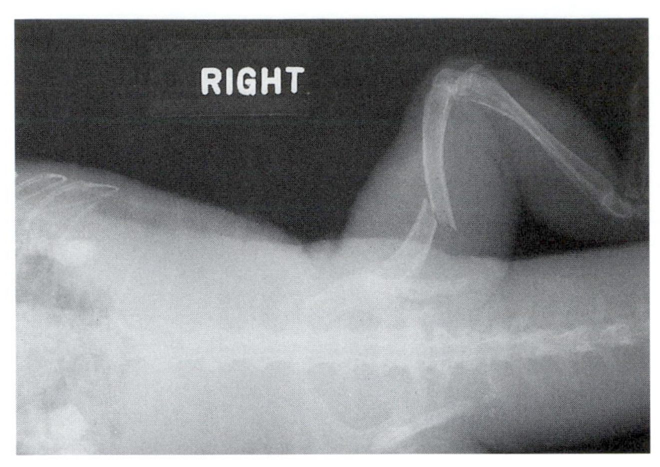


a

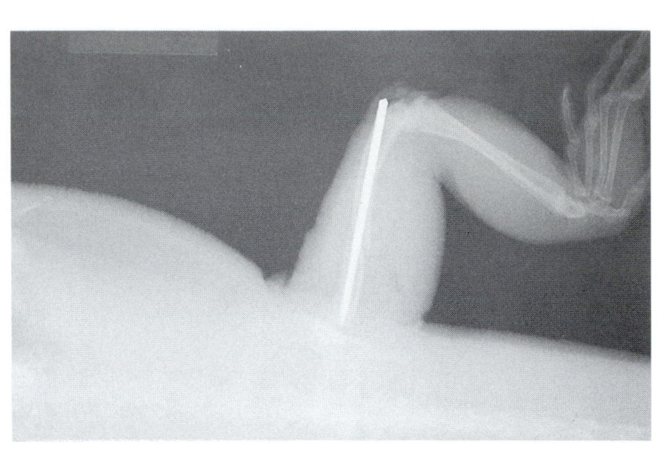

b

**Figure 9.5a & b.** Preoperative and postoperative radiographs of a right midshaft femoral fracture sustained by a half-grown green iguana. A stainless steel intramedullary pin was used to repair this fractured bone.

## HYPERTHERMIA (EXCESSIVELY HIGH BODY TEMPERATURE)

Hyperthermia can occur when an iguana's body is overheated by malfunctioning heating devices or when it is confined in a closed place, such as a transparent cage or automobile, that is exposed to sunlight.

Signs of hyperthermia are the following:

- Profound lethargy to the point of collapse and unresponsiveness
- A nonspecific change of skin color from a brighter green or golden orange to a more somber greyish- or brownish-green
- Diarrhea
- Vomiting

To treat hyperthermia, do the following:

- Remove the iguana from the source of heat.
- To decrease its body temperature, cool the iguana under running tepid tap water.
- In severe cases, take the iguana to a veterinarian for evaluation and treatment.

## HYPOTHERMIA (EXCESSIVELY LOW BODY TEMPERATURE)

Hypothermia can occur when an iguana's body temperature is exposed to abnormally cold environmental temperatures. If exposure is severe and prolonged, the iguana's immunity to infection will be greatly diminished; thus it will be more prone to a variety of bacterial, fungal, and viral diseases.

The clinical signs of hypothermia are nonspecific; they include the following:

- Extreme lethargy to the point of torpor
- Nonresponsiveness to external stimuli
- Skin color change from a brighter green or golden orange to a more somber greyish- or brownish-green

To treat hypothermia, do the following:

- Warm the iguana's environment to a range of between 26.7–31.1 °C (80–88 °F).
- If it is severely chilled, place the iguana in a container of tepid water to more effectively restore its deep-core body temperature to a more normal level of approximately 27–28 °C (~80–83 °F). Increase the iguana's internal body temperature **gradually**, and be cognizant of how much it is increasing.
- If there is evidence of infection, a veterinarian must treat the iguana aggressively with appropriate antibiotic therapy.

### Purposeful Cooling for Restraint or "Anesthesia"

Purposeful cooling should not be employed when attempting to restrain or "anesthetize" because (1) cooling reduces an iguana's immunity to infective microorganisms; and (2) there is absolutely no evidence that cooling renders a reptile insensitive to pain—it only makes it impossible for the animal to **react** to painful stimuli. Therefore, on the basis of humane treatment of animals, I discourage the practice of using refrigerator temperatures to restrain reptiles.

## SCOLIOSIS AND KYPHOSCOLIOSIS (VERTEBRAL DEFORMITIES)

Scoliosis is defined as the abnormal lateral (sideways) curvature of the vertebral column. Kyphoscoliosis is defined as a backward and lateral curvature of the vertebral column. These conditions are manifested in several different way with different degrees of severity: the vertebral curvature in some iguanas begins at the junction of the pelvis and tail; other iguanas with severe vertebral curvature have straight tails. When the vertebral column is massively affected, the iguana's entire body becomes permanently distorted. As the vertebral column becomes progressively deviated, the affected iguana's internal organs become increasingly crowded and compressed. Because of this compression, the physiological function of some internal organs, primarily the lungs and liver, may be severely impaired. As the lungs become increasingly compressed, respiration becomes more labored and difficult. The iguana then becomes exhausted, ceases to eat, declines in health, and eventually dies or must be humanely euthanatized. If their vertebral curvature is not too severe and does not cause internal organ compression and dysfunction, some iguanas can live normal lifespans. Examples of early, mild, and very severe scoliosis and kyphoscoliosis are shown in Figures 9.6a–c.

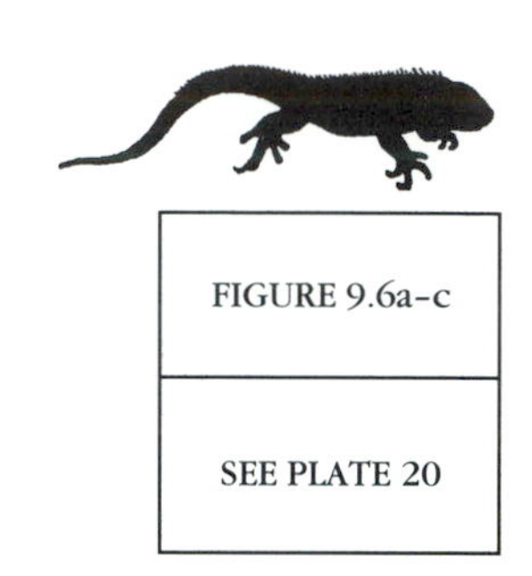


Although both of these conditions occur most often in older green iguanas, I have seen several very young green iguanas with these spinal deviations. Some of these iguanas had been fed nutritionally deficient diets; others had been fed ideal diets. Even the majority of iguanas suffering from very severe metabolic bone disease do not develop spinal curvature. One feature mimics similar disorders in humans: the majority of human patients affected with spinal curvature are girls and women; almost all cases of scoliosis and kyphoscoliosis in iguanas also occur in females. Therefore, the disparity in age of onset, the apparent lack of evidence that diet is responsible, and the skewed gender bias lead me to suspect that scoliosis and kyphoscoliosis might be, at least partially if not entirely, heritable (or otherwise sex-linked) in green iguanas.

**There is no practical and effective treatment for these vertebral curvatures. Because of the possibility that this condition is heritable, affected iguanas, or even unaffected iguanas whose offspring are affected, should not be used as breeders.**

## SEXUAL AGGRESSION BY MALE IGUANAS TOWARD THEIR OWNERS

After several years of being fed by, cared for, and interacting closely with its owner, it is not unusual for a close bond to form between an iguana and this special person in its life. However, between some mature male iguanas and their women owners, an abnormally strong attachment is formed. Two of my colleagues and I have now documented nearly 50 cases of **unprovoked** sexual aggression in which male iguanas have displayed more than casual interest in their female owners. The first 18 cases were described by Frye, Mader and Centofanti (1991). Most often, this aggression has taken the form of stereotypical courtship displays commencing with head nodding, then continuing on with dewlap extension, chasing, and attempts to bite or actually biting, and finally hemipenial protrusion. Some of these astonished owners have observed their iguanas masturbating on objects and even ejaculating (Figure 9.7a). One iguana was given a child's pacifier to carry around in its mouth following each instance of masturbation and ejaculation (Figure 9.7b).

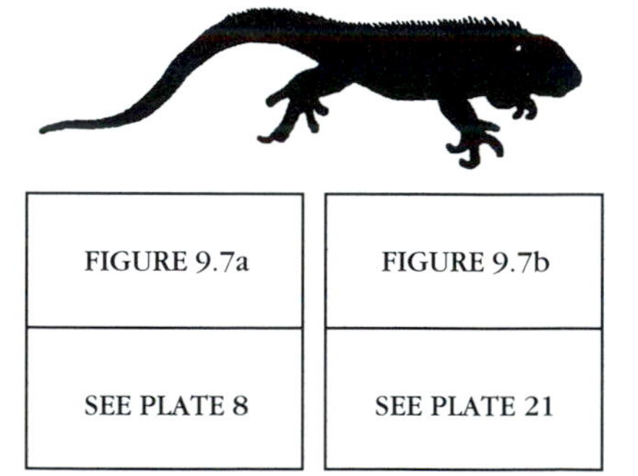

Most of these acts of aggression have involved relationships between iguanas obtained when they were very young and women of childbearing age with whom they have had unusually close contact. The women fed their iguanas at the same table where they dined, showered or bathed with them, and even permitted their iguanas to sleep in or on the same bed. All cases essentially involved adult male green iguanas who were raised as "only children" with no contact with any other male or female iguanas. Almost all of these cases occurred in households in which there were no adult male humans.

In every case investigated to the date of this writing, each of these aggressive displays occurred while the woman owner was menstruating or ovulating. The most likely cause for this remarkable behavior would be a pheromone (chemical, often hormonal cue), which is secreted during the human menstrual period and might be perceived by a male iguana. This (apparently) closely mimics a similar scentlike substance that is secreted by female iguanas, thereby acting as a stimulus for the male's sexual activity. Although it is possible that the scent-cue resembles that of another male iguana, it is unlikely because the behavior displayed by these aggressive males has, in every case, been sexual aggression, not territorial aggression. This has been demonstrated by the hemipenial erection, masturbation, and ejaculation—none of these components would be expected in male-to-male territorial competition because they would be counterproductive.

Although there is no specific treatment for this type of sexual aggression directed against human owners, the following can be done to ameliorate it:

- Simply confine the offending iguana to a cage or other enclosure.
- If caging is not acceptable, consider surgical intervention in the form of castration. This surgical procedure offers a humane, highly effective, and practical resolution to this problem. Generally, a male iguana calms down and ceases his aggressive attacks after approximately 2–4 weeks; most or all of the aggressive behaviors typical of a sexually mature male iguana eventually are abolished.

A striking consequence to castration is the change of color that is seen soon after the surgery. Previous to castration, many of the male iguanas upon which I operated had displayed their bright orange, gold, and bronze hues, but, within a few weeks after castration, these bright autumn colors faded and were replaced by the bright lime green that is characteristic of juvenile iguanas. However, the spines that constitute the dorsal crest remained long and luxuriant. Castration in an iguana requires a veterinary surgeon skilled in this procedure. In iguanas, the testes are intracoelomic; thus they are not contained in an external scrotum as they are in many mammals. They are located within the "abdominal" portion

FIGURE 9.7c

SEE PLATE 21

of the coelomic cavity and are intimately associated with both the aorta and posterior vena cava; and, because of this connection to these large vascular structures, they must be freed by delicately dissecting and carefully ligating them before they can be safely excised (Figure 9.7c). Because of the delicacy of the surgery and the necessity to operate literally "in a hole" (the testicles cannot be freed and withdrawn from their site adjacent to the vessels noted above), the operation requires much more time than that expended during either a canine castration or ovario-hysterectomy (spay) operation. Consequently, the fee for this highly specialized surgery is more than that charged for a similar canine or feline operation.

Not every adult male iguana exhibits this aggressive behavior; in fact, only a minority do. I recommend that castration be performed only on male iguanas that have already displayed overt—and serious—aggression. Unlike the situation with cats and some dogs that are neutered as a means of preventing unwanted male behavior, it is best to wait until a male iguana actually demonstrates that he is a candidate for neutering. There are no specific untoward side effects to this surgery.

An alternative to surgical castration is the use of an oral or injectable female hormone (medroxyprogesterone acetate in the long-acting "depot" form) which can be administered at intervals of 2–3 times yearly. This treatment may greatly diminish sexual displays and aggression. However, the dosage is empirical: it must be repeated; and it inherently is not as safe, sure, or free from unwanted side effects as is surgical castration.

## SKIN INFLAMMATION (DERMATITIS)

FIGURE 9.8a-d

SEE PLATE 22

Moist or dry dermatitis is a condition of the skin seen only occasionally in captive iguanas, but it can be serious.

Signs of moist or dry dermatitis are the following:

- Patches of obviously abnormal skin whose color differs markedly from the surrounding epidermis (Figure 9.8a).
- The skin may be jet black (Figures 9.8b & c).
- The skin is moist from sticky fluid which weeps out.
- As the skin is touched, it tends to slip away from the underlying muscular tissues, leaving them denuded (Figure 9.8d).
- Sometimes the affected skin is dry and has the unyielding texture of wood when touched with light finger-pressure.

You should wear protective disposable latex or vinyl plastic gloves (to avoid human infection) when touching an iguana who has dermatitis. An affected iguana should be taken to a veterinarian immediately for treatment.

## STOOL COLOR

Normally, the droppings of healthy green iguanas contain dark brown feces and a variable amount of chalky white urates. If the feces are red- or pink-colored and the urates are pink-hued, the cause must be elucidated. When bleeding occurs in the esophagus, stomach, or small intestines, the hemoglobin contained in the red blood cells is digested, and the stools become black and tarry. When bleeding occurs in the large intestine, rectum, or cloaca, the stools become plum red or bright red. Internal parasites, foreign bodies, or traumatic injuries also can cause such abnormal fecal colorations. Sometimes, an unusual color can be related to something in the food that was artificially colored with dye. Several concerned iguana owners have brought me their pets' "strange looking" stool specimens. The culprit was red dye which came from "hot dog"-type sausages that were fed as a treat. *Eugenia* leaves, beet tops, red swiss chard, and some other vegetables contain natural anthocyanins which, when eaten, color feces dark red. Some commercial iguana diets also are artificially colored with red, green, orange, or yellow food-coloring dyes to make them more attractive to iguanas—and probably also to the iguanas' owners. If blood is not found in the stool, abnormal color can be ignored. A "dip stick" test will reveal blood.

## TAIL DISORDERS

Dry gangrene of the tail occurs relatively often in captive green iguanas; it usually is spontaneous.

Dry gangrene can be caused by the following:

- Blunt or crushing injuries
- Pieces of retained old epidermis that have not been shed properly and which, after becoming wet, shrink and act like ligatures or tourniquets
- Vascular insufficiency due to injury or vascular thrombosis
- Miscellaneous infections

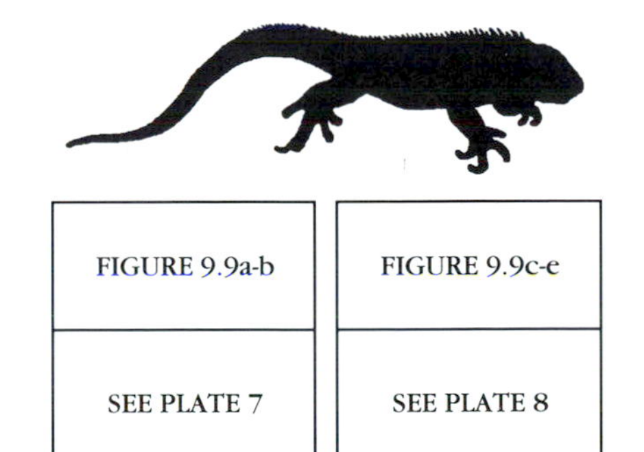


Spontaneously shed (autotomized) tails are easily treated. If the tail breaks off very close to the body, it usually regenerates. The new tail begins as a rounded bulge which soon elongates and tapers toward its end (Figure 9.9a & b). A regrown tail sometimes grows in an abnormal direction, or it may even have two or more branches (Figure 9.9c & d). After several cycles of being broken and then regenerating, a tail that is broken again may merely round over and not grow to a tapered point (Figure 9.9e). As the iguana matures, its tail becomes much less fragile and, therefore, is less easily autotomized.

Epidermal (sebaceous inclusion) cysts similar to those seen in some humans and in many dogs can affect green iguanas. These lesions are usually swellings that grow slowly and, when incised, are found to be filled with a greasy or waxy secretion. They may become infected and chronically abscessed and should be treated by a veterinarian.

The veterinarian would do the following to treat epidermal inclusion cysts:

- Open and drain the cyst contents.
- Flush with an aqueous wound-antiseptic such as 0.75% chlorhexidine diacetate.
- Pack with a water-soluble antibiotic ointment.
- If extensive, the affected portion of the tail would be amputated and allowed to regrow.

Treatment for many tail disorders in iguanas consists simply of amputating the tail above the site of injury or disease; then the tail will regenerate its lost portion within several months. The tail stump should not be sutured because suturing arrests regeneration. The regrown tail portion will be slightly shorter and less colorful than the original, and its scalation will not be quite the same as the original (Figure 9.9d); but it will function as well as ever as a balance organ, as a weapon with which it can defend itself, and, if given the opportunity to swim, as a propeller.

## URINARY BLADDER STONES (UROLITHS)

Iguanas affected with bladder stones (uroliths) usually are asymptomatic, or they may strain as if to defecate without producing stools. Uroliths often can be felt with the fingers as the posterior coelomic cavity is palpated gently. They are diagnosed with radiography (X-rays) (Figure 9.10a). **Development of urinary stones in green iguanas often can be traced to diets containing too much animal protein, particularly those in which dog, cat, or monkey chows form a significant portion.** Some uroliths form spontaneously and may be related to mineral imbalances. Although these stones may occasionally be passed from the urinary bladder, more often they must be removed surgically by a veterinarian because they can lodge in the opening to the urethra and obstruct the flow of urine into the urodeum portion of the cloaca. A cross-sectioned urinary stone is illustrated in Figure 9.10b.

Do the following to prevent the formation of urinary stones:

- Provide fresh water that is easily available and appealing to drink (see Chapter 3).
- Include calcium-rich green leaves in the diet.

It is now evident that the nutritional and physiological factors that contribute to the development of gout in iguanas are those that also promote urinary stones in iguanas.

**Figure 9.10b.** Illustration of the urinary bladder stone in Figure 9.10a. The stone has been sectioned to show its internal structure consisting of concentric rings of urate deposits.

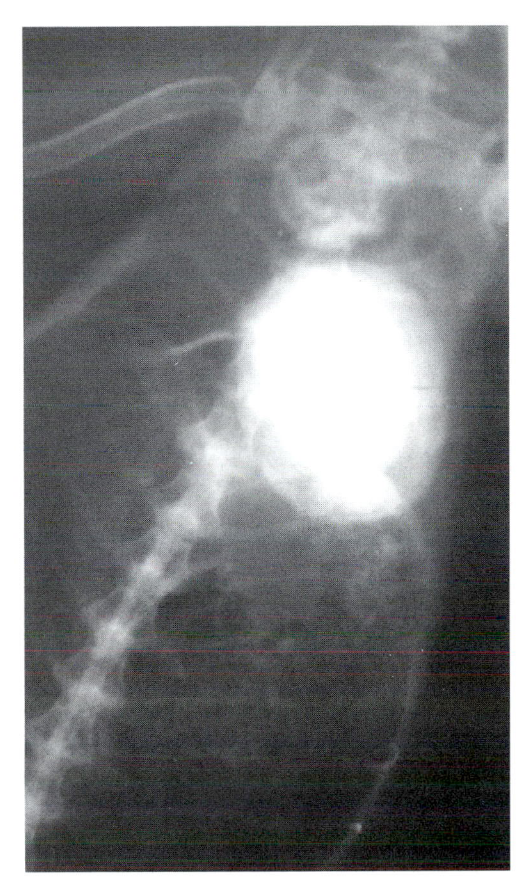

**Figure 9.10a.** Radiograph of a large urinary bladder stone that was removed surgically.

# CHAPTER 10

## REPRODUCTION

A major goal of many people who keep green iguanas in captivity is to induce them to reproduce. Although climatic conditions often prevent these tropical animals from being housed outdoors in simulated natural habitats, significant advances have been made in providing suitable indoor quarters that fulfill the many environmental requirements necessary for reproduction.

Much effort has been directed toward the induction of reproduction by using the releasing hormone GNRH (Phillips, et al., 1985, 1987). Tiny implanted osmotic pumps were used to deliver pulsed doses of the hormone. Not only was reproductive activity induced in the female iguanas, but male iguanas also were induced to cycle into their testicular activity and production of sperm merely by being exposed to GNRH-treated females. This demonstrates the actuality of induced testicular synchronization in males exposed to (hormone-treated) females.

### SEXUAL MATURITY

| FIGURE 10.1 |
| --- |
| SEE PLATE 3 |

**Most common green iguanas achieve sexual maturity between their third and fourth years; a few may achieve sexual maturity as early as the middle to end of their second year.** Even very small sexually mature males may try to copulate with much larger females (Figure 10.1). One study involving a colony of captive green iguanas indicated that *physiological* puberty is not always synchronous with the *physical* capability or the opportunity for breeding (Zug and Rand, 1987). An investigative study by Pratt, et al. (1994) found that, in addition to the mere formation of sperm and eggs, social, physiological, and morphological elements play major roles in the development of sexual maturity. Immature male green iguanas began developing several sexually dimorphic characteristics when they were as young as 14 months of age. These sexually dimorphic characteristics included such features as larger femoral pores, head, neck, and tail-base diameter; longer dorsal spines; increased testicular mass; and production of sperm. Pratt, et al. also found that sex-hormone levels began to exhibit a marked seasonality after the male iguanas reached 12 months of age. Larger male green iguanas that had higher concentrations of male sex steroid hormone developed their orange breeding color earlier and displayed more aggression than smaller males did. Interestingly, the testicular mass present in socially subordinate males was less than the testicular mass present in dominant males of *all size classes*. Female green iguanas (which had been kept under the same environmental regimen as the males) were 1–2 years older and 135–232% larger than males when they reached sexual maturity. Therefore, the attainment of sexual maturity is correlated with age and size: male green iguanas are younger and smaller, whereas female green iguanas are older and larger. Also, the females' sex hormone levels were not correlated with body size, as occurs in males.

All species of female iguanas lay eggs. Sexual maturity appears to occur earlier in well-fed captive females than it does in wild iguanas. Studies on a wild population of iguanas indicated that the modal age at which females achieved sexual maturity was 5 years old (Pratt, et al., 1994). Observations of captive female iguanas kept with sexually mature males revealed that most of these females mated and deposited fertile eggs when they were 3 or 4 years old, although some mated and produced eggs that hatched when they were as young as 2 years old. Whether the synchronization of males' and females' sexual maturity plays as great a role in captive iguanas as it does in more natural populations in the wild (as suggested by Rodda, 1992) is unclear because, when investigating "pet" iguanas, only captives were observed. Ideal conditions such as the provision of an appropriate diet, temperature, photoperiod, humidity, and freedom from predation pressure and territorial competition may (and probably do) greatly influence the onset of earlier sexual maturity in captive iguanas.

## COURTSHIP AND MATING

**A suitable environment and nonstressful social interaction encourage successful courtship and mating.**

Observations of wild populations of green iguanas yielded information that suggests that virtually all courtship and copulation occurs within defined territories (Cox and LeBoeuf, 1977; Distel and Veazey, 1982; Dugan, 1982a, 1982b; Dugan and Wiewandt, 1982; Rand, 1967; Rodda, 1992; Rodda and Grajal, 1990; and Stamps, 1977). These territorial prerogatives are essential to a male's reproductive success.

The subtleties of courtship are important factors which influence a female's choice of a mate and facilitate a female's receptivity (Burghardt, 1978; Rand, 1978; Rodda, 1992). Sometimes, the presence of a competing male stimulates an otherwise sluggish male with a flagging libido. The presence of more than one female also often stimulates courtship. This may be due to an augmentation of pheromonal (chemical or hormonal) scent cues, or it may be purely psychological. Exposure to unfiltered sunlight and a light shower are powerful stimulants to male courtship activity. Generally, the male must be perceived as being fit by any prospective female before she will accept his advances. Exceptions to this rule usually involve opportunistic matings by smaller and persistent males, and this is why many large male iguanas exhibit such hostility towards their smaller cage mates (of either gender).

Combat between competing males is relatively common when more than a single male occupies a delineated territory, but these combative encounters are only rarely fatal; they usually involve miscellaneous bites on or about the head, neck, and limbs. Deposed males should be removed from the confines of a dominant male's territory because the constant harassment will lead to its decline in health and fitness, starvation and, possibly, death.

## Stereotypical Male Courtship Behavior

Stereotypical male courtship behavior includes the following:

- Head bobbing.
- Extending and retracting the dewlap.
- Nuzzling and biting the skin of the female's neck.
- If two or more males are involved, they may go through mock (or real) battle with each other, with the winner claiming the female as his "prize."

During bouts of combat or courting that immediately precede copulation, males display their colors by extending and retracting their dewlaps, and exhibit much head-bobbing and high-stepping "body language." Chasing and biting of opponents frequently occur. In some instances, other iguanas within the home ranges of the combatants are rubbed with glandular secretions from the ventral portions of the combatants' thighs. During this mildly abrasive activity, a waxy substance that is thought to contain one or more chemical cues (pheromones) is applied to branches, rocks, and receptive female iguanas. This substance is produced by specialized integumentary glandular structures, called *femoral pores*, and serves to mark the territories and, occasionally, the female mates of successful or dominant male iguanas. Whether such scent marking of mates is purposeful or merely accidental is conjectural; it may occur only as a consequence of the thigh region of a mature male being moved over the surface of a female whereby some of the femoral pore secretion is deposited.

Another scent-laden waxy substance that is analogous to dried smegma is secreted at irregular intervals from both of the male's paired copulatory organs (*hemipenes*). When either the same or a different male iguana perceives the scent of these hemipenial plugs, the male who finds it usually reacts by displaying increased territorial behavior consisting of head bobbing and overt aggression towards other male iguanas within his "space." The male's tail base is larger than the female's tail base because the hemipenes are located in this site. Each hemipenis is connected to its respective right or left testicle by a vas deferens which leads from the testes (which are located within the body cavity anterior to the kidneys and adjacent to the adrenal glands, aorta, and posterior vena cava).

### Mating Behavior

Mating behavior typically involves the following:

- The male approaches the receptive female and climbs onto her back and straddles her (Figure 10.2a).
- In order to help him maneuver and partially restrain his mate, the male iguana grips the skin of the female's shoulder region with his teeth (Figure 10.2b). As a result, mated females often display skin wounds that bear mute witness to their amorous adventures (Figure 10.2c–d).
- The male then brings his cloacal vent into contact with that of the female.
- Once his cloacal vent is apposed to the female's, the male inserts one of his hemipenes into her cloacal vent and, after a period of time ranging from several to many minutes, ejaculation occurs (Figure 10.2e).

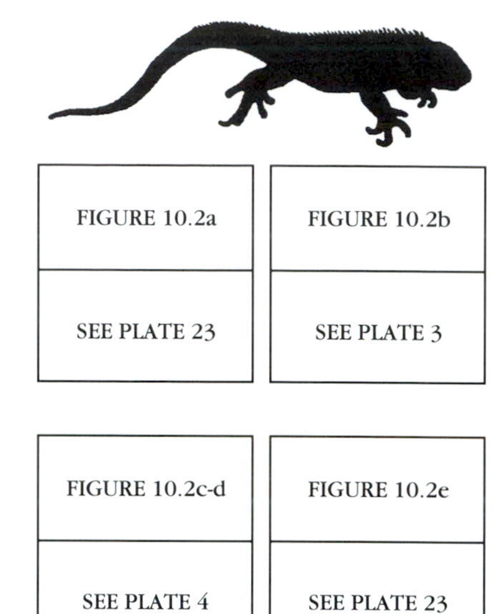

| FIGURE 10.2a | FIGURE 10.2b |
|---|---|
| SEE PLATE 23 | SEE PLATE 3 |

| FIGURE 10.2c-d | FIGURE 10.2e |
|---|---|
| SEE PLATE 4 | SEE PLATE 23 |

The excessive traumatic wounds sustained by some captive female iguanas may be a consequence of being unable to escape the attentions of an aggressive male; similar excessive mating-related trauma is unusual in wild iguanas (Rodda, 1992).

## MATING-INDUCED ANOREXIA (LOSS OF APPETITE)

Sexually mature male green iguanas, especially those housed with one or more females, tend to feed sparsely and may drink only sporadically during mating season which (depending upon the geographical latitude) extends from October through April in the latitudes close to the equator.

During courtship, after copulation, and later, while the fertilized eggs are maturing and accumulating their yolks and shells, female iguanas may or may not eat. However, they usually stop eating entirely during the last few weeks that their eggs are maturing. **This period of gravidity (pregnancy)-related anorexia (loss of appetite) is entirely normal. Because egg production is a stressful process for the females, during which they contribute much fat, protein, and calcium to their developing eggs, they should be healthy and in excellent condition prior to and during the mating season.**

## SPERM STORAGE (*AMPHIGONIA RETARDATA*)

Female iguanas can store living sperm in their reproductive tracts and use them to fertilize clutches of eggs several years after their last contact with a fertile male. This process is called *amphigonia retardata* and is common to many reptiles. By employing this reproductive strategy, physically fit male iguanas can sire offspring long after they have mated with a female and have left that particular breeding population. A beneficial factor is that both sexes do not have to expose themselves again to predation in order to reproduce.

## EGG DEVELOPMENT

Even female iguanas that have not mated recently—or have never mated—can produce eggs.

After fertilization (which occurs in the upper oviduct), the fertilized eggs receive their leathery eggshells as they pass down successive portions of the glandular oviduct. During this time of eggshell formation, the female iguana's blood-calcium concentration becomes substantially elevated, as it does during the yolking process (vitellogenesis); this marked hypercalcemia is entirely normal. The blood-calcium concentration returns to the usual level after the eggs have been deposited. If a female iguana does not deposit her eggs but resorbs them instead, a similar elevation of blood calcium occurs. The blood-calcium concentration returns to a normal level after the constituents of the eggs have been resorbed and redistributed to skeletal depots within the female's body.

| FIGURE 10.3a-b | FIGURE 10.3c |
|---|---|
| SEE PLATE 4 | SEE PLATE 24 |

The diagnosis of gravidity (pregnancy) in iguanas is relatively easy because the eggs can be seen as bulges within the abdominal cavity (Figures 10.3a–c). These eggs, which are still in the oviducts, can be felt by gently passing fingertips over them as the iguana's flanks are stroked just behind her ribcage. The eggs' shells are relatively soft and can be damaged by rough handling.

Before the female deposits her clutch, her belly swells substantially and the outline of several eggs often can be easily seen.

| FIGURE 10.4 |
|---|
| SEE PLATE 24 |

It was believed—and still is believed by some people—that actual embryonic development is only triggered by the eggs' exposure to atmospheric oxygen after they have left the oviduct and been deposited. I also believed this until I performed a salpingotomy and, via caesarian section, removed a clutch of 65 eggs from a large female green iguana that could not deliver her eggs naturally. When the eggs from this iguana were candled immediately after surgery, they were found to already have a well-developed network of embryonic blood vessels (Figure 10.4). Similarly, limb buds and a functioning heart were found in an embryo removed from a green iguana egg immediately after it was deposited

(Licht and Moberly, 1965). Within a few weeks, the embryonic and then the fetal heartbeat can be detected through the eggshell with an ultrasonic blood-flow detector (Figure 10.5).

## EGG DEPOSITION (OVIPOSITING)

The number of eggs deposited depends upon several criteria: for example, the age and size of the female; her nutritional condition and health status; the fertility of the male; and the taxonomic classification of the particular iguanid species. Generally, a captive female green iguana's first clutch contains 10–30 eggs. Older females in prime breeding condition often deposit more than 50 eggs at one time—and clutches of 65 or more eggs are not uncommon.

**The mere presence of a male iguana can induce the formation and deposition of eggs in a mature female iguana whether or not copulation has been successful. Females carrying eggs (whether the eggs are fertile or infertile) may commence searching for a suitable nesting site, then may begin excavating the substrate in the site with all four limbs even before abdominal swelling is evident. Within a week after this behavior is first observed, provide a nesting chamber so that the iguana will feel secure and will accept it as a suitable site for depositing her eggs. Make certain that the area is warm because that makes it more attractive to the gravid female.**

The time from mating to egg depositing in green iguanas is approximately 65 days.

After being satisfied that the nesting site is suitable, the female excavates a nest that may be only 45 cm (18 inches) to more than a meter (39 inches) deep, deposits her eggs, and covers them with the debris that was removed during construction of the nesting chamber. Following deposition, the female green iguana does not guard the nest containing her eggs (although she may return to it from time to time).

Actual egg depositing can require as much as 3 days to complete. Green iguana eggs measure approximately 15.4 mm (~⅝ inch) in diameter and are elongated, measuring approximately 35–40 mm (1⅜–1½ inches) long. Fertile eggs may be either smaller or larger than these figures because the size of the egg is related to the size, maturity, and nutrition of the female who produces them.

Depending upon the availability of suitable nesting sites and the nature of the substrate in which they are excavated, female green iguanas may deposit their eggs in a nest which they share with other wild female green iguanas (Nagy, 1989).

**Figure 10.5.** Monitoring the viability of an incubating iguana egg with an ultrasonic blood-flow Doppler. The embryo's heart beat can be detected with this instrument.

### How to Make a Nesting Environment

Use any of the following for a nesting chamber:

- Medium-sized dog house which has a hinged or removable roof
- Large **dark** plastic storage container
- Plastic garbage can with a suitable hole cut into its side slightly above the proposed level of the nesting litter material
- Non-resinous wooden box whose unfinished interior surface has been treated with polyurethane varnish and permitted to outgas (described in Chapter 2)

A board approximately 30 cm (12 inches) should be affixed across the entrance to prevent spillage of the nesting medium from the interior of the chamber. Make certain that there are no protruding nails that could injure the occupants.

Do the following to make the nesting medium:

- Fill the inside of the chamber with a mixture of clean, slightly moistened sand, vermiculite, pearlite, or sphagnum moss.
- Mix equal volumes (not weights) of nesting medium and chlorine-free water.
- After mixing, squeeze out as much of the water as possible; the nesting medium should be damp, but **never soggy** (Figure 10.6).

The eggs should be transferred and incubated in another container so that their embryonic development can be controlled more accurately.

## EGG INCUBATION TEMPERATURE

The warmth required for embryonic development can be provided by a commercial reptile egg incubator with the necessary heating and humidity controls (see Sources For Reptile-Related Products) or by a heating pad or other device placed beneath an incubation chamber. Be

**Figure 10.6.** Incubating green iguana eggs freshly uncovered to show their appearance. Healthy fertile eggs are white or a pale cream color and are not shrunken or wrinkled.

sure to monitor the temperature of the incubation medium in the **center** of the egg clutch frequently. A simple means for monitoring is to insert an appropriate thermometer into the center of the incubation medium and observe the temperature. Unless the heat-source temperature is changed, the temperature of the incubation medium should equilibrate and fluctuate very little from day to day.

Cover the incubating eggs with a few centimeters of moist incubation medium, and seal the incubation chamber with a sheet of glass, clear plastic, or plastic film to help retain the moisture and warmth.

The recommended incubation temperatures for green iguana eggs range from 30–32 °C (85–91 °F) (Banks, 1984; Hirth, 1963; Mendelssohn, 1980). These temperatures should not fluctuate more than plus or minus 1–2 degrees C (Hirth, 1963).

## EGG INCUBATION TIME

Egg incubation time is mainly a function of, and dependent upon, temperature. Each iguana genus has its own rather narrow range of incubation time; this can range from 59–84 days (Banks, 1984). The average egg incubation time for green iguanas is 65 days. Healthy fertile eggs are white or pale cream color, and are not shrunken or wrinkled.

## HATCHLINGS

The percentage of fertilized eggs which produce viable hatchlings depends upon the incubation conditions and, therefore, is variable; it ranges from 46–88% (Banks, 1984).

A hatchling "pips" (slits) the pliant eggshells from which it emerges with a tooth-like "caruncle" on the snout that soon disappears. After slitting the egg, a hatchling may remain within the open confines of the shell for a period of a few hours to over a day (Figure 10.7). During this time, the balance of the yolk contained within the yolksac is absorbed by the hatchling, and the umbilicus closes to leave a slit-like scar on the ventral belly that almost, but not totally, disappears after a few molts. Once it has left the confines of its eggshell, each hatchling becomes fully independent; there is no parental care for a newly hatched green iguana. After emerging from its egg, the hatchling excavates its way to the surface. Residual yolk nourishes the newly hatched iguana until it begins feeding 1–2 weeks after it has emerged from the nest.

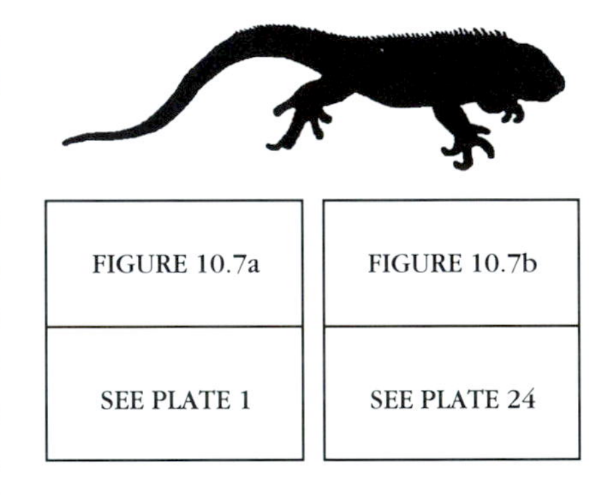

| FIGURE 10.7a | FIGURE 10.7b |
| --- | --- |
| SEE PLATE 1 | SEE PLATE 24 |

A hatchling green iguana is a miniature copy of its parents.

A case of monozygotic twinning was reported recently (Schilling, 1994). The twin iguanas were from a clutch of 58 eggs (31 of which were fertile) that were incubated at 29 °C (~84 °F) and hatched after 126 days. The twins shared a single yolksac.

## EGG RESORPTION AS RELATED TO BLOOD CALCIUM LEVELS

The eggs occasionally are resorbed before they can be laid. This is a natural means for recycling vital protein, and fat- and calcium-laden yolk. During the time of yolk and shell deposition, the female iguana's blood-calcium level is markedly elevated. Similarly, during the time when her eggs are resorbed, the female's blood calcium rises substantially above normal levels. An adult male iguana or non-gravid (not pregnant) female green iguana possesses a normal blood-calcium concentration of approximately 10.4–13.6 mg/dl. My veterinary colleague, Dr. Donald Burton, and Helen L. Benton (avid owner of 20 iguanas—to date), and I monitored female green iguanas whose blood was obtained at periodic intervals before, during, and after their eggs had become shelled, had matured, and were finally deposited. Some of the iguanas' blood-calcium determinations disclosed levels as high as 90 mg/dl. Other females which resorbed their eggs had blood-calcium levels as high as 151 mg/dl. Within a few weeks, all of these enormously high levels had returned to within normal limits.

These findings demonstrate **the ability iguanas have to mobilize calcium from, and sequester calcium in, their skeletal stores. Before female iguanas are treated medically for hypercalcemia, they should be evaluated carefully to ascertain whether they are either producing eggs or resorbing them.**

## COMPLICATIONS

After ovipositing, the female appears thin but, within a day or so, she usually commences eating regularly, and will regain her lost weight within a few weeks. If a female iguana continues to appear weak, depressed, or refuses to eat following ovipositing, she should be examined and evaluated by a veterinarian.

The most common complication of egg laying is obstruction of one or both of the oviducts through which the shelled eggs must proceed. This occurs when the eggs are overly large or misshapen.

Egg-depositing difficulties usually are the result of any of the following:

- Overly large eggs
- Misshapen or otherwise abnormal eggs
- Decomposed eggs whose necrotic contents induce intoxication in the female
- Narrowed pelvic-canal diameter due to previous metabolic bone disease
- Infection of the ovaries and/or oviduct(s)

- Low blood-calcium level
- Ruptured oviduct, sometimes with spillage of yolk into the coelomic cavity

Each of these conditions requires immediate veterinary evaluation and remedial care.

## SHOULD A FEMALE IGUANA BE "SPAYED"?

Whether they have or have not mated recently—or have never mated—female iguanas can produce eggs. The production of shelled eggs requires an immense amount of fat, protein, and calcium—all of which must be mobilized and drawn from stores in the females's body tissues. Consequently, the health of female iguanas that exhibit multiple clutching in successive years is jeopardized. However, they can be "spayed" in a fashion much like that performed on dogs and cats (Figure 10.8). This surgical procedure, called an ovariosalpingectomy, often greatly prolongs the life of a pet iguana because it prevents the repeated metabolic stress of producing eggs. The operation can be done soon after the female has achieved sexual maturity. The procedure, which requires general anesthesia, employs sterile surgical techniques identical to those used in humans and the more "conventional" small domestic animals. When performed under correct conditions, this surgery is safe and highly efficacious.

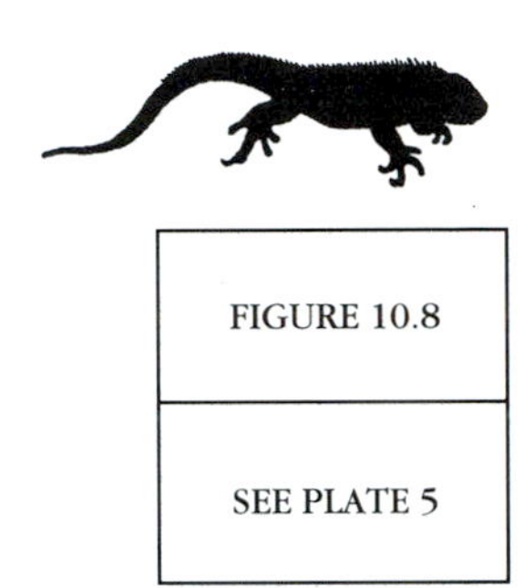

FIGURE 10.8

SEE PLATE 5

If your female iguana produces multiple clutches of eggs in a single year, and/or you are not interested in propagating iguanas in your home, discuss the merits of surgical sterilization with your veterinarian.

# CHAPTER 11

## WENDY'S OBSERVATIONS

*Author's comment*: In our book *Iguanas: A Guide to Their Biology and Captive Care*, the coauthor, Wendy Townsend, contributed a chapter relating her experiences with green iguanas. Many iguana owners told us how much they had enjoyed reading "Wendy's Observations." Thus, I am pleased to offer this information again.

❊ ❊ ❊ ❊ ❊

In this section I am going to tell about the green iguanas with whom I have been sharing my home. Most of these lizards were acquired as damaged or ailing animals, but with compassionate care quickly became fine pets. It is hoped that telling of my iguanas' behavior and activities will be interesting and sometimes endearing, and that many lessons about iguana care will be derived from these anecdotes. The accompanying Table 11.1 of iguana names and vital data is provided for ease in following the progress of each of these lizards.

For my tenth birthday gift, I was taken to a pet shop and allowed to pick out my first iguana, who later became known as Wiener. (She was

**TABLE 11.1 Wendy's Pet Iguanas**

| Name | Sex | SVL* | Age when received | # years in my group | Present status and SVL* |
|---|---|---|---|---|---|
| Wiener | F | 3 | 6 months | 10 years | Deceased; 14 |
| Iggly W. | M | 4 | hatchling | 4 years | Deceased; 15(e) |
| Skitz | M | 7 | 1 year (?) | 5 years | Healthy; 10 |
| Spot | M | 6 | 1 year | 10 years | Healthy; 16 |
| Peanut | M | 4 | 2 years | 7 years | Healthy; stunted @ 8 |
| Pete | M | 10 | 3 years | 7 months | Deceased; 12 |
| Debra | F | 9 | 3 years | 4 years | Deceased; 15 |
| Stumpy | M | 8 | 2 years | 2 years | Relocated; healthy |
| Pooky | F | 5 | 6 months | 7 years | Deceased; 14 |
| Snooky | F | 6 | 6 months | 9 years | Deceased; 15 |
| E.T. | F | 6 | 2 years | 1 year | Healthy; 13 |
| Queenie | F | 8 | 2 years | 1 year | Healthy; 13 |
| Goober | F | 3 | hatchling | 5 years | Healthy; 16 |
| Fishy | F | 7 | 10 months | 6 months | Healthy; 10 |
| Tiny Thing | ? | 3 | hatchling | 5 months | Healthy; 4 |
| Harry | ? | 3 | hatchling | 1 month | Healthy; 3 |

*SVL = snout to vent length in inches

named by my six-year-old cousin, who distorted the word "iguana" into "Wiener.") Wiener was the saddest of the group of juveniles at the pet shop. I wanted to "rescue" the lizard, which is why I chose an apparently weak animal.

Weeks later, I purchased Iggly, a healthy juvenile who became Wiener's companion. These two lizards never mated, perhaps because of insufficient year-round lighting and territory, and the absence of other iguanas. One Christmas, I left town for two weeks with my family. The two iguanas were left in the theoretical care of a sitter who did not replace a heat lamp when it went out. Our home in New York was too cold for iguanas without the supplementary heat source. Wiener was merely chilled, but Iggly was quite ill. A veterinarian examined the sick iguana and determined that euthanasia would be the kindest treatment.

I purchased Skitz from a fellow who was in the habit of continuously playing loud, raucous music within inches of the lizards' cage. Skitz's cage mate had died some weeks earlier. Her housing was filthy and cold, and her diet was lettuce and banana. Skitz is presently healthy, though she should be larger. She has not acclimated "emotionally," and remains nervous and fearful, spending much time in a hiding box.

I got Spot from a boy who was keeping the lizard in a bathroom with a light bulb for heat and a branch. Spot's diet had been fruit cocktail, lettuce and hamburger. He had soft, rubbery bones and an "S"-shaped spine. He is now quite large, and has had no health problems.

Peanut belonged to a woman who had been feeding him romaine lettuce, banana and other fruits, with yogurt being the only protein and calcium source. Peanut's keeper had had him for two years, during which time his growth was minimal, probably due to insufficient diet and lack of sunshine (or its substitute). Peanut has grown a meager four inches in five years. His continued lack of growth may be due to stress caused by Spot, though they're kept visually separate most of the time, as well as irreparable damage done during his development. In spite of his poor growth, Peanut feeds well and is active and strong. Spot, on the other hand, has grown very large. Both lizards are the same age, and are sexually mature.

Peanut seems perpetually desirous of mating, but will probably never be accepted by a female. Spot has always wanted to kill Peanut, and flies into a rage at the slightest glimpse of him. As if unaware of his tiny size, Peanut constantly struggles to fight with Spot. Such an encounter would last three seconds ending with Peanut's head pulverized. Peanut is even more eager to mount any female. Given a moment's access to the group (with Spot out of the room), Peanut is right on top of the nearest female, desperately trying to breed. The selective females will have nothing to do with little, inadequate Peanut, and dispatch him quickly with a kick from a back leg. It becomes necessary to remove Peanut from the group for he'll persist in his amorous approaches until his would-be mate seriously injures or kills him.

I adopted Pete and Debra from a man who was keeping these lizards in a mildewy, unclean bathroom. Pete and Debra were underweight, and both had a fungal skin infection which ran the length from forearmpit to midtail. Healthy diet, warm, clean housing and application of Neosporin® to the infected skin helped the two iguanas gain weight and recover in a matter of days. Pete and Debra were given free range of one room while Spot, Pooky, Snooky, and I shared another. Pete and Spot were ever aware of each other, and faced off constantly in the "neutral" territory between rooms. Debra insisted on going into Spot's area even after I returned her to Pete's many times. Though Spot never injured Pete, his intimidating presence wore him down. When Debra was 7 years old, she laid 39 eggs and died within 24 hours.

Stumpy came from a couple who fed him cat food and lettuce. This iguana was named for what remained of his tail, which had atrophied, probably after a breakage, and dropped off. He was extremely emaciated and had gnarled, brittle forelimbs. With care, he improved immensely during the first year. The healthier he became, the more he strove to challenge Spot and establish his own territory. Stumpy reached a point when his improvement leveled off as more of his energy was being spent on "normal male activities." Within the second year, I located an excellent new home for him where he could rule and not suffer Pete's fate. I had difficulty parting with Stumpy as he was a remarkably delightful pet. Stumpy's initial adoption and eventual relocation were accomplished through the Southwestern Herpetological Society.

Pooky and Snooky were both healthy youngsters and were gifts from a friend. When Pooky was 5, she laid 36 eggs. One egg gave her difficulty, and was passed three days later, brown and overly large. Before this last egg she was treated with injectable vitamins, an appetite stimulant, electrolyte solution and antibiotics—all recommended by a veterinarian. Two years later, Pooky laid 43 eggs and collapsed despite rehydration and other efforts to replenish her. Snooky produced three annual consecutive batches of eggs with no complications. The fourth pregnancy brought on an oviduct infection. Though she was treated with antibiotics, fluids, tube feedings and surgery, she died.

E.T. and Queenie came via special overnight delivery from an ill-informed but conscientious, keeper. With their apparent declining health, this keeper wanted to relocate the iguanas. Both were undersized for their age, and both had a couple of swollen joints. E.T. has a severe overbite due to his lower jaw which had softened after having been broken some time before. Both iguanas are wonderful pets, and have been growing rapidly. E.T. has laid 13 eggs while being kept with Peanut but these were not fertile.

E.T. has an immense appetite, and prefers to be hand-fed, particularly because her deformed jaw is a hindrance to a hearty feeding if left alone with a meal.

I obtained Goober as a hatchling from a pet shop. She had a broken arm that none of the employees would deal with. Now she almost outweighs Spot, though she still has a "trick" wrist where the break had been. Goober is a remarkably outgoing, even aggressive lizard. She will tolerate being petted and picked up only if she's in the "mood." Consistent with Goober's "whimsy," she is always curious and runs over to get in on most every activity in the room. She is a marvelous, impressive lizard—and is sometimes fun to playfully tease.

I bought Fishy from a pet shop at cost because she was too thin, excessively restless, and had a large abscess on her jaw. A tooth had broken, becoming lodged inside her mouth, causing the abscess. The pet shop employees were having difficulty with this, and had actually exacerbated the problem as the entrance to the abscess was inside the mouth and not on the outer lip, where they were lancing. Careful removal of the tooth and abscess were later accomplished and several puréed meals were administered during recovery. Fishy is presently in excellent condition.

Tiny Thing was the yellow-orange color of a pencil when I obtained him. A few barely green scales indicated that his normal color should be bright green. Tiny had been chewed on by the crickets he was supposed to eat, and there were two conspicuous bites on his back. Pet shop employees had been cramming wax worms down his throat because he wouldn't eat voluntarily. They had to have been certain Tiny would die, because they gave him to me. "Here, you take him. He'll never make it." Tiny was so bad off the proprietor didn't have the conscience to tap me, the bleeding heart, for even a few bucks. (A month earlier I bought Fishy from this shop.) I took the pitiful thread of an iguana home and set him up in a 7-gallon tank with a little potted pothos with trailing vines for his comfort. Before putting Tiny to bed, I soaked him in the bathroom sink in tepid water. This was to remove the fecal staining around his vent, which is typical of sick iguanas. While Tiny soaked, I puréed some papaya, a little kale and marmoset chow, plus enough water to make a thick liquid. After straining the mixture, I drew a 1.0 cc syringe full, with the intention of forcing Tiny to eat. To my surprise, he needed no forcing, and lapped up the meal in its entirety. The next morning, calcium carbonate and Nutri-Cal® were added to his breakfast, and then Tiny and I went outside for some sunshine therapy. Because a little iguana would easily overheat, I put Tiny on a "flotilla" of a kale leaf in a plastic tub of water. Within 20 minutes, the lizard defecated an undigested wax worm. Later, he started turning green. The next day, Tiny ate several sweet, pink flowers from a guava tree (*Psidium* sp.) and pieces of his kale flotilla. It took three days with two putrid bowel movements daily for Tiny to cleanse himself of what he had been forcefed. Half his diet those days was overripe papaya to help encourage his digestive processes. Three weeks later, Tiny shed his epidermis, and the cricket bites were nearly gone. Neosporin® creme was initially applied to the bites and, later, liquid vitamin E was used on them to serve as an emollient.

Tiny now eats the same food as the other iguanas. With his inquisitive ways and infant-like appearance, Tiny wins the hearts of the people he meets.

For the most part, I have managed to hire acceptable iguana sitters while I travel out of town. During Tiny's recuperation, he made three trips via airplane with me. Because of his need for daily attention, I didn't leave him for the sitter to tend with the other lizards. Being all of three inches SVL and especially fragile, it could hardly be reasonable to sack and box Tiny and put him through as "special baggage." Therefore he traveled in a lightweight cotton sock pinned to my undergarment. I had to be careful not to shoulder a bag or hug a family member closely upon arrival, as Tiny could be crushed. Much of my family finds Tiny's means of travel a source of relative hilarity.

I often forget how healthy Tiny has become, and he has reminded me a few times by nearly slipping away. Though Tiny is exceptionally tame, a sudden movement can cause him to flee. Once I put him to bask on a densely foliated potted bush on a sun deck. A pelican flew overhead, closer than the gulls and terns that had passed earlier, and Tiny dove for cover into the core of the bush. Another time, a more serious incident warned me to keep a better watch on Tiny. My two cats have never paid much attention to the lizards, even little Peanut. It was Tiny's agile movements and wispy tail that were irresistible to one of the cats that nearly killed him.

The responsibility for a pet iguana's injury or death usually rests on the keeper. Finding the piece of Tiny's tail and then his mauled, fur-encrusted, barely living body behind a shelf was a most unpleasant reminder of this. A month later, nearly two inches of his tail had grown back, and the scars were almost gone.

Every spring as I was growing up, our Volkswagen bug was loaded to capacity with "stuff," including a cat, various snakes and lizards and two or more iguanas. Each reptile traveled in his or her own pillow case for the long trip from New York City to Northern Michigan where we spent the summer. Great care was taken to place the animals where they would have ample air circulation and would not overheat or be crushed by shifting objects. The iguanas stayed secure in their pillowcases for the duration of the trip. (Road travels lasting longer than 24 hours require a little time out of the bag for water, though feeding is not recommended until a final destination is reached.)

The iguanas' Michigan home was a large cage in the studio-garage of a cabin on a lake. Each morning, the doors which made up one side of the building were opened, and direct sunlight reached the lizards for much of the day. A spot light bulb in a reflector fixture was set up for added warmth. Throughout the summer, many neighbors from around the lake would come by to look at the iguanas, sometimes asking questions, other times watching quietly. During these summers, I busied myself both with the abundant local wildlife and my own pets. On sunny days, I took the iguanas, one at a time, out on the dock.

Wiener especially liked to bask on the bow of a big wooden boat which was anchored nearby. I kept an eye on the lizard as she would dive into the water to cool down, or if she spotted a dog. Wiener could see dogs and people moving a hundred yards away, and if they came closer, she'd flatten out and prepare to dive. The gulls flying overhead did not trouble her once she had grown fairly large. The lake was clear, shallow near shore, and had a fine, sandy bottom which gave good visibility to Wiener's graceful swimming. She usually swam towards shore where she would dig and nibble at the sand. Wild blueberry bushes and dandelions grew there on the beach, and I would pick these for her. Often, Wiener would climb one of the huge pine trees, which I let her do, until her body almost got out of reach.

Michigan nights get cold, especially late in the summer. On these nights (when they were big enough to "kick back" if I rolled over), I put Wiener and Iggly in my sleeping bag so they'd keep warm. Like anything else the iguana becomes accustomed to, they came to expect such nighttime accommodations. After Iggly died, Wiener continued to sleep in my bed year-round, lying with limbs extended back against her body, sound asleep by my side. At sunrise, she woke up and found her way to her basking site.

When I went to live in the dormitory at the University of Miami, Florida, pets were not allowed. The biology department was pleased to provide a large wood-and-glass enclosure for Wiener, which I set up with branches and lights. I had a key to the room where she lived, and picked her up almost every night to bring back to my room. Initially, my roommate was a bit fearful of Wiener. Within a week, we were tossing coins over who got to have the lizard for the night. Of course, people knew about the iguana going back and forth from lab to dorm under my jacket, but "looked the other way," because I was a freshman and probably looked as homesick as I was.

When Iggly died, I purchased my first and last wild-caught adult iguana. He seemed to acclimate, and fed well. Though he appeared physically healthy, much of the time he seemed remote or depressed—until his first summer in Michigan. The very day I took the lizard outside for sunshine and a swim, he went wild when I tried to take him back indoors. He never calmed down that day, and frantically dug at his cage until his nose was bloodied. I slathered on the Neosporin® and put him in a canvas laundry bag in the cool bedroom which faced the woods. I wanted him to "chill out" for an hour while I prepared new accommodations for this wild animal who appeared to have snapped out of his depressed state, probably realizing his captivity and not liking it one bit.

I went to check on the lizard a half hour later. He had torn the canvas bag, torn the screen on the window which faced the deep woods, and was never found despite much searching and posting of signs. For many nights I had miserable fantasies about the unfortunate iguana's demise. If a raccoon, owl, or car didn't get him, the winter did. Oddly, that summer there had been an article in the local newspaper: "The iguana: Man's best friend?" According to the article, several iguanas had been reported to the animal shelter as missing. One lizard was found in a garden, and several people came to claim it.

The most humorous iguana moment my parents recall—and retell—was when Iggly got down from his perch, high-stepped his way into the living room and went on to the kitchen. He approached Felix, our cat, who was eating, and bobbed vigorously, intimidating the cat into abandoning her food. Iggly then ate the cat's meal and promptly returned to his room, while Felix, we and our dozen or so dinner guests looked on. Probably our guests still tell this story now and then, too.

My grandparents have a home in rural Indiana, the cabin in Michigan, and a winter home in the Bahamas. Every year since childhood, I've made no fewer than three trips to visit my family in these places. With some effort, travel and vacations with pet iguanas are possible. Over the years of taking iguanas "on the road" or arranging for their care at home, Iggly's death has been the only tragedy.

Travel abroad with pet iguanas is difficult, if not impossible, but within the United States, iguanas can be transported via airplane with minor inconvenience. When I transplanted from New York to California, I moved six boas, three pythons and five iguanas. Here is the procedure for air travel with iguanas.

Call the airline you're using and tell the agent you need to transport one (spare yourself complications) iguana. The reasons for calling ahead are: (a) there will be a "handling fee" for each "special package"; and (b) some planes don't have cargo compartments with temperature control. If the airline is notified of your package, they will book you onto a plane with a proper compartment. Transport only one iguana per cloth sack or sturdy pillowcase, with the open end tied shut. Up to three large lizards in their sacks will fit comfortably in a large dog kennel or similar sturdy traveling case with good ventilation. Your lizard's case won't come out on a conveyor with the regular luggage, but will be handled separately. Animals other than cats or dogs are not allowed in the passenger area. Do not put a lizard into any box or bag that will go through the security x-ray.

Because I moved frequently during the first few years while living in California, I had an iguana cage built on wheels. I chose some apartments over others for the sunshine the lizards would receive in their room. In each apartment, I put down indoor-outdoor turf to protect the carpeting. At this point, I will mention that while iguanas are well suited to apartment living, not all landlords will allow them. If renting, it is advised that iguana keepers maintain a "low profile" until it is determined that neighbors and building managers don't mind the lizards. In all but one previous rental, my iguanas were tolerated. Fortunately, I was already planning to move on when I received a 30-day notice: "They go, or you go!" Apparently, a neighbor had seen the lizards basking, and complained to the landlord.

When Goober was little, she and I shared the living room of one apartment while the other lizards had the bedroom. Spot had yet to figure out that Goober was female, so I took care to keep the bedroom door shut, for Spot knew Goober was under the same roof. He could not risk the little iguana mating with one of his females, so he was always alert to a chance to "eliminate" her, which he got one day when a neighbor came to the door, interrupting a feeding and my attention. A small apartment does not allow sufficient retreat for one lizard being chased by another, so Spot nearly tore Goober's head off. I rinsed the wound with Betadine® and water, and confined the injured lizard to a clean glass tank with paper towel and a water bowl. The next day, the veterinarian came and did excellent stitchwork. One year later, Goober and Spot became "best of friends," and the scar is nearly invisible.

Within a population of wild green iguanas, field biologists have occasionally observed adult females to interrupt and disperse a mating pair. Other than this, there seems to be little evidence to suggest that while female iguanas are selective of the males they will mate with, they don't appear to actively claim and guard chosen males. Within my iguana room, it would seem that Goober may be doing precisely this. During the mating season her aggression towards the three other females is heightened. She is particularly nasty to Queenie. As it has turned out, Queenie was Spot's first "choice," though he will eventually pair with each female in turn. (Over the years, Spot has been in the habit of "starting" with the young ones.) Goober repeatedly drives the females away from both Spot and his primary basking site, and then positions herself close to him, periodically bobbing to assert her claim. When a meal is presented, no competition or aggression is observed as all four lizards eat simultaneously and without event.

The social dynamics—and needs—of a population of iguanas, whether captive or wild, are complex, and shift with the number and maturity of individuals and the season. I am careful to provide sufficient hot spots and retreats for the "bullied" iguanas in the room.

Once Goober escaped to the outdoors while we were living in the Venice Beach area. An indoor search revealed a hole in the wall behind the refrigerator. After six weeks and much searching, Goober turned up on the neighbor's porch, contentedly basking in the morning sun. She appeared to have grown an inch or two. Clearly, the sunshine and choice forage of hibiscus and fig were good for her. Nevertheless, releasing or allowing pet iguanas to roam outdoors unattended is irresponsible and must be discouraged. If your iguana should escape, I have included a few suggestions which may increase the chances for finding your pet.

Look up. An iguana will most likely head up a tree or whatever he can climb, so thoroughly scan treetops and roofs, keeping in mind the iguana's ability to remain motionless and camouflaged. Take regular midday strolls around your home, as your pet may be basking or foraging within yards of where he got out. Be mindful of unusual episodes of dog barking as a clue to an iguana's location.

There is a fair chance a neighbor may come across a stray iguana, so either post a few signs describing the lizard as a harmless pet, or go around and tell neighbors personally. If the lost iguana is of notable size, informing police, humane society and animal control departments shouldn't be disregarded. Check the lost-and-found sections of local newspapers. Also, check with local pet shops as exotic strays are periodically found and taken to one of these.

One is hard pressed to present to a tame pet iguana an object which will frighten him. Even so, it seems each lizard can have his own "pet-peeve." Spot adores blueberries, courteously ruptured and offered by hand, one at a time. (If a blueberry is presented unruptured, Spot mouths it until it bursts.) However, if a dish of berries, more than two, is brought into his view, a violent, fearful flight ensues. This same response is elicited by the bottoms of a pair of my moccasins, which have round black nobs arranged on a pale leather sole. Perhaps he perceives blueberry pairs and dark beads as the eyes of a predator. Goober is indifferent to blueberries, singly or collectively, as are the other iguanas; however, she, alone, responds in a frightened manner to humans with white or gray hair or wearing hats, and sometimes to strangers. Occasionally, I forget about her anxieties and enter the room with a towel wrapped around my wet hair. Goober becomes wide-eyed and flies into the wall, scrambling for escape or cover from whatever the hair-towel represents. Pooky had the same problem with small children. Debra couldn't stand the sight of a snake; but this makes sense, as snakes are natural predators to iguanas. Still, Spot, Goober, Snooky and Pooky have never cared, one way or the other, about snakes. This behavior can probably be explained by some aspect of the imprinting process during each iguanas' development. In any case, I wonder what the blueberries, towels, or white-haired people represent that apparently terrify each lizard.

The iguana's eyes are very expressive and telling of his moment-to-moment sensation status. Both the rim of the eyelid and the pupil change shape and dilate, according to wariness, fear, inquisitiveness, anger, hunger and recognition, among other conditions. It is particularly moving to sit quietly and still with a baby iguana and establish eye contact with the little lizard. As he is beginning to get used to the human face, in his eyes, the expression of fear is almost completely replaced by what one might call wonder. When he grows up, his look becomes a look of familiarity and—I hope—contentment.

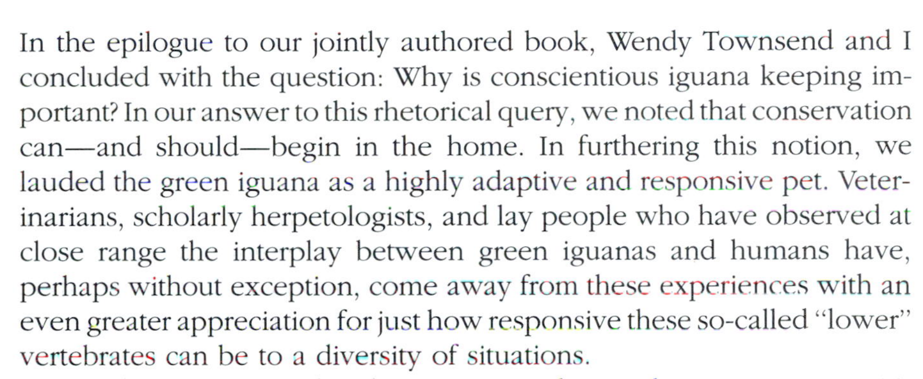

# EPILOGUE

In the epilogue to our jointly authored book, Wendy Townsend and I concluded with the question: Why is conscientious iguana keeping important? In our answer to this rhetorical query, we noted that conservation can—and should—begin in the home. In furthering this notion, we lauded the green iguana as a highly adaptive and responsive pet. Veterinarians, scholarly herpetologists, and lay people who have observed at close range the interplay between green iguanas and humans have, perhaps without exception, come away from these experiences with an even greater appreciation for just how responsive these so-called "lower" vertebrates can be to a diversity of situations.

With conservational and environmental issues becoming more critical, increased public awareness of—even affection for—the green iguana seem timely and appropriate. As all of us should know, preserving the green iguana (and other species as well) will include preserving their various habitats; among these are the rainforests. To that end, I urge the readers of this book to make a contribution to the International Iguana Society and/or to the Nature Conservancy's International Program for the Preservation of Rainforests. Gordon Rodda, in his review of Frye and Townsend (1993), suggested that pet dealers who benefit from the sale of iguanas and the ancillary products sold for their captive care should be encouraged to contribute (in a tithe-like fashion) a portion of their profits earned from these sales to the conservation organizations named above. Whether such an altruistic challenge is met with action remains to be seen, but I share Dr. Rodda's enthusiasm for his innovative proposition.

In addition to the practical environmental reasons for appreciating the green iguana, there is enormous value in showing kindness and respect towards all animals. Pet green iguanas can teach humans to be observant and compassionate, and they are fascinating fellow animals with whom we share the planet.

It is my desire that, after reading this book, you will be inspired to provide your green iguana with the appropriate habitat and correct nutritious diet, and you will endeavor to make its life in captivity as stress-free and disease-free as possible.

# APPENDIX A

## NORMAL PHYSIOLOGICAL VALUES OF *IGUANA IGUANA*

| Hematological tests | Normals | Absolute |
|---|---|---|
| White blood cell count | 4,500–10,000/MM$^3$ | |
| Red blood cell count | 0.8–2.0 × 10$^6$/MM$^3$ | |
| Hematocrit; packed cell volume | 24–37% | |
| Differential white blood cell count: | | |
| Lymphocytes | 40–65% | 1,600–8,000 |
| Heterophils | 30–45% | 1,200–4,000 |
| Azurophils | 15–25% | 600–1,250 |
| Monocytes | 1–4% | 50–500 |
| Eosinophils | 0–2% | 0–250 |
| Basophils | 1–4% | 50–500 |

| Chemistry values | |
|---|---|
| Glucose (mg/dl) | 65.0–155.0 |
| Uric acid (mg/dl) | 0.5–3.2 |
| Total protein (g/dl) | 4.5–8.0 |
| Albumin (g/dl) | 2.0–3.5 |
| Globulin (g/dl) | 3.5–5.5 |
| AST (SGOT) (units/dl) | 24.0–45.0 |
| ALT (SGPT) (units/dl) | 18.0–30.0 |
| LDH (units/dl) | <380 |
| Amylase (units/dl) | <450 |
| Creatinine phosphokinase (units/dl) | <100 |
| Calcium (mg/dl) | 10.5–13.6 |
| Phosphorus (mg/dl) | 5.3–6.8 |
| Sodium (mEq/l) | 152.0–164.0 |
| Potassium (mEq/l) | 2.5–3.8 |
| Blood urea nitrogen | unreliable in reptiles |
| Creatinine | unreliable in reptiles |

# APPENDIX B

## CONVERSION TABLES

### LINEAR MEASUREMENTS

1 millimeter = 0.039 inch
1 meter = 3.281 feet

1 inch = 25.4 millimeters
1 foot = 0.305 meter

### VOLUMETRIC MEASUREMENTS

1 liter = 33.815 fluid ounces
1 liter = 1.057 quarts
1 liter = 0.264 gallon
1 liter = 1,000 milliliters
1 liter = 10 deciliters
1 deciliter = 100 milliliters

1 fluid ounce = 29.573 milliliters
1 fluid ounce = 0.3 liter
1 pint = 0.473 liter
1 quart = 0.946 liter
1 U.S. gallon = 3.785 liters
1 U.S. gallon
= 128 ounces
= 0.83 British Imperial gallons
1 British Imperial gallon
= 4.546 liters
= 1.2 U.S. gallon

1 milliliter = 15–20 drops
5 milliliters = 1 teaspoon
3 teaspoons = 1 tablespoon
2 tablespoons = 1 ounce
1 teacup = 180 milliliters
1 glass = 240 milliliters
1 measuring cup = 240 milliliters (1/2 pint)

30 milliliters = 1 fluid ounce
473 milliliters = 1 pint
946 milliliters = 1 quart

### MEASUREMENTS OF MASS

#### METRIC

1 microgram = 1/1000 milligram
1 milligram = 0.035 ounce
1 gram = 1/454 pound
1 gram = 1,000 milligrams
1 kilogram = 2.205 pounds
1 kilogram = 1,000 grams
1 mg/kg = 0.454 mg/lb

#### AVOIRDUPOIS

1 ounce (Av) = 31.1 grams
1 pound = 0.454 kilogram
= 454 grams
1 mg/lb = 2.2 mg/kg

#### APOTHECARY

1 grain = 60 mg (0.06 gm)
15 grains = 1 gram

**Temperature Conversion Chart**

| Celsius Degree | Fahrenheit Degree | Celsius Degree | Fahrenheit Degree | Celsius Degree | Fahrenheit Degree |
|---|---|---|---|---|---|
| 0 | 32.0 | 17 | 62.6 | 34 | 93.2 |
| +1 | 33.8 | 18 | 64.4 | 35 | 95.0 |
| 2 | 35.6 | 19 | 66.2 | 36 | 96.8 |
| 3 | 37.4 | 20 | 68.0 | 37 | 98.6 |
| 4 | 39.2 | 21 | 69.8 | 38 | 100.4 |
| 5 | 41.0 | 22 | 71.6 | 39 | 102.2 |
| 6 | 42.8 | 23 | 73.4 | 40 | 104.0 |
| 7 | 44.6 | 24 | 75.2 | 41 | 105.8 |
| 8 | 46.4 | 25 | 77.0 | 42 | 107.6 |
| 9 | 48.2 | 26 | 78.8 | 43 | 109.4 |
| 10 | 50.0 | 27 | 80.6 | 44 | 111.2 |
| 11 | 51.8 | 28 | 82.4 | 45 | 113.0 |
| 12 | 53.6 | 29 | 84.2 | 46 | 114.8 |
| 13 | 55.4 | 30 | 86.0 | 47 | 116.6 |
| 14 | 57.2 | 31 | 87.8 | 48 | 118.4 |
| 15 | 59.0 | 32 | 89.6 | 49 | 120.2 |
| 16 | 60.8 | 33 | 91.4 | 50 | 122.0 |

For temperatures not listed above use the following formulae:
°Celsius to °Fahrenheit: (°C)9/5 + 32
°Fahrenheit to °Celsius: 1.8 × °C + 32 or (°F − 32°)5/9

# APPENDIX C

## SOURCES FOR REPTILE-RELATED PRODUCTS

These products are listed for the reader's convenience, but are not necessarily endorsed by the author.

### COMMERCIAL IGUANA DIETS

**Five Star Iguana Diet**
8805 Dee Ellen Lane
Riverview, FL 33569
1-800-747-0557

**Iguana Diet**
Fluker Laboratories
Division of Fluker Farms
1-800-735-8537

**Iguana Vegi Formula**
Ocean Nutrition Corp.
San Diego, CA 91950

**Mill Creek Farms Iguana Diet**
Mill Creek Farms
Montgomery City, MO 63361
1-800-354-2832

**Nutri Grow Iguana Diet**
American Reptile, Inc.
118 So. Main Street
Dry Ridge, KY 41035
1-606-824-9950

**Nutri'guana**
Feather Gourmet
10275 Old Placerville Road, Suite 5
Sacramento, CA 95827
1-800-732-1533

**Pretty Pets Iguana Diet**
Pretty Bird International
5810 Stacy Trail
Stacy, MN 55079
1-800-356-5020

**Reed's Iguana and Tortoise Chow**
Tetra Terrafauna
3001 Commerce Street
Blacksburg, VA 24060

**Ziegler Brothers' Iguana Mash**
About Birds
P.O. Box 387
Hebron, IL 60034-0387
1-815-648-4078

**Zupreem Iguana Diet**
Premium Nutritional Products
5500 Southwest Seventh Street
Topeka, KS 66606
1-800-345-4767

### LIGHTS

**Champion Lighting & Supply Co.**
1407 Bethlehem Pike
Flourtown, PA 19031
1-800-673-7822

**Chromalux Full Spectrum Lamps**
Lumiram Corporation
P.O. Box 297
Mamaroneck, NY 10543
1-914-698-1205

**Duro-Lite Lamps, Inc.**
9 Law Drive
Fairfield, NJ 07004

**Duro-Test Lighting**
1-800-688-5826

**Hagen Life-Glo Full-Spectrum Lamps**
Rolf C. Hagen (U.S.A.) Corp.
Mansfield, MA 02048

**M. Pencar Associates**
137-75 Geranium Avenue
Flushing, NY 11355
1-800-788-5781

**Repta-Sun Long-Life Full-Spectrum Lights**
Fluker Labs
Division of Fluker Farms
Baton Rouge, LA
1-800-735-8537

Reptile Light Sources
Energy Savers Unlimited, Inc.
Harbor City, CA
1-310-784-2770

**Ultraviolet Resources International**
13000 Athens Avenue
Cleveland, OH 44107
1-800-247-3251

**Vita-Lite Full-Spectrum Lights**
Sally M. Butts, Sales Representative
P.O. Box 134
Laytonville, CA 95454
1-800-984-8742

**Zoo Med Laboratories**
3100 McMillan Road
San Luis Obispo, CA 93401

## HEATING DEVICES AND ENVIRONMENTAL REGULATORS

**Energy Savers Unlimited**
Harbor City, CA
1-310-784-2770

**Kane Manufacturing Co., Inc.**
P.O. Box 774
Des Moines, IA 50303
1-800-247-0038

**Lyon Electric Co., Inc.**
2765 Main Street
Chula Vista, CA 91911
1-619-585-9900

**Modular Environmental Controls**
Div. Helix Magnetics, Inc.
8535 Commerce Avenue
San Diego, CA 92121
1-619-566-8335

**Pearlco Ceramic Heat Bulbs**
Eastern U.S. Representative:
Habitat Creators
1-516-736-9587
Western U.S. Representative:
RAM Network
1-818-345-0434

**Proportional Micro-Climate Thermostats**
Bob Clark
12316 Val Verde Drive
Oklahoma City, OK 73142
1-405-749-0797

**Repticare Ceramic Heat-Emitter**
ZooMed Laboratories, Inc.
3090 McMillan Road
San Luis Obispo, CA 93401

**Reptile Heating Mats**
Kane Manufacturing Co., Inc.
P.O. Box 774
Des Moines, IA 50303
1-800-247-0038

**Reptovators**
O.T.B., Inc.
405 Baltimore Avenue
Derby, KS 67037
1-316-788-7088

**Stanfield Electric Heat Pads**
1-800-255-0316

**Thermal Regulators**
Custom Reptile Network
12 High Avenue
Nyack, NY 10960
1-914-353-5034

**Thief of Hearts**
509 N. Street
Wichita, KS 67203
1-316-943-3443

## REPTILE EGG INCUBATORS

**Reptilife® Incubation System**
Lyon Electric Co., Inc.
2765 Main Street
Chula Vista, CA 91911
1-619-585-9900

**Reptovators**
O.T.B., Inc.
405 Baltimore Avenue
Derby, KS 67037
1-316-788-7088

**Thief of Hearts, Inc.**
509 N. Street
Wichita, KS 67203
1-316-943-3443

## IGUANA HARNESSES AND LEASHES

**Real Animal Friends**
R.A.F. Trading Corp.
101 Albany Avenue
Freeport, NY 11520
1-516-223-7600

**T-Rex Comfort Leash**
Ocean Nutrition
225 W. 15th Street
National City, CA 91950
1-619-336-4728

## MISCELLANEOUS PRODUCTS

**23% Calcium Gluconate (Glucoboronate) Solution U.S.P. (106.9 mEq/100 ml)**

American Veterinary Pharmaceuticals
Division of American Veterinary Products, Inc.
Fort Collins, CO 80524

Sanofi American Health
Subsidiary of Sanofi, Inc.
Overland Park, KS 66210

**Green Iguana Video**
Hardin Productions
6942 Abrams, Suite 103
Dallas, TX 75231
Tel: 1-214-750-7770
Fax: 1-214-750-1180

**Hydroponic Supplies**
Hydro-Fresh Farm
P.O. Box 511
San Martin, CA 95046

**Iguanas, Supplies, Food, Lights, etc.**
David Blair's Critter Corner, Inc.
316 W. Mission, #117
Escondido, CA 92025
1-619-746-5422

**Intensive Care System**
ThermoCare® Intensive Care Systems
ThermoCare, Inc.
P.O. Box 6069
Incline Village, NV 89450
1-702-831-1201

**Soft Paws®**
Soft Paws, Inc.
303 Paddington St.
Lafayette, IN 70503
1-318-232-4575
(available from veterinarians who can demonstrate how they are applied)

# APPENDIX D

## DIRECTORY OF HERPETOLOGICAL SOCIETIES OF THE UNITED STATES

This directory is compiled from the *Reptile and Amphibian Magazine*, *Herpetological Review*, the Northern Ohio Association of Herpetologists, and various other publications.

### ALASKA

Fairbanks Herpetocultural Society
%Dr. Betsy Rodger
Mt. McKinley Animal Hospital
800 College Road
Fairbanks, AK 99701
Tel: 907-452-6104

### ARIZONA

Arizona Herpetological Association
P.O. Box 66712
Phoenix, AZ 85082-6712
Tel: 602-894-1625
Membership: 300

International Society for the Study of Dendrobatid Frogs
%Ed Tunstall
2320 Palomino Drive
Chandler, AZ 85224

International Venomous Snake Society
%Tom Marcellino
P.O. Box 4498
Apache Junction, AZ 85278-4498
Tel: 602-984-6017
Membership: 250

National Turtle & Tortoise Society
P.O. Box 66935
Phoenix, AZ 85082-6935

Southern Arizona Herpetological Association
%Tom Boyden
4521 West Mars Street
Tucson, AZ 85704

Tucson Herpetological Society
P.O. Box 31531
Tucson, AZ 85751-1531

### ARKANSAS

Arkansas Herpetological Society
%Floyd Park
Route 2, Box 16
Hensley, AR 72065

### CALIFORNIA

American Federation of Herpetoculturists
P.O. Box 300067
Escondido, CA 92030-0067
Tel: 619-747-4948
Fax: 619-747-5224
Membership: 4200

Bay Area Amphibian & Reptile Society
Palo Alto Junior Museum
1451 Middlefield Road
Palo Alto, CA 94301

California Turtle & Tortoise Club Executive Board
P.O. Box 7300
Van Nuys, CA 91409-7300
Tel: 818-993-1551
Membership: 2300

California Turtle & Tortoise Club TOOSLO Chapter
P.O. Box 14222
San Luis Obispo, CA 93406
Tel: 209-481-5222
Membership: 207

Chameleon Information Network
13419 Appalachian Way
San Diego, CA 92129
Tel: 619-436-7978
Fax: 619-484-2669
Membership: 950

Desert Tortoise Preserve Committee
P.O. Box 453
Ridgecrest, CA 93555

Horned Lizard Conservation Society of Southern California
16377 Rancherias Road
Apple Valley, CA 92307
Membership: 400

International Gecko Society
P.O. Box 370423
San Diego, CA 92137-0423
Tel: 619-655-8668
Fax: 619-655-8428
Membership: 750

Island Empire Herpetology Society
San Bernardino County Museum
2024 Orange Tree Lane
Redlands, CA 92373

North Bay Herpetological Society
6366 Commerce Blvd., #216
Rohnert Park, CA 94928
Tel: 707-575-4170
Membership: 150

Northern California Herpetological Society
P.O. Box 1363
Davis, CA 95617-1363
Reptile & Amphibian Rescue Network
29575 Pacific Coast Highway
Malibu, CA 90265

Sacramento Turtle & Tortoise Club
%Felice Rood
25 Starlit Circle
Sacramento, CA 95831
Tel: 916-421-1134

Sacramento Valley Herpetological Society
%Bob Pedder
6007 Watt Avenue
North Highlands, CA 95660

San Diego Herpetological Society
P.O. Box 4036
San Diego, CA 92164-4036
Tel: 619-691-9055
Membership: 300

San Diego Turtle & Tortoise Society
13963 Lyons Valley Road
Jamul, CA 92935-9607

San Joaquin Herpetological Society
P.O. Box 1104
Clovis, CA 93612-1104

Shasta Snake Society
P.O. Box 171
Douglas City, CA 96024

Southern California Herpetological Association
P.O. Box 2932
Santa Fe Springs, CA 90670

Southwestern Herpetologists Society
P.O. Box 7469
Van Nuys, CA 91409
Membership: 780

Varanid Information Exchange
8726D S. Sepulveda Blvd. #243
Los Angeles, CA 90045

Venomous Snake Society
P.O. Box 691454
Los Angeles, CA 90069

## COLORADO

Colorado Herpetological Society
P.O. Box 150381
Lakewood, CO 80215
Tel: 303-757-5988
Membership: 120

Northeast Colorado Herpetological Society
%Roger Klingenberg, D.V.M.
6247 West 10th
Greeley, CO 80631

Rocky Mountain Herpetological Society
%Charles Sarkisian
5362 N. Nevada Avenue, #201
Colorado Springs, CO 80918

## CONNECTICUT

Connecticut Herpetological Society
%George Whitney, D.V.M.
860 Oakwood Road
Orange, CT 06477

Eastern Seaboard Herpetological League
%Michael Uricheck
77 Faber Avenue
Waterbury, CT 06704

Southern New England Herpetological Association
470 Durham Road
Madison, CT 06443

## DELAWARE

Delaware Herpetological Society
Ashland Nature Center
Brackenville & Barley Mill Rd.
Hockessin, DE 19707

## DISTRICT OF COLUMBIA

American Society of Icthyologists & Herpetologists
National Museum of Natural History
Washington, DC 20560

## FLORIDA

American Society of Ichthyologists & Herpetologists
Florida State Museum
University of Florida
Gainesville, FL 32611

Central Florida Herpetological Society
P.O. Box 3277
Winter Haven, FL 33885
Tel: 813-294-2235
Fax: 813-299-8844
Membership: 1200

Florida Panhandle Herpetological Society
%The Zoo
5801 Gulf Breeze Parkway
Gulf Breeze, FL 32561

Florida West Coast Herpetological Society
%John Lewis
1312 S. Evergreen Avenue
Clearwater, FL 33516

Gainesville Herpetological Society
P.O. Box 7104
Gainesville, FL 32605

Gopher Tortoise Council
%C. Small
Dept. of Biology
University of Central Florida
400 Central Park Blvd.
Orlando, FL 32816
Membership: 100

Herpetological League
Dept. of Biology
University of Miami
Coral Gables, FL 33124

Palm Beach County Herpetological Society
13837 54th Lane North
Royal Palm Beach, FL 33411
Tel: 407-964-8375
Membership: 50

South Marion Herpetological Society
P.O. Box 1817
Belleview, FL 34421
Tel: 904-245-2614
Membership: 30

Suncoast Herpetological Society
P.O. Box 2725
Dunedin, FL 34697

Tampa Bay Herpetological Society
%3310-A Carlton Arms Drive
Tampa, FL 33614

## GEORGIA

Georgia Herpetological Society
P.O. Box 464778
Lawrenceville, GA 30246
Tel: 404-653-9966
Membership: 140

Georgia Herpetological Society
P.O. Box 76744
Atlanta, GA 30358

Troup County Association of Herpetologists
%C.W. Dodgen
801 Grant Street
LaGrange, GA 30240

## IDAHO

Idaho Herpetological Society
P.O. Box 6329
Boise, ID 83707

## ILLINOIS

Central Illinois Herpetological Society
1125 W. Lake Avenue
Peoria, IL 61614
Tel: 309-685-5661
Membership: 100

Chicago Herpetological Society
2060 N. Clark Street
Chicago, IL 60614
Tel: 312-281-1800
Fax: 312-549-5199
Membership: 2000

## INDIANA

Hoosier Herpetological Society
P.O. Box 40544
Indianapolis, IN 46240-0544

Mid-Mississippi Valley Herpetological Society
%Mike Ladoto
925 Park Place Drive
Evansville, IN 47713

## IOWA

Iowa Herpetological Society
P.O. Box 166
Norwalk, IA 50211

## KANSAS

Kansas Herpetological Society
%Olin Karch
1112 Rural Street
Emporia, KS 66801

Kaw Valley Herpetological Society
Route 1, Box 29B
Eudora, KS 66025

Society for the Study of Amphibians & Reptiles
P.O. Box 626
Hays, KS 67601-0626
Tel: 913-623-4258
Fax: 913-625-8890

## KENTUCKY

Central Kentucky Herpetological Society
P.O. Box 12227
Lexington, KY 40581-2227

## LOUISIANA

Louisiana Herpetological Society
5025 Tulane Drive
Baton Rouge, LA 70803

Reptile Defense Fund
P.O. Box 16042
Baton Rouge, LA 70893

## MARYLAND

Maryland Herpetological Society
Natural History Society of Maryland
2643 N. Charles Street
Baltimore, MD 21218
Tel: 410-235-6116

Western Maryland Herpetological Society
P.O. Box 134
Boonsboro, MD 21713
Membership: 60

## MASSACHUSETTS

Massachusetts Herpetological Society
P.O. Box 1082
Boston, MA 02103

New England Herpetological Society
P.O. Box 1082
Boston, MA 02103
Tel: 617-789-5800
Membership: 280

Western Massachusetts Herpetological Society
Science Museum
236 State Street
Springfield, MA 01103

## MICHIGAN

Great Lakes Herpetological Society
%Tropical Fish Pond, Inc.
4308 North Woodward
Royal Oak, MI 48072

Michigan Society of Herpetologists
321 West Oakland Avenue
Lansing, MI 48906

## MINNESOTA

Minnesota Herpetological Society
Bell Museum of Natural History
10 Church Street, S.E.
Minneapolis, MN 55455

## MISSISSIPPI

Southern Mississippi Herpetological Society
P.O. Box 10047
Gulfport, MS 39505

## MISSOURI

St. Louis Herpetological Society
P.O. Box 220153
Kirkwood, MO 63122

## NEBRASKA

Nebraska Herpetological Society
Biology Department
University of Nebraska-Omaha
Omaha, NE 68182
Tel: 402-554-2369
Fax: 402-554-3532
Membership: 70

## NEVADA

Northern Nevada Herpetological Society
P.O. Box 21282
Reno, NV 89515-1282

## NEW MEXICO

Chihuahuan Desert Herpetological Society
%Paul Hyder
Dept. of Biology
New Mexico State University
Las Cruces, NM 88003

New Mexico Herpetological Society
Dept. of Biology
University of New Mexico
Albuquerque, NM 87131

## NEW YORK

Long Island Herpetological Society
476 N. Ontario Avenue
Lindenhurst, NY 11757
Tel: 516-884-5447
Membership: 300

New York Herpetological Society
Box 1245, Grand Central Station
New York, NY 10163-1245
Membership: 400

New York Turtle & Tortoise Society
163 Amsterdam Avenue, Suite 365
New York, NY 10023
Fax: 718-275-3307
Membership: 2000

Upstate Herpetological Association
HC 68 Box 30B
Springfield Center, NY 13468
Tel: 607-264-3441
Membership: 250

## NORTH CAROLINA

North Carolina Herpetological Society
State Museum of Natural Sciences
P.O. Box 29555
Raleigh, NC 27626-9555

## OHIO

Greater Cincinnati Herpetological Society
%Museum of Natural History
1720 Gilbert Avenue
Cincinnati, OH 45202

Greater Dayton Herpetological Society
%Museum of Natural History
2629 Ridge Avenue
Dayton, OH 45414

Mid-Ohio Herpetological Society
%Helen L. Benton
1556 Tremont Road
Columbus, OH 43212
Tel: 614-488-6747
Membership: 100

Northern Ohio Association of Herpetologists
Dept. of Biology
Case Western Reserve University
Cleveland, OH 44106

Society for the Study of Amphibians & Reptiles
Department of Zoology
Miami University
Oxford, OH 45056

Toledo Herpetological Society
%Sandy Allen
1587 Jermain Drive
Toledo, OH 43606-4056
Tel: 419-475-0521
Membership: 85

## OKLAHOMA

Oklahoma Herpetological Society
Oklahoma City Chapter
Route 1, Box 59
Goodwell, OK 73939

Oklahoma Herpetological Society
Tulsa Chapter
%Tulsa Zoo
5701 E. 36th Street, N.
Tulsa, OK 74115
Tel: 918-669-6235

## OREGON

Oregon Herpetological Society
%Steven Aveldson
8435 Derbyshire Lane
Eugene, OR 97405

## PENNSYLVANIA

Eastern Seaboard Herpetological League
%Charles Bell
5050 Wynnefield Avenue, #305
Philadelphia, PA 19131

Lehigh Valley Herpetological Society
P.O. Box 9171
Allentown, PA 18105-9171

Philadelphia Herpetological Society
%Mark Miller
9573 Walley Avenue
Philadelphia, PA 19115-3009
Tel: 215-464-3561
Membership: 840

Pittsburgh Herpetological Society
%Pittsburgh Zoo
1 Hill Road
Pittsburgh, PA 15206
Tel: 412-361-0835
Membership: 200

Susquehanna Herpetological Society
%Sam Burleigh
211 S. Market Street
Muncy, PA 17756

## RHODE ISLAND

Rhode Island Herpetological Association
30 Metropolitan Road
Providence, RI 02908
Tel: 401-751-2807
Membership: 150

## TENNESSEE

International Iguana Society, Inc. (U.S. Membership)
Dept. of Biology
Southern College
Collegedale, TN 37315
Fax: 615-238-2435
Membership: 500

Tennessee Valley Herpetological Society
P.O. Box 360
Ooltewah, TN 37363

## TEXAS

Association of Amphibian & Reptilian Veterinarians
%Dr. Michelle Frahm
Gladys Porter Zoo
500 Ringold Street
Brownsville, TX 78520
Membership: 1000

East Texas Herpetological Society
P.O. Box 34028
Houston, TX 77234-4028
Tel: 713-484-3925
Fax: 713-922-9858
Membership: 300

Greater San Antonio Herpetological Society
%W. Rowe Elliott
134 Aldrich Street
San Antonio, TX 78227

Lubbock Turtle & Tortoise Society
%Joe Cain
5708 64th Street
Lubbock, TX 79424

North Texas Herpetological Society
P.O. Box 1043
Euless, TX 76039

South/Central Texas Herpetological Society
%Neils Saustrup
1405 Rabb Road
Austin, TX 78704
Tel: 512-447-8083
Membership: 200

South Texas Turtle & Tortoise Society
%James Maples, Jr.
927 Wilson
Alice, TX 78332

Texas Herpetological Society
Hutchinson Hall of Science
31st at Canton
Lubbock, TX 79410

## UTAH

Utah Association of Herpetologists
195 West 200 North
Logan, UT 84321-3905
Tel: 801-752-0297
Membership: 135

Utah Herpetological Society
P.O. Box 9361
Salt Lake City, UT 84109

## VIRGINIA

Blue Ridge Herpetological Society
P.O. Box 727
Brookneal, VA 24528
Tel: 804-376-5229
Membership: 100

Dragon Patch Herpetology Club
913 East Main Street
Salem, VA 24513

Herpetocultural Society of Virginia
P.O. Box 3535
Virginia Beach, VA 23454

Virginia Herpetological Society
%Joseph Mitchell
Dept. of Biology
University of Richmond
Richmond, VA 23173

Washington Herpetological Society
12420 Rock Ridge Road
Herndon, VA 22070
Membership: 40

## WASHINGTON

Pacific Northwest Herpetological Society
P.O. Box 70181
Bellevue, WA 98007-0181

## WISCONSIN

Int'l Society for the Study of
Dendrobatid Frogs
%Dale Bertram, M.D.
One Virginia Terrace
Madison, WI 53705

Wisconsin Herpetological Society
P.O. Box 366
Germantown, WI 53022-0366
Membership: 150

## WYOMING

Wahsatch Alliance of Herpetoculturists
%T.A.H.
P.O. Box 1907
Casper, WY 82606

# APPENDIX E

## INTERNATIONAL HERPETOLOGICAL AND SPECIAL INTEREST IGUANA GROUPS

### ARGENTINA

Asociacion Latino-Americana Ictiologo y Herpetologo
%Dr. M.A. Freiberg
Museo Argentina Ciencias Naturales
Avenida Angel Gallardo 470
Buenos Aires
Argentina

### AUSTRALIA

Australian Affiliation of Herpetological Societies
%Dr. H. Ehmann
School of Biological Sciences
Sydney Technical College
Broadway, N.S.W. 2007
Australia

Australian Herpetologist's League
G.P.O. Box 864
Sydney, N.S.W. 2001
Australia

Victorian Herpetological Society
16 Suspension Street
Ardeer, Victoria
Australia

### AUSTRIA

Austrian Herpetological Society
%Hans Esterbauer
Johann Puch Strasse 27/III/5
4403 Steyr
Austria

### BELGIUM

Belgian Herpetological Society
%Edward Rheinhard
Schranshoflei 1B
2830 Bonheiden/Rymenam
Belgium

Carapace
Rue de Tubize 128a
1440 Braine le Chateau
Belgium

Centre d'Observation Belge des Reptiles et Amphibiens
%A. Goethals
Avenue General Medecin Derache, 153
1050 Brussels
Belgium

R.A.N.A. Belgium
Avenue du Bois-lá-Haut 21
1330 Rixensart
Belgium

Terra, Herpetologic Society
%F. Vanderstraeten
Wolterslaan 93
9110 Gent-Sint-Amandsberg
Belgium

### CANADA

Association of Reptile Keepers
Sapperton RPO
New Westminster, British Columbia V3I 5P7
Canada

Ontario Herpetological Society
P.O. Box 244
Port Credit, Ontario L5G 4L8
Canada

Reptile Breeding Foundation
P.O. Box 1450
Picton, Ontario K0K 2T0
Canada

Venomous Animal Society of Canada
%S. Allen
11 Knightsbridge Road, No. 1010
Bramalea, Ontario L6T 3X4
Canada

### COSTA RICA

Pro Iguana Verde Foundation
Apartado 692-1007
San José
Costa Rica
Tel: 506-31-6756
Fax: 506-32-1950

### DENMARK

Nordisk Herpetologisk Forening
%U. Olsen
Ørnevej 6
4040 Jyllinge
Denmark

## ESTONIA

Estonian Herpetological Society
%Peeter Poldsam
Havi 9-5
3600 Pärnu
Estonia

## FRANCE

R.A.N.A. France
Les Treilles
16150 Chabanais
France

Société Herpetologique de France
%Université de Paris VII
Laboratoire d'Anatomie comparée
2 Place Jussieu
75230 Paris cedex 05
France

Village des Tortue
Soptom
BP 24
Gonfaron
France

## GERMANY

Deutschen Gesellschaft für Herpetologie und Terrarienkunde
%Dr. W. Bohme
Zoologisches Forschungsinstitut A. Koenig
Adenauerallee 150-164
5300 Bonn 1
Germany

Die Arbeitsgemeinschaft Für Leguane in der DGHT; Publishes *IGUANA* (in German)
%Dr. Gunther Köhler
Im Mittelfeld 27
63075 Offenbach/Main
Germany
Tel: 011-49-69-64986266
Fax: 011-49-69-64986571

Harz Herpetological Society
%Herbert Rösler
Ferdinand Freiligrath Strasse 51
06502 Thale/Harz
Germany

Herpetofauna
Postfach 1110
Stuttgarter Strasse 35
7056 Weinstadt 1
Germany

Interessen-Gemeinschaft Schildkrotenschutz
%R. Windolf
Katharina-Eberhard Strasse 12-14
8013 Haar bei München
Germany

Isis Gesellschaft für Biologische Aquarien und Terrarienkunde
%J. Woolmann
Schwanthalerstrasse 123
8000 München 2
Germany

Kulturbund der DDR (Zentraler Fachausschuss Terrarisktik)
1030 Berlin
PSF 34
Germany

North German Herpetological Society
%Andrej Koralewski
Georgstrausse 8
44534 Lünen
Germany

Westfalen Herpetological Society
%Olaf Kannchen
Bambergstrasse 11
59192 Bergkamen/Westfalen
Germany

## HUNGARY

Hungarian Herpetological Society
%Tamás Fehér
2013 Pomaz
Rosza U8
Hungary

## INDIA

Center for Herpetology
Madras Crocodile Bank
Post Bag 4
Mamallapuram, Tamil Nadu 603104
India
Tel: 011-91-44-4113-46332
011-91-44-491-0910
011-91-4113-42511

Madras Snake Park Trust
Deer Sanctuary
Guindy, Madras 600 022
South India

## ITALY

Centro Carapax
CP 34, 58024 Massa Marittima (GR)
Italy

Italian Herpetological Society
%Luciano Mariotto
Via Lencavallo 57/c
10154 Torino
Italy

## JAPAN

Herpetological Society of Japan
%Dr. R.C. Goris
Sugao 9480-7
Miyamae ku, Kawasaki-shi 213
Japan

The Japan Snake Institute
%Dr. Y. Sawai
Yabuzuka-honmachi, Nittagun
Gunmma Prefecture 379-23
Japan

## THE NETHERLANDS

Chelonian Documentation Center
%J.H. de Pon
P.O. Box 125
8700 AC Bolsward
The Netherlands

Dutch Snake Society
%Jaap Koolij
Langervelderweg 137
2211 AG Noordwijkerhout
The Netherlands

Nederlandse Schildpadden Vereniging
Papelaan 18
2522 EJ Voorschoten
The Netherlands

Nederlandse Studiegroep Anolissen
F. van Leeuwen
2e Boerhavestraat 5hs
1091 AK Amsterdam
The Netherlands

Nederlandse Vereniging voor Herpetologie en Terrariumkunde
%E.F. Elzenga
Burg. H. van Konijnenburglaan 46
3925 XB Scherpenzeel
The Netherlands

Societas Europaea Herpetologica
%Dr. M.S. Hoogmoed
Rijksmuseum van Natuurlijke Historie
Postbus 9517
2300 RA Leiden
The Netherlands

## NEW ZEALAND

New Zealand Herpetological Society
%A.J. Howard
66 Don Buck Road
Massey, Auckland 8
New Zealand

New Zealand Herpetological Society
28 Spinella Drive
Glenfield, Auckland
New Zealand

## POLAND

Polish Herpetological Society
%Andrzej Kovelew
Choldna 15/1301
00891 Warszawa
Poland

## PUERTO RICO

Chelonia-Sociedad para el estudio de los Quelonios
%J.L. Pinero
P.O. Box 22061, UPR Station
San Juan, 00931
Puerto Rico

## RUSSIA

Moscow Herpetological Society
Reptile Curator
Moscow Zoopark
B. Gruzinskaya 1
123820 Moscow
Russia

## SCOTLAND

Scottish Herpetological Society
5 Florabank Road, Haddington
East Lothian
Scotland EH41 3LJ
Tel: 011-16-20-825061
Membership: 60

Scottish Herpetological Society
%John Spence
273 Allison Street
Glasgow G42 8AB
United Kingdom

## SINGAPORE

Singapore Herpetological Society
Reptile House
Singapore Zoological Society
80 Mandai Lake Road
Singapore 2572
Singapore

## SOUTH AFRICA

Herpetological Association of Africa
%National Museum
P.O. Box 266
Bloemfontein 9300
South Africa
Tel: 011-51-479609
Fax: 011-51-479681
Membership: 330

## SWEDEN

Swedish Herpetological Society
Department of Zoology
University of Göteborg
400 33 Göteborg
Sweden

## SWITZERLAND

Schildkroten-Informationsdienst
%H.H.D. Falk
Bachserstrasse 10
8174 Stadel b. Niederglatt/ZH
Switzerland

## UNITED KINGDOM

Association for the Study of Reptiles & Amphibians
%Cotswold Wildlife Park
Burfold, Oxon OX8 4JW
United Kingdom

British Chelonia Group
%Miss F. McGrattan
10 Clyde Park, Redland
Bristol BS6 6RR
United Kingdom

British Herpetological Society
%Zoological Society of London
Regents Park
London NW1 4RY
United Kingdom
Membership: 1000

Cleveland Herpetological Society
%Peter Castle
8 Linton Road, Normanby
Middlesbrough, Cleveland TS6 0HZ
United Kingdom

Essex Reptiles & Amphibians Society
6 Chestnut Way, Tiptree
Colchester, Essex CO5 0NX
United Kingdom
Tel: 011-16-21-819675
Membership: 100

International Herpetological Society
%A.J. Mobbs
65 Broadstone Avenue, Walsall
West Midlands WS3 1JA
United Kingdom
Tel: 011-19-22-477281
Membership: 850

London Herpetological Society
%James Montgomery
3 Anstey Lodge
81 Wellington Road
Enfield/Middlesex EN1 2QS
United Kingdom

North East Herpetological Society
%Alan Mason
10 Clapham House
100 John Dobson Street
Newcastle Upon Tyne
United Kingdom

North Tyneside Herpetological Society
%Raymond Dryden
58 Mitford Gardens
High Howdon/Wallsend
North Tyneside NE28 0QT
United Kingdom

Northern Herpetological Society
%Ian Burn
29 Coquetdale
Amble, Northumberland
United Kingdom

South West Herpetological Society
%Jon Flynn
9 Sandpath Road, Kingsteignton
Newton Abbot/Devon TQ12 3BG
United Kingdom

Southwestern Herpetological Society
%F.B. Gibbons
Acanthus 59
St. Marychurch Road
Torquay, Devon T01 3HG
United Kingdom

The Tortoise Trust
BM Tortoise
London WC1N 3XX
United Kingdom
Tel: 011-12-67-211578
Membership: 2500

Three Counties Reptilians
34 King John's Road
North Warnborough, NR. Hook,
Hampshire RG29 1EJ
United Kingdom
Tel: 011-12-56-702543
Membership: 60

Wirral Herpetological Society
4 Elm Park Road
Wallasey, Wirral L45 5JH
United Kingdom

## UNITED STATES

International Iguana Society
(International Membership)
Finca Cyclura
Rt. 3, Box 328
Big Pine Key, FL 33043

# APPENDIX F

## ON-LINE COMPUTER SPECIAL INTEREST GROUPS

Herpetology Network
℅Mark F. Miller
P.O. Box 52261
Philadelphia, PA 19115-7261
Voice: 215-464-3561
Modem: 215-464-3562
Fax: 215-464-3561

America Online
1 800 827 6364

PRODIGY
Bulletin Board "Pets"
Exotic, Iguanas
1 800 767 3664

# GLOSSARY

| | |
|---|---|
| **ambient** | environmental, surrounding (temperature). |
| **anomaly** | an abnormal condition or conformation involving an organ. |
| **anorexia** | loss of appetite; refusal to feed. |
| **aorta** | the large arterial vessel that carries blood to the abdominal organs, rear limbs, and tail. |
| **appendicular skeleton** | pertaining to the limbs and their appendages. |
| **aquatic** | living in, on, or near the water. |
| **arachnid** | spiders, scorpions, mites, ticks, and other eight-legged arthropods. |
| **arboreal** | living or climbing in trees. |
| **atrophy** | decrease in size of tissue or an organ. |
| **axial skeleton** | pertaining to skull, vertebral column, and pelvis. |
| **bask** | to warm the body in sunlight or beneath a source of radiant energy. |
| **bioactive** | having an effect on living tissues in an organism. |
| **calcareous** | chalky; possessing a high calcium content. |
| **cancellous (trabecular) bone** | spongy bone; bony tissue characterized by its spaces, often filled with bone marrow. |
| **carnivorous** | flesh-eating. |
| **carrion** | dead and decaying flesh. |
| **caruncle** | the tooth-like temporary structure with which a hatchling iguana slits its eggshell preliminary to its exit. |
| **caudal** | pertaining to the tail end. |
| **cloaca** | the common vault into which the alimentary and genitourinary systems terminate via their own tubes or ducts. |
| **conspecific** | belonging to the same species. |
| **constipation** | difficulty or inability to pass feces. |
| **copradeum** | the portion of the terminal digestive tract that empties into the cloaca. |
| **cortical bone** | the dense and outermost portion of bone. |
| **cranial** | relating to the skull (head) end of an animal. |
| **dewlap** | a skin-covered flattened flap-like organ connected to the skin of the iguana's lower jaw. |
| **dorsal** | relating to the back. |
| **dorsoventral** | relating to the upper and lateral surfaces of the body or body part. |
| **dysecdysis** | difficult or faulty shedding of the epidermis. |
| **dyspnea** | difficult or labored breathing. |
| **ecdysis** | the process of molting or shedding the epidermis. |

**ectothermic** body temperature regulated by the environmental temperature rather than by heat which is produced internally.

**electrolytes** various ions required by cells to regulate the electric charge across the cell membrane; in respect to this book, physiologic ions contained in tissue or body fluids.

**endogenous** originating or produced within an organism, a tissue, or a cell.

**etiology** the cause or origin of disease.

**exogenous** originating outside an organism.

**flora** plants.

**folivore** leaf-eating.

**gavage** washing or placing a substance into a hollow organ via a tube or other device.

**geophagy** earth or soil eating.

**gingival** referring to the gums.

**granuloma** an inflammatory lesion containing an infectious, parasitic, or foreign object; usually surrounded by dense connective tissue; often follows an abscess.

**halogen** a sodium salt containing bromine, chlorine, fluorine, or iodine. Some plants can concentrate these compounds from the soil in which they grow.

**herbivorous** plant or vegetable eating.

**hydroponic** technique for growing plants in a water-nutrient solution rather than in soil.

**hyperparathyroid** overactive secretion by the parathyroid glands.

**hyperplasia** abnormal cell number.

**hypertonic** having a higher osmotic pressure of two solutions; a solution which has a greater than a physiologic or isotonic concentration.

**hypertrophy** abnormal cell or organ size; non-tumorous enlargement of organ or tissue as a result of increase in size rather than number of cells.

**hypervitaminosis** a specific vitamin overdosage.

**hypotonic** having the lower osmotic pressure of two solutions; a solution which has a less than a physiologic or isotonic concentration.

**hypovitaminosis** pertaining to a specific vitamin deficiency.

**iatrogenic** a condition caused by a treatment.

**idiopathic** of unknown cause or etiology.

**ileus** obstruction of the intestines; can be caused by a physical object or by a failure of normal peristaltic movement.

**inanition** partial or complete starvation resulting from a lack of food.

**indigenous** native.

**ingesta** swallowed food.

**insectivorous** insect-eating.

**inspissated** abnormally dry.

**integument** skin.

**intussusception** the invagination or telescoping of the duodenum into the stomach or one segment of intestine into an adjacent segment.

**invertebrate** lacking a backbone or vertebral column.

| | |
|---|---|
| **isotonic** | having the same concentration; with respect to physiologic solutions that are compatible with living tissues. |
| **keratin** | a constituent of epidermis and integumentary shell plates. |
| **lateral** | relating to the side or flank. |
| **lithophagy** | stone or rock eating. |
| **maceration** | softening of a solid by the action of water or other aqueous solution. |
| **mandible** | the lower jaw. |
| **mastication** | chewing. |
| **metazoa** | multicellular animals. |
| **metabolites** | constituents of food or metabolism used or excreted by an organism. |
| **microflora** | bacterial and protozoan inhabitants of the intestine. |
| **motility** | ability to move; used here in the context of moving gastrointestinal contents through the alimentary tract. |
| **necropsy** | examination of a corpse. |
| **neoplasm** | new growth; a tumor. |
| **nephrotoxic** | chemically damaging to the kidneys. |
| **neuropathy** | a disease or an abnormality of the nervous system. |
| **obstipation** | partial or complete obstruction to the passage of feces through the intestine. |
| **omnivorous** | eating both flesh and plant material. |
| **osteomalacia** | softening of the bones. |
| **osteopenia** | insufficiently mineralized bone. |
| **parathyroid** | one or more pairs of glandular structures whose hormone secretion, parathormone, is responsible for calcium and phosphorus metabolism. |
| **pathogen** | a disease-causing organism. |
| **pheromone** | a chemical scent or cue secreted by one organism to which another organism of the same species responds either physiologically or psychologically. Many pheromones mediate or facilitate a sexual response in members of the opposite sex. |
| **photoperiod** | daily exposure to light; in this book's context, duration of amount of light related to amount of dark. |
| **physiologic (fluids)** | fluids mimicking those that are present in an organism; compatible with the natural-occurring fluids characteristic of an organism. |
| **plasma** | the fluid portion of unclotted blood. |
| **postmortem** | after death. |
| **proctodeum** | the terminus (end) of the alimentary tract. |
| **puree** | finely chopped or strained food. |
| **pyogranuloma** | a chronic inflammatory pus-filled enlargement. |
| **radiography** | diagnostic X-ray imaging. |
| **renal** | relating to the kidneys. |
| **rostral** | relating to the beak or nose. |
| **savannah** | a flat, sparsely forested grassland of a tropical or subtropical region. |

| | |
|---|---|
| **sequester** | to take up and concentrate a compound or chemical from the environment and store in the tissues; in this book's context, a plant or animal concentrating and storing mineral salts contained in soil. |
| **slurry** | a soft, finely ground, nearly liquid suspension of a material suspended in an aqueous agent. |
| **snout-to-vent length** | the linear measurement of the distance from an iguana's snout to its flap-like cloacal vent; usually expressed in centimeters. |
| **squamate** | referring to animals which possess scales. |
| **subcutaneous** | relating to beneath the skin. |
| **taxonomy** | the naming of or identification of a group of organisms or objects. |
| **terrestrial** | land-living. |
| **thermoregulate** | regulating body temperature. |
| **torpor** | state of mental or physical inactivity; sleepiness; sluggishness. |
| **tympany** | bloating; the retention of gastrointestinal gas. |
| **umbilicus** | navel, "belly button." |
| **urates** | urinary salts of uric acid—usually sodium, potassium or ammonium. |
| **urodeum** | that portion of the terminus (end) of the urinary excretory system that empties into the common cloaca. |
| **urolith** | urinary bladder stone. |
| **vena cava** | the large, thin-walled vein that carries blood from the rear limbs, tail, and abdominal visceral organs to the heart. |
| **ventral** | relating to the belly. |
| **xeric** | extremely dry. |
| **xeroderma** | pathologically dry, thickened, and scaly skin. |

# BIBLIOGRAPHY AND SUGGESTED READING


Allen, M. E. (1989, January 13–15). Dietary Induction and Prevention of Osteodystrophy in an Insectivorous Reptile *Eublepharis macularius*: Characterization by Radiography and Histopathology. *Proc. III Int. Coll. Pathol. Reptiles Amphibians*. Orlando, FL.

———. (1989). The Effect of Three Light Treatments on Growth in the Green Iguana, *Iguana iguana*. *Proc. Am. Assoc. Zoo Vet. Ann. Mtng.*, p. 64.

———, and Capen, C. C. (1976). Fine Structural Changes of Bone Cells in Experimental Nutritional Osteodystrophy of Green Iguanas. *Virch. Arch.*, B. *20*:169–184.

———. (1976). Ultrastructural Evaluation of Parathyroid and Ultimobranchial Glands in Iguanas with Experimental Nutritional Osteodystrophy. *Gen. Comp. Endocrinol.*, *30*(2):209–222.

———, Oftedal, O. Y., and Knapka, J. (1982). Manipulation of Calcium and Phosphorus Levels in Live Prey. In: *Proc. of NE Section on Amer. Assoc. Zoos, Parks, and Aquar.*

———, and Werner, D. I. (1990). Management of the Green Iguana (*Iguana iguana*) in Central America. *Proc. 1990 Am. Assoc. Zoo Veterinarians*, 19–25.

Altman, R., et al. (1972). Turtle-Associated Salmonellosis: II. The Relationship Between Pet Turtles to Salmonellosis in Children in New Jersey. *Am. J. Epidem.*, *95*:518–520.

Anonymous. (1993). A Quick Guide to Some Common Brassicas. *IľM Practitoner*, *15*(7):5.

Arnett, J. R. (1979). Breeding the Fiji Banded Iguana. *Int. Zoo. Yrbk.*, *19*:78–79.

Auffenberg, W. (1982). Feeding Strategy of the Caicos Ground Iguana, *Cyclura carinata*. In: *Iguanas of The World: Their Behavior, Ecology and Conservation*. G. M. Burghardt and A. S. Rand (Eds.), pp. 84–116. Park Ridge, NJ; Noyes Publishing.

Baker, E. F., et al. (1972). Epidemiological Aspects of Turtle-Associated Salmonellosis. *Arch. Environ. Health*, *24*:1–9.

Bakhuis, W. L. (1982). Size and Sexual Differentiation in the Lizard *Iguana iguana* on a Semi-Arid Island. *J. Herpetol.*, *16*:322–325.

Banks, C. B. (1984). Reproductive History of a Captive Colony of *Iguana iguana*. *Acta Zoo. et Path. Antverpiensia*, *78*:101–114.

Barnard, J. B., Oftedal, O., Barbosa, P., Mathias, C., Allen, A., Citino, S., Ullrey, D., and Montali, R. (1991). The Response of Vitamin-D-deficient Green Iguanas (*Iguana iguana*) to Artificial Ultraviolet Light. *Proc. Am. Assoc. Zoo Vet. Ann. Mtng.*, 147–150.

Barnard, S. M., and Upton, S. J. (1994). *A Veterinary Guide to the Parasites of Reptiles*, Vol. 1 Protozoa. Malabar, FL; Krieger Publishing Co., Inc.

Barnes, C. B. (1984). Reproduction History of a Colony of Captive Common Iguanas (*Iguana iguana*). *Acta Zool. et Pathol. Antverpiensia*, *78*:101–114.

Barten, S. L. (1981). The Induction of Voluntary Feeding in Captive Snakes. *Bull. Chi. Herp. Soc.*, *16*(1):1–5.

Beltz, E. (1989). *Care in Captivity: Husbandry Techniques for Amphibians and Reptiles*. Chicago, IL; Chicago Herpetological Soc.

Blair, D. (1991). West Indian Rock Iguanas: Their Status in the Wild and Efforts to Breed them in Captivity. *Proc. Northern California Herpetological Society Captive Propagation and Husbandry Conference. Special Publ. No. 6*:54–66.

Boam, G. W., et al. (1970). Subcutaneous Abscesses in Iguanid Lizards. *J.A.V.M.A.*, *157*:617–619.

Boever, W. J., and Williams, J. (1975). *Arizona* Septicemia in Three Boa Constrictors. *Vet. Med/Small Anim. Clin.*, *70*:1357–1359.

Boycott, J. A., et al. (1953). *Salmonella* in Tortoises. *J. Path. & Bact.*, *65*:401–411.

Boyer, T. H. (1991). Common Problems and Treatment of Green Iguanas (*Iguana iguana*). *Bull. Assoc. Amphib. and Rept. Veterinarians*, *1*(1):8–11.

———. (1991). Green Iguana Care. *Bull. Assoc. Amphib. and Rept. Veterinarians*, *1*(1):12–14.

Brattstrom, B. H. (1974). The Evolution of Reptilian Social Behavior. *Am. Zoologist*, *14*:35–49.

Britton, S. W., and Klein, R. F. (1939). Emotional Hyperglycemia and Hyperthermia in Tropical Mammals and Reptiles. *Am. J. Physiol.*, *125*:730–734.

Burchfield, P. M. (1973). Rhinoceros Iguanas. *Gladys Porter Zoo Newsl.*, *2*:6.

Burghardt, G. M. (1978). Of Iguanas and Dinosaurs: Social Behavior and Communication in Neonate Reptiles. *Amer. Zool.*, *17*(1): 177–190.

———, Greene, H., and Rand, A. S. (1977). Social Behavior Hatchling Green Iguanas: Life at a Reptile Rookery. *Science, 195*:(4279):689–691.

———, and Rand, A. S. (1985). Group Size and Growth Rate in Hatchling Green Iguanas (*Iguana iguana*). *Behav., Ecol., Sociobiol., 18*(1):101–104.

Cambre, R. C., et al. (1980). Salmonellosis and Arizoniosis in the Reptile Collection at the National Zoological Park. *J.A.V.M.A., 177*(9):800–803.

Capen, C. C., and Marten, S. L. (1983). Calcium-Regulating Hormones and Diseases of the Parathyroid Glands. In: *Textbook of Veterinary Internal Medicine, 2nd Ed.* S. J. Ettinger (Ed.), pp. 1561–1565. Philadelphia; W. B. Saunders.

Carey, W. M. (1973). Some Notable Longevity Records for Captive Iguanas. *Int. Zoo Yrbk., 13*:154–155.

———. (1975). The Rock Iguana, *Cyclura pinguis*, on Anegada, British Virgin Islands, with Notes on *Cyclura ricordi* and *Cyclura cornuta* on Hispaniola. *Bull. Florida State Mus. Biol. Sci., 19*:498–502.

Carothers, J. H. (1984). Sexual Selection and Sexual Dimorphism in Some Herbivorous Lizards. *American Naturalist, 124*:244–254.

Carpenter, C. C. (1982). The Aggressive Displays of Iguanine Lizards. *In*: *Iguanas of The World: Their Behavior, Ecology and Conservation.* G. M. Burghardt and A. S. Rand (Eds.), pp. 84–116. Park Ridge, NJ; Noyes Publishing.

Case, T. J. (1982). Ecology and Evolution of the Insular Gigantic Chuckawallas, *Sauromalus hispidis* and *Sauromalus varius*. *In*: *Iguanas of The World: Their Behavior, Ecology and Conservation.* G. M. Burghardt and A. S. Rand (Eds.), pp. 84–116. Park Ridge, NJ; Noyes Publishing.

Chome, B. B. (1992). Zoonoses of House Pets Other than Dogs, Cats, and Birds. *Pediatic Infect. Dis. J., 11*:479–487.

Clark, H. F., and Karzon, D. T. (1972). Iguana Virus, a Herpes-Like Virus Isolated from Cultured Cells of a Lizard, *Iguana iguana*. *Infect. & Immun., 5*:559–569.

Combs, G. F., Jr. (1994). Clinical Implications of Selenium and Vitamin E in Poultry Nutrition. *Veterinary Clinical Nutrition, 1*(3):133–140.

———, and Combs, S. (1986). Biochemical Functions of Selenium, Chapter 6. *In*: *The Role of Selenium in Nutrition*, pp. 206–265. New York; Academic Press.

Cox, C. R., and Le Boeuf, B. J. (1977). Female Incitation of Male Competition: A Mechanism in Sexual Selection. *American Naturalists, 111*:317–335.

Dacke, C. G. (1979). *Calcium Regulation in Sub-Mammalian Vertebrates.* New York; Academic Press.

Dearing, M. D. (1993). An Alimentary Specialization for Herbivory in the Tropical Whiptail Lizard, *Cnemidophorus murinus*. *J. Herpetol., 27*(1):111–114.

Derikson, W. K. (1976). Lipid Storage and Utilization in Reptiles. *Amer. Zool., 16*:711–723.

de Vosjoli, P. (1992). *The General Care and Maintenance of the Green Iguana.* Lakeside, CA; Advanced Vivarium Systems.

Distel, H., and Veazey, J. (1982). The Behavioral Inventory of the Green Iguana, *Iguana iguana*. *In*: *Iguanas of the World: Their Behavior, Ecology and Conservation*, G. M. Burghardt and A. S. Rand (Eds.), pp. 250–270. Park Ridge, NJ; Noyes Publishing.

Drummond, H., and Burghardt, G. M. (1982). Orientation and Dispersing Hatchling Green Iguanas, *Iguana iguana*. *In*: *Iguanas of the World: Their Behavior, Ecology and Conservation.* G. M. Burghardt and A. S. Rand (Eds.), pp. 271–291. Park Ridge, NJ; Noyes Publishing.

Dugan, B. (1982a). The Mating Behavior of the Green Iguana, *Iguana iguana*. *In*: *Iguanas of the World: Their Behavior, Ecology and Conservation.* G. M. Burghardt and A. S. Rand (Eds.), pp. 320–339. Park Ridge, NJ; Noyes Publishing.

———. (1982b). A Field Study of the Headbob Displays of Male Green Iguanas (*Iguana iguana*): Variation in Form and Context. *Animal Behavior, 30*:327–338.

———, and Wiewandt, T. V. (1982). Socio-Ecological Determinants of Mating Strategies in Iguanine Lizards. *In*: *Iguanas of the World: Their Behavior, Ecology and Conservation.* G. M. Burghardt and A. S. Rand (Eds.), pp. 303–319. Park Ridge, NJ; Noyes Publishing.

Dunson, W. A. (1968). Salt Gland Excretion in the Pelagic Sea Snake, *Pelamis*. *Am. J. Physiol., 215*:1512–1517.

———. (1969a). Electrolyte Excretion by the Salt Glands of the Galapagos Marine Iguana. *Am. J. Physiol., 216*:995–1002.

———. (1969b). Reptilian Salt Glands. *In*: *The Exocrine Glands.* S. Y. Botelho, et al. (Eds.), pp. 89–103. Philadelphia; Univ. Pennsylvania Press.

DuPonte, M. W., et al. (1978). Activation of Latent *Salmonella* NS *Arizona* Organisms by Dehydration in Red-eared Turtles, *Pseudemys scripta elegans*. *Am. J. Vet. Res., 39*:529–530.

Duval, J. J. (1983). Recommendations for the Captive Management of West Indian Rock Iguanas (*Cyclura*). *Proc. VI Symp. Captive Propagation and Husbandry.* Thurmont, MD. pp. 181–196.

Etheridge, R. E. (1982). Checklist of Iguanaine and Malagasy Iguanid Lizards. *In*: *Iguanas of the World: Their Behavior, Ecology and Conservation.* G. M. Burghardt and A. S. Rand (Eds.), pp. 7–37; Park Ridge, NJ; Noyes Publishing.

Farnsworth, R. J., Brannian, R. E., Fletcher, K. C., and Klassen, S. (1986). A Vitamin E-Selenium Responsive Condition in a Green Iguana. *J. Zoo An. Med., 17*:42–45.

Fitch, H. S., and Henderson, R. W. (1977). Age and Sex Differences, Reproduction and Conservation of *Iguana iguana*. *Milwaukee Publ. Mus. Contrib. Biol. and Geol.*, *13*:1–21.

———. (1978). Ecology and Exploitation of *Ctenosaura similis*. *Univ. Kansas Sci. Bull.*, *51*:483–500.

Flanigan, W. F. (1973). Sleep and Wakefulness in Iguanid Lizards, *Ctenosaurus pectinata* and *Iguana iguana*. *Brain Behavior and Evolution*, *8*:401–436.

Fowler, M. E. (1975). Toxicities in Exotic and Zoo Animals. *Vet. Clinics of North America*, *5*(4):690–691.

———. (1986). Metabolic Bone Disease. *In*: *Zoo and Wild Animal Medicine*. M. E. Fowler (Ed.), pp. 55–76. Philadelphia; W. B. Saunders, Co.

Fox, L. R. (1975). Cannibalism in Natural Populations. *Ann. Rev. Ecol. Syst.*, *6*:87–106.

Frank, N. (1992, January–February). Green Iguanas: Their Care and Captive Husbandry. *Reptile and Amphibian Magazine*, pp. 30–32.

Frye, F. L. (1973). *Husbandry, Medicine and Surgery in Captive Reptiles*. Bonner Springs, KS; Veterinary Medical Publishing Co., Inc.

———. (1981). *Biomedical and Surgical Aspects of Captive Reptile Husbandry. 1st Ed.* Edwardsville, KS; Veterinary Medicine Publishing Co., Inc.

———. (1986). Feeding and Nutritional Diseases. *In*: *Zoo and Wild Animal Medicine*, 2nd Ed. M. E. Fowler (Ed.), pp. 139–151. Philadelphia; W. B. Saunders.

———. (1991a). *Biomedical and Surgical Aspects of Captive Reptile Husbandry, 2nd Ed.* Malabar, FL; Krieger Publ. Co., Inc.

———. (1991b). *A Practical Guide for Feeding Captive Reptiles*. Malabar, FL; Krieger Publ. Co., Inc.

———. (1994a). *Reptile Clinician's Handbook: A Compact Clinical and Surgical Reference*. Malabar, FL; Krieger Publ. Co., Inc.

———. (1994b). Ultrasonic Doppler Blood Flow Detection in Small Exotic Animal Medicine. *Seminars in Avian and Exotic Pet Medicine*, *3*(3):133–139.

———. (1995a). Nutritional Considerations. *In*: *Health and Welfare of Captive Reptiles*. C. Warwick, F. L. Frye, and J. B. Murphy (Eds.), pp. 82–97. London, UK; Chapman & Hall.

———. (1995b). Salmonellosis in Pet Reptiles and their Owners. *Reptiles Magazine*, *3*(1):26–42.

———, and Calvert, C. (1989a). Preliminary Information on the Nutritional Content of Mulberry Silk Moth (*Bombyx mori*) Larvae. *J. Zoo Wildl. Med.*, *20*(1):73–75.

———. (1989b, September 14). The Feeding of *Bombyx mori* as Prey Insects for Captive Lizards: A Quantum Improvement Over *Gryllus* spp., *Tenebrio molitor*, or *Galleria* spp. *Abstr. First World Congr. Herpetol.* Section S-4. Canterbury, England. Rutherford College, University of Kent.

———. (in press). The Nutritional Content of Calcium-Supplemented Mulberry Silk Moth (*Bombyx mori*) Larvae. *HerpetoPathologica*.

———, Centofanti, B. V., and Harris, J. M. (1991, September 27–30). Successful Treatment of Iatrogenic (Diet-Related) Hypervitaminosis-D and Hypercalcemia in Four Iguanas *Iguana, iguana*. *Proc. IV Int. Col. Pathol. Rep. & Amphib.*, Bad Nauheim, Germany.

———, Mader, D. R., and Centofanti, B. V. (1991). Interspecific (Lizard:Human) Sexual Aggression in Captive Iguanas (*Iguana iguana*): I. A Preliminary Compilation of Eighteen Cases. *Bull. Assoc. Amphib. and Rept. Veterinarians*, *1*(1):4–6.

———, and Himsel, C. A. (1988). The Proper Method for Stethoscopy in Reptiles. *Vet. Med.*, *83*(12):1250–1252.

———, and Townsend, W. (1993). *Captive Iguanas: A Guide to their Biology and Captive Care*. Melbourne, FL; Krieger Publ. Co., Inc.

Garner, R. J. (1961). *Veterinary Toxicology*, 2nd Ed., pp. 299–395. Baltimore, MD; The Williams and Wilkins Co.

Gerhmann, W. B. (1987). Ultraviolet Irradiances of Various Lamps Used in Animal Husbandry. *Zoo Biology*, *6*:117–127.

Gibbons, J. R. H., and Watkins, I. F. (1982). Behavior, Ecology, and Conservation of South Pacific Banded Iguanas, *Brachylophus*, Including a Newly Discovered Species. *In*: *Iguanas of the World: Their Behavior, Ecology and Conservation*. G. M. Burghardt and A. S. Rand (Eds.), pp. 418–441. Park Ridge, NJ; Noyes Publishing.

Glaser, C. A., Angulo, F. J., and Rooney, J. A. (1994). Animal-Associated Opportunistic Infections Among Persons Infected with the Human Immunodeficiency Virus. *Clin. Infect. Dis.*, *18*:14–24.

Grant, C. (1937). Herpetological Notes with New Species from the American and British Virgin Islands. *J. Dept. Agric., Univ. P. Rico*, *21*:503–522.

Grzimek, B. (Ed.). (1972). *Grzimek's Animal Life Encyclopedia*, Vol. 6, Reptiles. New York; Van Nostrand Reinhold Co.

Günther, R., and Tetzlaff, I. (1990). Lange Lebensdauer eines Grünen Leguans, *Iguana iguana*. *Der Zoologiscshe Garten*, *60*(6):346–348.

Haast, W. E. (1969). Hatching Rhinoceros Iguanas, *Cyclura cornuta*, at the Miami Serpentarium. *Int. Zoo Yrbk.*, *9*:49.

Habermalz, D., and Pietzsch, O. (1973). Identification of *Arizona* Bacteria. A Contribution to the Problem of *Salmonella* Infections Among Reptiles and Amphibians in Zoological Gardens. *Ztlbl. Bakteriol. Parasitenkd. Hyg. Abt. I Orig. A*, *225*:323–342.

Halloran, B. P., and Castro, M. E. (1989). Vitamin D Kinetics In Vivo: Effect of 1,25-Dihydroxyvitamin D Administration. *Am. J. Physiol.*, *256*:E686–691.

Hardin, B. (1994). *Green Iguanas: The Video Guide to Care and Breeding*. Dallas, TX; Hardin Productions.

Harris, D. M. (1982). Preliminary Observations on the Ecology of *Iguana iguana*, in Northern Columbia. *In*: *Iguanas of the World: Their Behavior, Ecology and Conservation*. G. M. Burghardt and A. S. Rand (Eds.), pp. 150–161. Park Ridge, NJ; Noyes Publishing.

Hinshaw, W. R., and McNeil, E. (1944). Gopher Snakes as Carriers of Salmonellosis and Paracolon Infections. *Cornell Vet.*, *24*:248–254.

Hinshaw, W. R., and McNeil, E. (1946). Paracolon Type 10 from Captive Rattlesnakes. *J. Bacteriol.*, *51*:397–398.

Hinshaw, W. R., and McNeil, E. (1947). Lizards as Carriers of Salmonella and Paracolon Bacteria. *J. Bacteriol.*, *53*:715–718.

Hirth, H. F. (1963). Some Aspects of the Natural History of *Iguana iguana* on a Tropical Strand. *Ecology*, *44*:613–615.

Hoff, G. L., and Hoff, D. M. (1984). *Salmonella* and *Arizona*. *In*: *Diseases of Amphibians and Reptiles*. G. L. Hoff, F. L. Frye, and E. R. Jacobson (Eds.), pp. 69–82. New York; Plenum Book Co.

Hoff, G. L., and White, F. H. (1977). *Salmonella* in Reptiles: Isolation from Free-Ranging Lizards (Reptilia, Lacertilia) in Florida. *J. Herpetol.*, *11*:123–129.

Howard, C. J. (1980). Notes on the Maintenance and Breeding of the Common Green Iguana (*Iguana iguana iguana*) at Twycross Zoo. *In*: *The Care and Breeding of Captive Reptiles*. S. Townson, N. J. Millichamp, D. G. D. Lucas, and A. J. Millwood (Eds.), *Brit. Herpetol. Soc.*, pp. 47–50.

Hulbert, L. C., and Oehme, F. W. (1961). *Plants Poisonous to Livestock*. Manhattan, KS; Kansas State University.

Innis, C. (1994). Considerations in Formulating Captive Tortoise Diets. *Bull. Amphib. Reptil. Veterinarians*, *4*(1):8–12.

Ippen, R. (1965). Considerations on the Comparative Pathology of Bone Diseases in Reptiles. *Zentralbl. Alleg. Path.*, *108*:424–434.

Iverson, J. B. (1977). *Behavior and Ecology of the Rock Iguana, Cyclura carinata*. Ph.D. Dissertation, University of Florida, Gainesville.

———. (1980). Colic Modifications in Iguanine Lizards. *J. Morphology*, *163*:79–93.

———. (1982). Adaptations to Herbivory in Iguanine Lizards. *In*: *Iguanas of the World: Their Behavior, Ecology and Conservation*. G. M. Burghardt and A. S. Rand (Eds.), pp. 60–83. Park Ridge, NJ: Noyes Publishing.

Jackson, C. G., and Jackson, M. M. (1971). The Frequency of *Salmonella* and *Arizona* Microorganisms in Zoo Turtles. *J. Wildl. Dis.*, *7*:130–132.

Jackson, M. M., et al. (1969). Investigation of Enteric Bacteria on the Testudinata-1: Occurrence of the Genera *Arizona*, *Citrobacter*, *Edwardsiella*, and *Salmonella*. *Bull. Wildl. Dis. Assoc.*, *5*:328–329.

Jackson, O. F., and Cooper, J. E. (1981). Nutritional Diseases. *In*: *Diseases of the Reptilia*, Vol. 2. J. E. Cooper and O. F. Jackson (Eds.), pp. 409–428. London; Academic Press.

———. (1980). The Action of Vitamin A on Adult Epidermis and Dermis. *In*: *The Physiology and Pathophysiology of the Skin*. Vol. 6, A. Jarrett (Ed.), pp. 2059–2091. London; Academic Press.

Jes, H. (1987). *Lizards in the Terrarium*. Hauppauge, NY; Barron's Educational Series.

Kästle, W. (1962). Kalk als Zusatznahrung für Eschsen. *Aquar. Terrar. Zeitschr.*, *15*:62.

Kaufmann, A. F. (1962). Granulomatous Oöphoritis in a Turtle. *J. Am. Vet. Med. Assoc.*, *53*:860–862.

———. (1972). Turtle-Associated Salmonellosis. *Am. J. Epidemiol.*, *95*:521–528.

———, and Morrison, Z. (1966). An Epidemiologic Study of Salmonellosis in Turtles. *Am. J. Epidemiol.*, *84*:364–370.

———, et al. (1967). *Salmonella* Excretion by Turtles. *Pub. Health Reports*, *9*:840–842.

Kennedy, M. E. (1973). Salmonella Isolations from Snakes and Other Reptiles. *Can. J. Comp. Med.*, *37*:325–326.

Kok, M. W. (1988). Successful Breeding with *Iguana iguana*. *Lacerta*, *46*(8):115–121.

Koopman, J. P., and Janssen, F. G. J. (1973). The Occurrence of Salmonellas and Lactose-Negative Arizonas in Reptiles in the Netherlands, and a Comparison of Three Enrichment Methods Used in Their Isolation. *J. Hyg.*, *71*:363–371.

Köhler, G. (1991a). Der Grüner Leguan, *Iguana iguana* (Linnaeus). *In*: *Amphib.-Rept. Kartei*.

———. (1991b). *Der Grüne Leguan*. Liesingstrasse 11, 6450 Hanau, Germany; Verlag Gunther Köhler.

Lewis, C. B. (1944). Notes on *Cyclura*. *Herpetologica*, *2*:92–8.

Licht, P., and Moberly, W. R. (1965). Thermal Requirements for Embryonic Development in the Tropical Lizard, *Iguana iguana*. *Copeia*, *1965*(4):515–517.

Loftin, H., and Tyson, E. (1965). Iguanas as Carion Eaters. *Copeia*, *1965*(4):515.

Lonnberg, E. (1902). On Some Points of Relation Between the Morphological Structure of the Intestine and the Diet of Reptiles. Bihang Till K. Vet. Ajad. Handl. Band 28, Afd. IV, No. 8, pp. 3–50.

Lowenstein, M. S., et al. (1971). Salmonellosis Associated with Turtles. *J. Infect. Dis.*, *124*:433.

McBee, R. H. (1971). Significance of the Intestinal Microflora in Herbivory. *Ann. Rev. Ecol. Syst.*, *1*:65–176.

———, and McBee, V. H. (1982). The Hindgut Fermentation in the Green Iguana, *Iguana iguana*. *In*: *Iguanas of the World: Their Behavior, Ecology and Conservation*. G. M. Burghardt and A. S. Rand (Eds.), pp. 77–83. Park Ridge, NJ; Noyes Publishing.

McCoy, R. H., and Seidler, R. J. (1973). Potential Pathogens in the Environment; Isolation, Enumeration, and the Identification of Seven Genera of Intestinal Bacteria Associated with Small Green Pet Turtles. *Appl. Microbiol.*, *25*:534–538.

McInnes, H. M. (1971). *Salmonella saintpaul* Infection of Sheep with Lizards as Possible Reservoirs. *New Zealand Vet. J., 19*:28.

Mendelssohn, H. (1980). Observations on a Captive Colony of *Iguana iguana*. *In*: *Reproductive Biology and Diseases of Captive Reptiles*. J. B. Murphy and J. T. Collins (Eds.), pp. 119–123. Society for the Study of Amphibians and Reptiles.

Miller, E. R. (1985). Mineral X Disease Interactions. *J. An. Sci., 60*:1500–1507.

Miller, T. J. (1987). Artificial Incubation of Eggs of the Green Iguana (*Iguana iguana*). *Zoo Biol., 6*:225–236.

Mitchell, J. C. (1986). Cannibalism in Reptiles: A Worldwide Review. *S.S.A.R. Herp. Circular* No. 15.

Montgomery, G. G. (Ed.). (1978). *The Ecology of Arboreal Folivores*. Washington, DC; Smithsonian Institution Press.

Mora, J. M. (1989). Eco-behavioral Aspects of Two Communally Nesting Iguanines and the Structure of Their Shared Nesting Burrows. *Herpetologica, 45*(3):293–298.

———. (1991a). Comparative Grouping Behavior of Juvenile Ctenosaurs and Iguanas. *J. Herp., 25*(2):244–246.

———. (1991b). Cannibalism in the Ctenosaur Lizard, *Ctenosaura similis*, in Costa Rica. *Bull. Chicago Herp. Soc., 26*(9):197–198.

Nagy, K. A. (1973). Behavior, Diet, and Reproduction in a Desert Lizard, *Sauromalus obesus*. *Copeia, 1973*:93–102.

———. (1977). Cellulose Digestion and Nutrient Assimilation in *Sauromalus obesus*, a Plant-eating Lizard. *Copeia, 1977*:355–362.

———. (1982). Energy Requirements of Free-Living Iguanid Lizards. *In*: *Iguanas of the World: Their Behavior, Ecology and Conservation*. G. M. Burghardt and A. S. Rand (Eds.), pp. 49–59. Park Ridge, NJ: Noyes Publishing.

Nockels, C. F. (1988). Increased Vitamin Needs During Stress and Disease. *Proc. Georgia Nutrition Conf. Feed Indust.*, 9–16.

Otis, V. S., and Behler, J. L. (1973). The Occurrence of Salmonellae and *Edwardsiella* in the Turtles of the New York Zoological Park. *J. Wildl. Dis., 9*:4–6.

Packard, M. J., Packard, G. C., and Boardman, T. J. (1982). Structure of Eggshells and Water Relations of Reptilian Eggs. *Herpetologia, 38*:136–155.

Pagon, S., et al. (1976). Occurrence of *Salmonella* in Healthy Snakes and Snake Cadavers: Isolation of a New *Salmonella* Species Belonging to the Sub-genus IV (*S.* IV 18:Z36, Z38). *Ztbl. Bakteriol. Parasitenkd. Hyg.* Abt. I Orig. A, *236*:464–471.

Paul-Murphy, J., Mader, D. R., Kock, N., and Frye, F. L. (1987). Necrosis of Esophageal and Gastric Mucosa in Snakes Given Oral Dioctyl Sodium Sulfosuccinate. *Proc. Am. Assoc. Zoo. Vets.*, 474–477.

Parra, R. (1978). Comparison of Fore and Hindgut Fermentation in Herbivores. *In*: *The Ecology of Arboreal Folivores*. G. G. Montgomery (Ed.), pp. 205–209. Washington, DC; Smithsonian Institution Press.

Peters, U. (1982). The Breeding of Endangered Species. *Int. Zoo News, 176*:29/2:7–13.

Phillips, J. A., Alexander, N., Karesh, W. B., Millar, R., and Lasley, B. L. (1985). Stimulating Male Sexual Behavior with Repetitive Pulses of GnRH in Female Green Iguanas, *Iguana iguana*. *J. Exp. Zool., 234*:481–484.

———, and Lasley, B. L. (1987). Modification of Reproductive Rhythm in Lizards via GnRH Therapy. *Ann. NY Acad. Sci., 519*:128–136.

———, Garel, A., Packard, G. C., and Packard, M. J. (1990). Influence of Moisture and Temperature on Eggs and Embryos of the Green Iguanas (*Iguana iguana*). *Herpetologica, 46*(2):238–245.

Porter, K. R. (1972). *Herpetology*. Philadelphia; W. B. Saunders Co.

Porter, W. P. (1967). Solar Radiation Through the Living Body Walls of Vertebrates with Emphasis on Desert Reptiles. *Ecol. Monogr., 37*:273–296.

Pratt, N. C., et al. (1994). Functional Versus Physiological Puberty—an Analysis of Sexual Bimaturity in the Green Iguana, *Iguana iguana*. *An. Behav., 47*:1101–1114.

Putz, R. (1982). Erfahrungen bei der Haltung und Zucht des Grünen Leguans *Iguana iguana iguana*. *Herpetofauna, 4*(20):21–25.

Rand, A. S. (1967). Adaptive Significance of Territoriality in Iguanid Lizards. *In*: *Symposium of Lizard Ecology*. W. M. Milstead (Ed.), pp. 106–115. Columbia, Missouri; University of Missouri Press.

———. (1968a). A Nesting Aggregation of Iguanas. *Copeia, 1968*:552–561.

———. (1968b). The Temperature of Iguana Nests and their Relation to Incubation Optima and to Nesting Sites and Season. *Herpetologica, 28*:252–253.

———. (1978). Reptilian Arboreal Folivores. *In*: *The Ecology of Arboreal Folivores*. G. G. Montgomery (Ed.), pp. 115–122. Washington, DC; Smithsonian Institution Press.

———. (1991). Digging Iguanas. *Zoolife Magazine*, Winter Issue.

———, and Dugan, B. A. (1980). Iguana Egg Mortality Within the Nest. *Copeia, 1980*:531–534.

———, Dugan, B. A., Monteza, H., and Vianda, D. (1990). The Diet of a Generalized Folivore: *Iguana iguana* in Panama. *J. Herp., 24*(2):211–214.

———, and Greene, H. W. (1982). Latitude and Climate in the Phenology of Reproduction in the Green Iguana, *Iguana iguana*. *In*: *Iguanas of the World: Their Behavior, Ecology and Conservation*. G. M. Burghardt and A. S. Rand (Eds.), pp. 142–149. Park Ridge, NJ: Noyes Publishing.

Ricklefs, R. E., and Cullen. (1973). Embryonic Growth of the Green Iguana, *Iguana iguana*. *Copeia*, 296–305.

Rodda, G. H. (1991). Sexing *Iguana iguana*. *Bull. Chicago Herp. Soc.*, *26*:173–175.

———. (1992). The Mating Behavior of *Iguana iguana*. *Smithsonian Contributions to Zoology*, 534. 44 pp.

———, and Burghardt, G. M. (1985). *Iguana iguana* (Green Iguana) Territoriality. *Herpetological Rev.*, *16*:112.

———, and Grajal, A. (1990). The Nesting Behavior of the Green Iguana, *Iguana iguana*, in the Llanos of Venezuela. *Amphibia-Reptilia*, *11*:31–39.

Roman, J. A. V. (1978, October 31–November 15). Reproduction and Management of Dominican Iguanas, *Cyclura cornuta* and *Cyclura ricordi* in the National Zoological Gardens. Unpublished manuscript. Presented at the 9th Congress of the Spanish-American Union of Zoos; Mayaguez, Puerto Rico.

Rosenstein, B. J., et al. (1965). A Family Outbreak of Salmonellosis Traced to a Pet Turtle. *New Engl. J. Med.*, *272*:960–961.

Rossi, J. (1994). Soft Paws® for Green Iguanas, *Iguana iguana*. *Bull. Amphi. Rept. Vet.*, *4*(1):4.

Rost, D. R., and Young, M. C. (1984). Diagnosing White-Muscle Disease. *VM/SAC*, *80*:1286–1287.

Ryan, M. J. (1982). Variation in Iguanine Social Organization: Mating Systems in Chuckawallas (*Sauromalus*). *In*: *Iguanas of the World: Their Behavior, Ecology and Conservation*. G. M. Burghardt and A. S. Rand (Eds.), pp. 380–390. Park Ridge, NJ; Noyes Publishing.

Schilling, R. (1994). Breeding of *Iguana iguana rhinolopha*. *Iguana*, *13*:35–38.

Schmidt-Nielsen, K. (1964). *Desert Animals*. pp. 225–251. New York: Oxford University Press.

———, and Frange, R. (1958). Salt Glands in Marine Reptiles. *Nature*, (London, England) *182*:783–785.

Schröder, H.-D., and Karasek, E. (1977). Toxicity of Salmonellae Isolated from Reptiles. pp. 87–91. *XIX Int. Symp. Erkrankheiten Zootiere*. Berlin, GDR; Akademie-Verlag.

Schuchman, S. M., and Taylor, D. O. N. (1970). Arteriosclerosis in an Iguana (*Iguana iguana*). *J. Am. Vet. Med. Assoc.*, *157*:614–616.

Shaw, C. E. (1954). Captive Bred Cuban Iguanas (*Cyclura maclaeyi maclaeyi*). *Herpetologica*, *10*:73–78.

———. (1969). Breeding the Rhinoceros Iguana (*Cyclura cornuta cornuta*) at San Diego Zoo. *Int. Zoo Yrbk.*, *9*:45–48.

Sherbrooke, W. C. (1990). "Rain-Harvesting" Behavior in the Texas Horned Lizard (*Phrynosoma cornutum*). *J. Herpetol.*, *24*(3):302–308.

Sieberling, R. J., et al. (1975). Evaluation of Methods for the Isolation of *Salmonella* and *Arizona* Organisms from Pet Turtles Treated with Antimicrobial Agents. *Appl. Microbiol.*, *29*:240–245.

Sokol, O. M. (1967). Herbivory in Lizards. *Evolution*, *21*:192–194.

Sokol, O. M. (1971). Lithophagy and Geophagy in Reptiles. *J. Herp.*, *5*:69–71.

Stamps, J. A. (1977). Social Behavior and Spacing Patterns in Lizards. *In*: *Biology of the Reptilia*, *Vol. 7*, pp. 265–334. London; Academic Press.

———. (1983). Reptilian Herbivores, A Review of Iguanas of the World. *Science*, *220*:1145–1146.

Stebbins, R. C., and Cohen, N. W. (1973). The Effect of Parietalectomy on the Thyroid and Gonads in Free-Living Western Fence Lizards *Sceloporus occidentalis*. *Copeia*, *1973*:662–668.

Szarski, H. (1962). Some Remarks on Herbivorous Lizards. *Evolution*, *16*:529.

Tan, R. J. S., et al. (1978). Intestinal Bacterial Flora of the Household Lizard, *Gecko gecko*. *Res. Vet. Sci.*, *24*:262–263.

Templeton, J. R. (1964). Nasal Salt Excretion in Terrestrial Lizards. *Comp. Biochem. Physiol.*, *11*:223– 229.

Throckmorton, G. S. (1976). Oral Food Processing in Two Herbivorous Lizards, *Iguana iguana* (Iguanidae) and *Uromastix aegyptius* (Agamidae). *J. Morph.*, *148*:363–390.

Tonge, S., and Bloxam, Q. (1984). Captive Reproduction of Rhinoceros Iguana (*Cyclura c. cornuta*) in Indoor Accommodation. *Acta Zoo et Path. Antverpiensia*, *78*:115–128.

Troyer, K. (1982). Transfer of Fermentative Microbes Between Generations in a Herbivorous Lizard. *Science*, *216*:540–542.

———. (1984a). Structure and Function of the Digestive Tract of Herbivorous Lizard, *Iguana iguana*. *Physiol. Zool.*, *57*(1):1–8.

———. (1984b). Diet Selection and Digestion in *Iguana iguana*: The Importance of Age and Nutrient Requirements. *Oecologica*, *61*:201–207.

Trust, T. J., et al. (1981). Importation of Salmonellae with Aquarium Species. *Can. J. Microbiol.*, *27*:500–504.

———. (1987). Small Differences in Daytime Body Temperature Affect Digestion of Natural Food in an Herbivorous Lizard (*Iguana iguana*). *Comp. Biochem. Physiol., [A]*, *87*:623–626.

Tucker, J. M., and Kimball, M. H. (1961). *Poisonous Plants in the Garden*. Davis, CA; University of California Agricultural Extension Service.

U.S. Department of Agriculture. (1958). *16 Plants Poisonous to Livestock in the Western States*. Farmer's Bulletin No. 2106. Washington, DC.

Van Aperen, W. (1969). Notes on the Artificial Hatching of Iguana Eggs, *Iguana iguana* at Melbourne Zoo. *Int. Zoo Yrbk.*, *9*:44–45.

Van Devender, R. W. (1982). Growth and Ecology of Spiny-Tailed and Green Iguanas in Costa Rica, with Comments on the Evolution of Herbivory and Large Body Size. *In*: *Iguanas of the World: Their Behavior, Ecology and Conservation*. G. M. Burghardt and A. S. Rand (Eds.), pp. 162–183. Park Ridge, NJ; Noyes Publishing.

Wallach, J. D. (1966). Hypervitaminosis D in Green Iguanas. *J. Am. Vet. Med. Assoc.*, *149*:912–914.

———. (1971). Environmental and Nutritional Diseases of Captive Reptiles. *J. Am. Vet. Med. Assoc.*, *159*:1632–1643.

———, and Hoessle, C. (1968). Fibrous Osteodystrophy in Green Iguanas. *J. Am. Vet. Med. Assoc.*, *153*:863–865.

Wells, J. G., et al. (1974). Evaluation of Methods for Isolating *Salmonella* and *Arizona* Organisms from Pet Turtles. *Appl. Microbiol.*, *27*:8–10.

Werner, D. I. (1982). Social Organization and Ecology of Land Iguanas, *Conolophus subcristatus*, on Isla Fernandina, Galápagos. *In*: *Iguanas of the World: Their Behavior, Ecology and Conservation*. G. M. Burghardt and A. S. Rand (Eds.), pp. 342–365. Park Ridge, NJ: Noyes Publishing.

———. (1988). The Effect of Varying Water Potential on Body Weight, Yolk and Fat Bodies in Neonate Green Iguanas. *Copeia*, *1988*:406–411.

———, and Miller, T. J. (1984). Artificial Nests for Female Green Iguanas. *Herp. Rev.*, *15*(2):57–58.

———, Baker, E. M. del C. Gonzalez, E., and Sosa, I. R. (1988). Kinship Recognition and Grouping in Hatchling Green Iguanas. *Behav. Ecol. Sociobiol.*, *21*(2):83–89.

Wiewandt, T. (1977). *Ecology, Behavior, and Management of the Mona Island Ground Iguana, Cyclura stejnegeri*. Ph.D. Dissertation. Cornell University, Ithaca, NY.

———. (1982). Evolution of Nesting Patterns in Iguanine Lizards. *In*: *Iguanas of The World: Their Behavior, Ecology and Conservation*. G. M. Burghardt and A. S. Rand (Eds.), pp. 119–141. Park Ridge, NJ; Noyes Publishing.

Wilke, H. (1981). Die Situation von *Cyclura cornuta cornuta* Bonnaterre in Zoologische Gärten, ihre Natürlichen Lebensbedingungen und der einer Übertragung auf die Tiere des Zoo Frankfurt. *A. M. Zool. Garten N. V., Jena*, *51*:3/4S:177–190.

Witmer, M. (1994). Letter to the editor. *Notes from NOAH*, *22*(1):15–16.

Zeigel, R. F., and Clark, H. F. (1969). Electron Microscopy Observations on a New Herpes-Like Virus Isolated from *Iguana iguana* and Prolonged in Reptilian Cells *in vivo*. *Infect. & Immun.*, *5*:570–582.

Zug, G. R., and Rand, A. S. (1987). Estimation of Age in Nesting Female *Iguana iguana*: Testing Skeletochronology in a Tropical Lizard. *Amphibia-Reptilia*, *8*:237–250.

Zwart, P. (1960). *Salmonella* and *Arizona* Infections in Reptiles in the Netherlands. *Antionie Leeweunhoek*, *26*:250–254.

Zwart, P., and Van de Watering, C. C. (1969). Disturbances of Bone Formation in the Common Iguana (*Iguana iguana* L.): Pathology and Etiology. *Acta Zoo et Path. Anat.*, *48*:333–356.

Zweifel, R. G. (1961). Another Method of Incubating Reptile Eggs. *Copeia*, *1961*:112–113.

# INDEX